Palgrave Studies in European Political Sociology

Palgrave Studies in European Political Sociology addresses contemporary themes in the field of Political Sociology. Over recent years, attention has turned increasingly to processes of Europeanization and globalization and the social and political spaces that are opened by them. These processes comprise both institutional-constitutional change and new dynamics of social transnationalism. Europeanization and globalization are also about changing power relations as they affect people's lives, social networks and forms of mobility. The Palgrave Studies in European Political Sociology series addresses linkages between regulation, institution building and the full range of societal repercussions at local, regional, national, European and global level, and will sharpen understanding of changing patterns of attitudes and behaviours of individuals and groups, the political use of new rights and opportunities by citizens, new conflict lines and coalitions, societal interactions and networking, and shifting loyalties and solidarity within and across the European space. We welcome proposals from across the spectrum of Political Sociology and Political Science, on dimensions of citizenship; political attitudes and values; political communication and public spheres; states, communities, governance structure and political institutions; forms of political participation; populism and the radical right; and democracy and democratization.

More information about this series at
http://www.palgrave.com/gp/series/14630

Laura Landorff

Inside European Parliament Politics

Informality, Information and Intergroups

palgrave
macmillan

Laura Landorff
Department of Culture
and Global Studies
Aalborg University
Aalborg, Denmark

Palgrave Studies in European Political Sociology
ISBN 978-3-030-04205-9 ISBN 978-3-030-04206-6 (eBook)
https://doi.org/10.1007/978-3-030-04206-6

Library of Congress Control Number: 2018962360

Cover image: Lucky Dice
Cover credit: Bombay Mix/Alamy Stock Photo

This Palgrave Macmillan imprint is published by the registered company Springer Nature Switzerland AG
The registered company address is: Gewerbestrasse 11, 6330 Cham, Switzerland

Acknowledgements

My research on the European Parliament's Intergroups started with a term paper that I wrote as an M.A. student during the European Studies research project semester at Aarhus University in 2009 and ends now with the publication of this book. It has been an exciting, eventful, precious, and at times challenging journey. At this point, I would like to express my deepest thanks to a number of people who supported me during this time.

I am deeply indebted to my interview partners who dedicated their precious time to my research project. Without you, this book would have not been possible. Moreover, I wish to thank the European Parliament for granting me with a study visit in 2012 and thus, for supporting my research on-site.

I would like to express my sincere appreciation to my former supervisors Ulrike Liebert (University of Bremen), Margrit Schreier (Jacobs University Bremen), Ann-Christina Lauring Knudsen (University of Aarhus) and Niilo Kauppi (University of Jyvaskylä) for their valuable guidance, advice and helpful comments throughout the Ph.D. process. I am very grateful and honoured to have been supported by such an international, multi- and interdisciplinary team of scholars.

The Bremen International Graduate School of Social Sciences (BIGSSS) has been my academic home from September 2011–2016. I am very thankful for the academic, institutional and administrative support I received at all times. The BIGSSS Ph.D. scholarship allowed me several field stays in the European Parliament as well as numerous conference and summer school participations where I presented my research and received valuable comments on my work. In particular, I wish to thank Arndt Wonka, coordinator of the research field on Global Governance and Regional Integration at BIGSSS. Your constructive feedback and continuous encouragement meant a lot. Moreover, a special thanks goes to my former Ph.D. colleagues at BIGSSS who became dearest friends, in particular to Anna Hokema, Ines Spieler, Juliane Klein and Caterina Bonora. *Tusind tak* for your great company and continuous support. I also like to extend my gratitude to Herwig Reiter for the extensive exchange on qualitative research and data analysis during numerous workshops at BIGSSS.

Furthermore, I am very grateful to the German Academic Exchange Service (DAAD) for funding my research stay at the University of Strasbourg, France in the autumn of 2013. In addition, I like to thank the Aarhus University Research Foundation (AUFF) for financing my stay as a visiting Ph.D.-student at Aarhus University in the autumn of 2014.

I also wish to extend my gratitude to my former professors and colleagues at the School of Culture and Society/European Studies at the University of Aarhus, in particular to Ann-Christina Lauring Knudsen, Lisanne Wilken, Christoffer Kølvraa, Hagen Schulz-Forberg and Christina Fiig. I also like to thank Knud Erik Jørgensen at the Department of Political Science. Thank you very much for your inspiration, encouragement and promotion. You planted a seed for this book as well as for my own personal development as a researcher.

I am also very grateful to my new academic home at the Department of Culture and Global Studies at the University of Aalborg. In particular, I like to thank my colleagues Lise Rolandsen Agustin, Søren Dosenrode, Wolfgang Zank and Anita Nissen for their valuable comments on earlier drafts of this book. Moreover, I wish to thank the Head of Department, Marianne Rostgaard, as well as the Vice Head of Department, Lise-Lotte Holmgreen. Thanks to their support, I was able to enjoy a writing retreat at the beautiful site of Klitgården Refugium to finish this book.

My deepest gratitude goes to my parents for all their support and love, for raising me to be the person that I am. This book is dedicated to you.

Contents

Abbreviations

AEM	Association Européenne des Élus de Montagne (Association of Elected Representatives from Mountain Regions)
AER	Assembly of European Regions
AFCO	Committee on Constitutional Affairs
AFET	Committee on Foreign Affairs
AGRI	Committee on Agriculture and Rural Development
ALDE	Alliance of Liberals and Democrats for Europe
AREV	Assemblée des Régions Européennes Viticoles (Assembly of European Wine Regions)
ATD	Agir Tous pour la Dignité
BUDG	Committee on Budgets
CAAT	Centre for Alternatives to Animal Testing
CAP	Common Agricultural Policy
CARDOC	Centre archivistique et documentaire du Parlement européen, Luxembourg
CEMR	Council of European Municipalities and Regions
CoR	Committee of the Regions
CFSP	Common Foreign and Security Policy
CMO	Common Market Organisation
CNAOC	Confédération Nationale des Producteurs de Vins et Eaux-de-Vie de Vin à Appellations d'Origine Contrôlées
COD	Co-decision procedure/Ordinary Legislative Procedure
CPMR	Conference of Peripheral Maritime Regions
CSO	Civil Society Organisation
CULT	Committee on Culture and Education
CV	Curriculum Vitae

DE	Germany
DEVE	Committee on Development
DG	Directorate-General
DG AGRI	Directorate-General for Agriculture and Rural Development
DG ENER	Directorate-General for Energy
DG ENV	Directorate-General for Environment
DG MARE	Directorate-General for Maritime Affairs and Fisheries
DG MOVE	Directorate-General for Mobility and Transport
DG REGIO	Directorate-General for Regional and Urban Policy
DG RTD	Directorate-General Research and Innovation
DG SANCO	Directorate-General for Health and Consumers
EBCD	European Bureau for Conservation and Development
ECON	Committee on Economic and Monetary Affairs
ECR	European Conservatives and Reformists Group
ECSC	European Coal and Steel Community
EDF	European Disability Forum
EFBWW	European Federation of Building and Woodworkers
EFD	Europe of Freedom and Democracy Group
EFT	European Transport Workers' Federation
ELDR	European Liberal Democrat and Reform Party
ELO	European Landowners' Organisation
EMI	European Metropolitan network Institute
EMPL	Committee on Employment and Social Affairs
ENAR	European Network against Racism
ENVI	Committee on Environment, Public Health and Food Safety
EP	European Parliament
EPP-ED	Group of the European People's Party (Christian Democrats) and European Democrats in the European Parliament
ETUC	European Trade Union Confederation
ETUI	European Trade Union Institute
EU	European Union
EUREAU	European Federation of National Associations of Water Services
FACE	European Federation of Associations for Hunting and Conservation of the EU
FEMM	Committee on Women's Rights and Gender Equality
FI	Finland
FR	France
GATT	General Agreement on Tariffs and Trade
GB	Great Britain
Greens/EFA	The Greens/European Free Alliance in the European Parliament
GUE/NGL	European United Left—Nordic Green Left—European Parliamentary Group

HSI	Humane Society International
ICT	Intra-Corporate Transfer
IFAW	International Fund for Animal Welfare
IT	Italy
ITRE	Committee on Industry, Research and Energy
IUCN	International Union for Conservation of Nature
JURI	Committee on Legal Affairs
LGBTI	Lesbian, Gay, Bisexual, Transgender and Intersex
LIBE	Committee on Civil Liberties, Justice and Home Affairs
LU	Luxembourg
MEP	Member of European Parliament
MP	Member of Parliament
NGO	Non-Governmental Organisation
OLP	Ordinary Legislative Procedure
PECH	Committee on Fisheries
PETI	Committee on Petitions
Ph.D.	Doctor of Philosophy
PL	Poland
REACH	Registration, Evaluation, Authorisation and Restriction of Chemicals
REGI	Committee on Regional Development
RO	Romania
S&D	Group of the Progressive Alliance of Socialists & Democrats in the European Parliament
SE	Sweden
SME	Small and Medium-Sized Enterprise
TRAN	Committee on Transport and Tourism
US	United States
WTO	World Trade Organisation

List of Figures

List of Tables

CHAPTER 1

Introduction

The European Parliament (EP) is the only directly elected institution of the European Union (EU). Thus, it is of utmost importance for the legitimacy of the Union. It is a transnational representative body that works as part of an institutional triangle consisting of the European Commission and the Council of the European Union,[1] which distinguishes it from other legislative institutions (Judge & Earnshaw, 2008). In its current 8th parliamentary term (2014–2019), the EP has 751 members from 28 EU member states, representing over 500 million EU citizens (European Parliament, 2017). In this way, the EP is one of the largest parliaments in the world (Judge & Earnshaw, 2008).[2] Established in 1952 as the Common Assembly of the European Coal and Steel Community (ECSC)—as unelected, consultative body—the EP has come a long way 'in a historically short period of time' (Corbett, Jacobs, & Neville, 2016, p. 451; Hix, Raunio, & Scully, 2003). Since the 1970s, the Parliament's budgetary, legislative and control competencies have been gradually enhanced with every treaty reform reaching its apex—for the time being—with the ratification of the Lisbon Treaty in 2009.[3] Post-Lisbon, the EP is co-legislator with the Council in 85 policy areas, for instance in the areas of economic governance, consumer protection, environment and energy (Burns, 2016; European Parliament, 2018). This means that the majority of EU laws is adopted jointly by these two institutions (Burns, 2016). Moreover, it acts as 'genuine bicameral budgetary authority' deciding on equal footing with the Council on the EU's

L. Landorff, *Inside European Parliament Politics*,
Palgrave Studies in European Political Sociology,
https://doi.org/10.1007/978-3-030-04206-6_1

budget (Burns, 2016, p. 158). Finally, the EP further advanced its control functions, for instance, its influence on the selection of the European Commission president, and thus on the 'most powerful executive office in the EU' by initiating the *Spitzenkandidaten* process prior its elections in 2014 (Hobolt, 2014, p. 1528). Thus, today the EP is a key player within the EU institutional system, and one of the most influential parliaments in the world.

The EP is a young parliament that has been directly elected for the first time in 1979 and thereafter every five years. It is a dynamic parliament that increased its size from 410 seats in its very first term (1979–1984) to 751 in the 8th term (2014–2019). The EP stands out for its own, unique organisational complexities and multilingual and multinational features operating in three different locations (Brussels, Strasbourg and Luxembourg) and in 24 official working languages (European Parliament, 2015a). In line with the EP's special characteristics, its members represent a new type of politician who is different from nominated delegates working in international organisations or elected parliamentarians in national legislatures (Kauppi, 2003). As representatives, Members of European Parliament (MEPs) have 'important responsibilities towards multiple 'constituencies'', i.e. towards their voters at home, their national political parties and their EP political groups (Scully & Farrell, 2003, p. 285). Consequently, MEPs are subject to various, at times competing demands from voters, from colleagues in the EP, from parties at national, regional and local level, from interest groups or 'their own sense of duty and ambition' (Katz, 1999, p. 61). This fluid nature, and the fact that its members are less hemmed in by domestic parties, voters and interests, allows the parliamentarians 'considerable leeway in choosing – at least initially – how they want to play things while they are in Strasbourg and Brussels' (Bale & Taggart, 2006, p. 11). As this book will show, the creation and maintenance of Intergroups by MEPs constitutes a brilliant example for this kind of leeway. The EP's transformation from an unelected, marginalised body within the EU's institutional triangle to a genuine co-legislator and budgetary authority makes the EP an interesting research object in the first place. In conjunction with the ongoing debate about the EU's democratic deficit and the continuous demands for parliamentary involvement in EU politics, it is more important than ever to gain an understanding of how parliamentarians from 28 member states with different national, political and cultural backgrounds practice and organise parliamentary work. In response, this book delivers an explorative study on Intergroups, more specifically on MEPs' engagement in Intergroups in the EP. Intergroups are informal cross-party, cross-committee groupings bringing together MEPs from different political groups, parliamentary committees and member states as well as representatives of civil society and other EU institutions in their meetings. The 7th EP (2009–2014) recorded 27 officially recognised Intergroups covering a wide range of themes from ageing and intergenerational solidarity to climate change, from trade unions to animal welfare, from disability to urban areas, to name just a few (European Parliament, 2013a). Numbers of members ranged from 12 MEPs (Intergroup 'Extreme Poverty and Human Rights') to 126 MEPs (Intergroup 'Climate Change, Biodiversity and Sustainable Development') (European Parliament, 2013a).

Research on Intergroups in the European Parliament so Far

Until now Intergroups or rather the informal dimension of EP politics have only been marginally addressed in the literature. So far contemporary research on the Parliament has concentrated on four inter-related areas: (1) work on the general development and functioning of the EP[4]; (2) research on the political behaviour and EP elections[5]; (3) research on the internal politics and organisation of the EP[6]; and (4) examination of the inter-institutional bargaining between the EP, the Council and the European Commission[7] (Hix et al., 2003, p. 193). Within these areas, only scattered accounts on Intergroups are provided. A precious few publications refer to them marginally in the context of: the EP's general development and functions (Corbett et al., 2016; Judge & Earnshaw, 2008); organised interest representation and (corporate) lobbying (Bouwen, 2003; Greenwood, 2003, 2007; Kohler-Koch, 1997); civil society (Dutoit, 2001, 2009; Mény, 2009); and political representation and the development of a European Party System (Andeweg, 1995). Thereby, the works by Jacobs and Corbett (1990), Jacobs, Corbett, and Shackleton (1992, 1995), Corbett et al. (2000, 2007, 2011, 2016) on the EP and Dutoit (2001) provide the most extensive, though rather descriptive, account of the evolution of Intergroups in the EP since 1979. Corbett et al. (2016) provide continuous updates on the history, objectives and working methods of selected Intergroups.[8]

In these works, the focus is predominately on Intergroups, and thus on the meso-level, while the reasoning of MEPs to engage in Intergroups is only briefly addressed (Corbett et al., 2011). The very recent works of Nedergaard and Jensen (2014) and Ringe, Victor, and Carman (2013) underline the increasing popularity and importance of Intergroups as study object in EP contemporary research.

With regard to informal governance, EP research has so far concentrated on the EP as an institution and its role in informal institution-building, institutional change and inter-institutional processes. The work of Farrell and Héritier (2003) shows how the co-decision process has led to the emergence of informal institutions and decision-making procedures; see also Héritier (2012), Reh, Héritier, Bressanelli, and Koop (2011), and Häge and Kaeding (2007) on the co-decision procedure. Crum (2012, p. 354) conceptualises the EP as a 'driving force in informal institution-building' in Common Foreign and Security Policy (CFSP). Hence, EP intra-institutional informal arrangements have been marginalised so far. In response, this book aims to open up the institutional black box of the EP, to get closer to the MEPs and beyond descriptions of the EP's formal, institutional structures at the same time, focusing on intra-institutional informal arrangements, such as Intergroups.

Research on the EP and EU institutions in general is accompanied by the problem that these institutions 'have no exact counterparts in national political systems' (Judge & Earnshaw, 2008, p. 10). Attempts to locate the EP within 'wider theories of legislatures' are characterised by the *suis generis* argument fuelled by the description of the EP as having unique characteristics and defying 'easy categorization' (Corbett et al., 2011, p. 2; Judge & Earnshaw, 2008, p. 24). By comparisons with the United States (US) Congress or national parliaments of the EU member states, scholars attempt 'to shake off the mantle of the 'sui generis' approach' and aim to demonstrate that 'the EP look[s] increasingly like a normal parliament with cohesive parties […]' (Hix, Noury, & Roland, 2007, p. 3; McElroy, 2007, p. 434). In this context, this book emphasises that Intergroups do not present a unique phenomenon to the EP as argued by Mény (2009). In contrast, there are counterparts in the parliaments of the EU member states, such as all-party groups in the British House of Commons or working/study groups in the French Senate as well as in the US Congress (Corbett et al., 2011; Crespo Allen, 1996; Landorff, 2010; Ringe et al., 2013). This adds to the argument that the

EP can be increasingly studied in a comparative perspective. Given, however, that it is parliamentarians from different member states gathering in Intergroups, they are, of course, unique as this is by definition not the case in national parliaments.

With regard to the present study, research on the political behaviour, the EP's internal politics and organisation are of particular relevance. Consequently, they are briefly reviewed in the following paragraphs.

Research on the political behaviour concentrated primarily on exploring MEPs' voting behaviour (e.g. Hix et al., 2007), on socialisation (e.g. Franklin & Scarrow, 1999; Scully, 2005), on roles (e.g. Bale & Taggart, 2006; Katz, 1999; Scully & Farrell, 2003). This research has contributed significantly to explaining institutional behaviour and outcomes. Hence, it is well known how parliamentarians vote (e.g. Hix et al., 2007), but it is little known about the processes preceding voting (Ringe, 2010). Thus, there has been less concentration on what MEPs do besides voting. This is, on (informal) practices,[9] conceptualised here as part of MEPs' behaviour, as 'what someone does' (Mérand, 2011, p. 182), as 'socially organized activities [and] competent performances' (Adler & Pouliot, 2011, pp. 6–7). However, in recent years, a rethinking takes place in terms of how to study EU institutions, actors and politics at large. The study of everyday (parliamentary) practices of European integration gains of importance. Pointing to anthropological studies on EU institutions,[10] Adler-Nissen (2016, p. 99) calls for a 'practice turn in EU Studies' to generate a deeper understanding of the everyday aspects of European integration 'from above' and 'from below'. In the context of the EP, Busby (2013) delivers an exciting and rich ethnographic study of MEPs everyday practices of European politics by focusing on the role of national party delegations. This book takes its place alongside these works and joins the call for a 'practice turn' in the study of the EU.

Research on the EP's internal politics and organisation has focused on the official organs (e.g. the political groups and parliamentary committees) and how these shape what the EP does. Thereby, academic interest in EP committees increased with the increase of EP legislative powers. This is reflected in studies on the composition of and assignments to the EP standing committees (e.g. Bowler & Farrell, 1995; McElroy, 2006; Neuhold, 2001; Yordanova, 2011, 2013; Whitaker, 2001, 2011), on report allocation in the EP (e.g. Kaeding, 2004; Mamadouh & Raunio, 2003), on the role of committees in the EP policymaking process and in consensus-building within the EP (e.g. Neuhold, 2001;

Ripoll Servent, 2015; Settembri & Neuhold, 2009), as well as on the role of national parties in committees (e.g. Westlake, 2011; Whitaker, 2001, 2011). These works have shown that the parliamentary committees constitute the EP's 'legislative backbone' (Westlake, 1995, p. 191). They are of utmost importance in fulfilling the Parliament's legislative, budgetary, oversight and agenda-setting tasks (Corbett et al., 2016). The 7th EP (2009–2014) had 20 standing committees which 'were divided functionally into different policy areas' (Burns, 2013, p. 166). In general, the EP committee system reflects the EU's legislative programme (Whitaker, 2011). The standing committees differ in their size. In the 7th EP, committee size ranged from 76 parliamentarians in the committee on Foreign Affairs (AFET) to 24 parliamentarians in the committee on Fisheries (PECH) (Corbett et al., 2011, p. 146). What is more, they differ in their prestige and strength as 'they are unevenly involved in the legislative process of the EU' constituting lawmaking committees, such as the committees on Constitutional Affairs (AFCO) and Budgets (BUDG) and non-lawmaking committees, such as the committee on Petitions (PETI) (Neuhold, 2001; Whitaker, 2011, p. 30). For an in-depth insight into different types of committees, see Settembri and Neuhold (2009). The majority of MEPs serves in one parliamentary committee and acts as substitutes in another (Corbett et al., 2011).[11] Despite their national and political heterogeneity, EP committees 'generally work very consensually, regardless of the issue at stake and the procedure applied' (Settembri & Neuhold, 2009, p. 147). They play a key role in EP politics as sources of policy expertise and 'as primary arenas of legislative deliberation and negotiation' (Ringe, 2010, p. 213). Hence, for parliamentarians, the EP committee system provides an opportunity to 'acquire and make use of existing expertise in specific policy areas' (Ringe, 2010, p. 21). Given the lack of a governmental or, respectively, permanent majority in the EP, the committees play a decisive role in forming the 'institution's position', in developing consensus and 'majorities on an issue-by-issue basis', and thus facilitate collective action (Corbett et al., 2016, p. 199; Yordanova, 2009, p. 254). Against this background, the Parliament has been regarded as an institution consisting of 'strong committees and weak parties' (Burns, 2016, p. 161).

Research on the EP's political groups, however, has shown that the gradual expansion of the EP's legislative competences 'led to a growing centralisation in the political groups' as well as to 'growing ideological compromises, as the parties were forced to "get things done"'

(Hix et al., 2007, p. 52; Lindberg, Rasmussen, & Warntjen, 2008). In the 7th EP, seven political groupings were formed covering an ideological spectrum from the radical left to the extreme right, including centre-left (S&D) to centre-right parties (EPP-ED), the liberals (ALDE), environmentalists and regionalists (Greens/EFA), and anti-Europeans and Eurosceptics (Burns, 2013, p. 166; Hix et al., 2007). Thereby, the centre-right Christian Democrats and Conservative European People's Party (EPP) and the centre-left Group of the Progressive Alliance of Socialists & Democrats (S&D) constituted not only the two largest transnational groups in the 7th EP but were also the two main dominating parties throughout the past six parliaments (Corbett et al., 2016). In contrast to national political groups, the political groups in the EP are of transnational character. They are far more heterogeneous than their national counterparts constituting aggregations of national party delegations (over 176 national parties in the 7th EP) and being composed of parliamentarians from different EU member states who share 'the same broad ideological convictions' (Burns, 2013, p. 165; Sabbati, 2014). Hence, in the EP, parties are not formed along national lines but 'around traditional socio-economic and ideological cleavages' (Hix et al., 2007, p. 217).

Research on the transnational political groups has concentrated on their development over time (e.g. Bardi, 1992; Raunio, 1997), their internal organisation and cohesion (e.g. Hix, Kreppel, & Noury, 2003; Hix & Lord, 1997), their role in the EP's legislative organisation and in the voting behaviour of MEPs (e.g. Hix et al., 2007; Kreppel, 2002), as well as on coalition formation within the EP (e.g. Hix & Høyland, 2013; Kreppel & Hix, 2003; Kreppel & Tsebelis, 1999), and their impact on the EP's legislative decision-making (e.g. Lindberg, 2008; Lindberg et al., 2008). These works have shown that the cohesion of the political groups has grown over time, 'especially since the early 1990s' (Hix, 2008, p. 1256). Thus, today the political groups are coherent organisations with defined policy goals and the ability 'to shape the behaviour of their members' (e.g. voting behaviour) (Hix et al., 2007, p. 52; Raunio, 1997). They play a central role in setting the parliamentary agenda, in the organisation of parliamentary committees, and thus in the establishment of a division of labour among MEPs, for instance through the allocation of rapporteurships as shown by the work of Yordanova (2011) and Kaeding (2004, 2005). Recently, research on the parliamentary committees and political groups has been accompanied by studies on certain central actors within committees and transnational groups, such as party group coordinators (Daniel & Thierse, 2017; Kaeding & Obholzer, 2012) or (shadow) rapporteurs (Benedetto, 2005; Hurka, Kaeding, & Obholzer, 2015; Yoshinaka, McElroy, & Bowler, 2010). In sum, the official structures of the EP are very well illuminated.[12] But there is very little on the life of the EP, 'looking beyond the description of its formal' and institutional structures (Priestley, 2008, p. xi).

Aim of the Book

Accordingly, the aim of the book is twofold:

Empirically, the ambition is to explore the phenomenon 'Intergroups' through the perceptions and interactions of MEPs in these cross-party, cross-committee groupings. The objective is to provide original and comprehensive, yet nuanced data on the meaning and motives MEPs attach to their Intergroup activities. The phenomenon 'Intergroup' shows that the EP as an institution 'does not do anything by itself; it is the people as everyday political agents who make' the EP happen (Kauppi, 2011, p. 150). Arguing that in the case of the EP and Intergroups individual choice might not be necessarily institutionally set, but influenced by the very person and his or her social characteristics, the social practices of MEPs, their perceptions and frames through which they interpret reality need to be analysed to deepen our understanding of how the EP works (Kauppi, 2005, 2011). Knowing that time is a scarce resource of MEPs and that parliamentary committees already cover some of the subjects mentioned above, one wonders: Why do MEPs dedicate their precious time to Intergroups? Why do they engage in something that is not an official body of the EP and thus, not part of the official legislative process? Institutional theory of political behaviour suggests that MEPs' behaviour is 'influenced primarily by three different sorts of career goals', namely: re-election, policy and office (Hix et al., 1999, p. 12). Thereby, re-election is presented as the main goal of MEPs, while policy and office goals are perceived as strategies to accomplish this goal. Taking into account Corbett et al. (2011) instancing personal, constituency and national concerns for MEPs' activities in Intergroups, this work assumes that MEPs as legislators display strategic and goal-oriented behaviour and that the engagement in Intergroups must have some benefits for MEPs. This aspect is further discussed in Chapter 2 outlining the theoretical framework of the study.

Theoretically, this work is inspired by the latest return of sociological concerns in EU studies. For an overview, see Favell and Guiraudon (2011), Kauppi (2013, 2018), and Zimmermann and Favell (2011). Consequently, it applies a political sociological approach to the EP to account for 'the informal practices, symbolic representation and power relations of social actors' (Jenson & Mérand, 2010, p. 74). In particular, it refers to scholars known under the label of the Strasbourg school emerging from French political science, e.g. Georgakakis and Rowell (2013), Georgakakis and Weisbein (2010), Kauppi (2011), Beauvallet and Michon (2010), and Beauvallet, Lepaux, and Michon (2013). In line with the Strasbourg school, this study draws on the analytical toolbox of the French sociologist Pierre Bourdieu, containing the three-interrelated concepts of field, capital and habitus, and their recent applications in European integration studies, to analyse the EP from a sociological perspective as a transnational field (Adler-Nissen, 2015; Busby, 2013; Kauppi, 2011). This means that the EP is conceptualised as a more or less structured space for action, as a field of struggles in which various agents, driven by their habitus, mobilise different forms of capital to position themselves vis-à-vis other agents in the field (Favell & Guiraudon, 2011). By employing a political sociological framework, political actions and strategies (including practices) of individuals are linked to structural locations and social characteristics to reveal how individuals shape structures (power relationships) within the parliamentary space and subsequently determine political outcomes (Kauppi, 2005).

Argument of the Book

Based on extensive fieldwork in the EP (including semi-structured interviews and observations) in combination with the statistical analysis of MEPs' sociopolitical characteristics, this book forwards the following argument with regard to MEPs engagement in Intergroups:

In line with its Bourdieusian-inspired theoretical framework, the study demonstrates how MEPs acquire different forms of capital, i.e. social capital (e.g. interpersonal relations), informational capital (e.g. expert, organisational and political knowledge) and political capital (e.g. reputation, prestige or posts) through their interactions in Intergroups. These forms of social resources are not perceived as independent from each other but as mutually reinforcing. Social capital is converted into informational capital by MEPs and both forms are used to gain political capital, which constitutes the specific resource of the political field. Thereby, this book argues that MEPs' engagement in Intergroups is primarily driven by their own policy goals, and the perception of an asymmetry of certain interests being marginalised on the parliamentary agenda to the advantage of others. As a result, this book shows further, how MEPs mobilise these acquired resources to foster opinion-formation in the Parliament, to shape EP policy outcomes as well as the parliamentary agenda in favour of the cause of the Intergroup. In this way, the engagement of MEPs in Intergroups becomes an example of an internal power struggle on the prerogative of interpretation of parliamentary practices and politics at the supranational level.

Relevance of the Book

In this way, the book has relevance along several lines and literatures: On the empirical level, the study sheds light on the informal dimension of legislative and procedural activities in the EP. This is highly relevant as 'the rules of the game of Brussels policymaking are not codified in law, [but] operate through informal processes relying on cultural competence and symbolic capital [...]' as the anthropologist Cris Shore argues in an interview on the necessity of ethnographic fieldwork in Brussels (Mundell, 2010, p. 2). Consequently, informal practices need to be considered in the assessment of EP politics and their impact on EU decision-making. The rising numbers of Intergroups pointing to the continuous and increasing engagement of MEPs in Intergroups show that there is much more going on in the EP than an exclusive focus on its official organs and formal procedures may reveal (see Chapter 3). In contrast, academic research on Intergroups and on MEPs' activities in Intergroups has only been marginally addressed in EP contemporary research and is close to non-existent. Through extensive field research, this study provides new insights and original empirical data.

In this way, the book simultaneously fills an existing gap in EP research and adds to research on parliamentary organisation at large. In opening up the institutional black box of the EP, zooming in on its members and providing further insights into how MEPs practice and organise their work beyond the formal structures, this study is of relevance to research on legislative organisation and accounts for research on the informal dimension of EU politics becoming ever more relevant

(Christiansen & Neuhold, 2012, 2013; Christiansen & Piattoni, 2004; Kleine, 2013). In addition, it is of high importance to the discussion of the EU's democratic deficit. Drawing on arguments made in legislative research, the question of how the EP can capitalise on for instance its rise in legislative powers within the EU institutional triangle and vis-à-vis the Council depends also 'upon how the internal organization of the EP itself is worked out' (Bowler & Farrell, 1995, p. 219). Given the rising numbers of Intergroups and MEPs' activities in Intergroups, these belong to the EP's internal organisation and thus, to the question of how the EP can take advantage of its rise in competences. Moreover, analysing how MEPs practice their mandate and studying the underlying meaning guiding these practices will deepen our understanding of how the EP works, why it works the way it does and thereby, deliver an input to the analysis of the democratic deficit in the EU as it reveals the practices that may (re-)produce this deficit.

On the theoretical and conceptual level, this study is relevant as its political sociological framework is informed by structural constructivism, which is a fairly new theoretical approach applied to EU studies (Kauppi, 2005). Adapting the Bourdieusian concepts of field, capital and habitus, which have been developed in the context of the French nation state society to a supranational institution, this study contributes to a refinement and specification of these concepts. In particular, this book argues that the Bourdieusian antagonist interpretation of the concept of field does not grasp the social reality and relations of MEPs in the EP. In this context, the study presents a reading of the concept that accounts for the consensus-style of EU decision-making as well as for the interplay between cooperation and competition present in EP politics. Moreover, this book offers a new interpretation of the concept of informational capital, which in the Bourdieusian coinage originally designated statistics. Applied to the EP and MEP's actions in Intergroups, this research offers an innovative modification of informational capital as comprising three different dimensions of knowledge: expert, organisational and political knowledge. Through these conceptual advancements, the book adds to the discussion on how a Bourdieu-inspired political sociology can be applied in EU studies. In advocating an interdisciplinary and multi-method research approach, this book promotes not only EU studies as 'an inherently interdisciplinary field', but also contributes further to the argument that research on EU affairs may benefit from 'drawing on analytical strategies and research methods derived from across the social sciences' (Favell & Guiraudon, 2011, p. 24; Lynggaard, Manners, & Löfgren, 2015, pp. 3–4).

In addition, this book goes beyond the two recent works on Intergroups by Ringe et al. (2013) and Nedergaard and Jensen (2014) along the following lines:

While Ringe et al. (2013) and Nedergaard and Jensen (2014) analyse Intergroups from a network theory perspective (Nedergaard & Jensen, 2014) or by means of social network analysis (Ringe et al., 2013) the present study takes an actor-centred political sociological perspective on MEPs' activities in Intergroups. This allows for a more holistic approach to the study of political behaviour or rather of political practices combining social characteristics, structural positions and actions of MEPs within one conceptual framework. Here, the aspects of social characteristics of MEPs, existing hierarchies and power struggles in the EP, are stressed to a greater degree than in Ringe et al. (2013) or Nedergaard and Jensen (2014).[13]

In contrast to Ringe et al. (2013)[14] and Nedergaard and Jensen (2014), the present study draws not only on qualitative interview data, but also on original and first-hand insights from observations gained through the personal attendance of Intergroup meetings in the EP, as well as from the analysis of Intergroup and EP Bureau minutes. As a result, this book offers additional insights on the institutionalisation of Intergroups over time (Chapter 3). Since interviews have been conducted with MEPs, EP officials and representatives of civil society, the study presents several perspectives on MEPs' engagement in Intergroups and thereby, explores the phenomenon from different angles as well as through different methods, aiming for a more holistic picture of MEPs in Intergroups. Additionally, this study devotes more attention to Intergroup chairs and members as different social groups within Intergroups as done in previous research by Ringe et al. (2013) and Nedergaard and Jensen (2014). In this way, the book reveals differences among Intergroup chairs and members with regard to the different forms of capital being sought and subsequently utilised by them in and through Intergroups. Moreover, by supplementing interview data with data generated through observational methods, this study calls more attention to the fact that attendance of Intergroup meetings is substantially lower than membership lists by the EP might suggest. This is an important insight when discussing Intergroups as an actual practice of MEPs.

A Sociological Approach to the European Parliament

Taking a sociological stance on the EP means not playing institutional approaches off sociological approaches and vice versa. It is more that sociological approaches allow us to pose different questions and to construct different research objects (see also Favell & Guiraudon, 2011). Hence, the focus of attention is set on what lies beneath the iceberg, to use the words of Fligstein (2008, p. 9) comparing the EU to an iceberg 'whose underlying structural foundations [...] are rarely studied by mainstream scholar of EU studies'. In particular, this book argues that EU institutionalism could benefit from sociological thinking in three aspects: with regard to the role of actors, their motives and the attention paid to social relations and structured practices.

Initially, actors have always played a major role in EU integration theories which is reflected in a wealth of actor-centred studies on EU institutions; see for instance, Gary Marks' call for an actor-centred approach to multilevel governance (Marks, 1996). The sociological perspective employed in this book criticises, however, the reduction of actors to either '*homo oeconomicus* who reacts to market signals' as conceptualised by rational-choice institutionalists or 'to place-markers in systems of norms' as conceptualised by constructivist institutionalists (Jenson & Mérand, 2010, p. 86). In contrast, it is argued that social features reinforce strategic choices and social actions. These social factors provide actors with choice and action with more 'varied foundations than a simple calculation of optimality' (Jenson & Mérand, 2010, p. 78). Moreover, by attributing an independent 'influence of norms on actors', constructivist institutionalists de-emphasise the 'social dimensions of strategy and the often conflict-ridden nature of relations among actors engaged in the construction of norms' (Jenson & Mérand, 2010, p. 79) A sociological perspective to actors argues for the concept of embedded agency (Kauppi, 2011). This means that social actions and strategic choice 'never take place in a social vacuum but rather in socially structured fields of action' (Kauppi, 2011, p. 156). The 'strategies of *homo sociologicus* are always socially embedded' (Jenson & Mérand, 2010, p. 79).

With regard to the motives of actors, EU institutionalism could benefit from an inclusive, reflexive ontology (see Kauppi, 2010). An inclusive ontology aims to go beyond the established dichotomies of an exclusive ontological framework, i.e. beyond the dualism between objectivism and subjectivism, institution and individual, calculation and socialisation. Hereby, a relational approach to the study of the EU is advocated that accounts for the interactive and dynamic character of its institutions, and the groups and individuals 'inhabiting them' and studies both actors and context in a dialectical, more holistic fashion (Kauppi, 2010, p. 19). In this way, an inclusive, reflexive ontology allows to explore nuances of empirical reality (Jenson & Mérand, 2010, p. 85).

With regard to social relations and structured practices, a sociological contribution to EU institutionalism points out 'that power structures' or, respectively, unequal power relations 'exist and have effects' on the creation of institutions (Jenson & Mérand, 2010, p. 87). Looking at the institutional rise of the EP over the past four decades, since 1979, it shows that the MEPs have been constantly involved in power struggles. Internally, members fought, e.g. for a Members' Statute. Externally, MEPs fought for enhanced legislative oversight and budget powers vis-à-vis the Council and the European Commission (Priestley, 2008). This empirical observation supports the pursuit of a political sociological approach that 'concentrates on the study of power and the junction of personality, social structure, and politics' (Adler-Nissen, 2009, p. 79).

In sum, the methodological strategy of the book is based on an inclusive, reflexive ontology (see Kauppi, 2010). It departs from the assumption that social reality is constructed through the dialectical relationship between structure and agency. Based on this methodological paradigm, the structural constructivist theory of politics informs this research (Kauppi, 2005). It is believed that reality is constructed by agents who, constrained by material and symbolic structures, struggle to accumulate social resources (Kauppi, 2003).

Research Methods and Data

Drawing on political sociology in the conceptual framework, a mixed methods approach combining quantitative and qualitative research methods is employed in this study (e.g. Johnson, Onwuegbuzie, & Turner, 2007). Given the lack of prior systematic empirical research on Intergroups and the interest in the perceptions, meanings and practices of MEPs, fieldwork is of central importance to this project. Drawing on qualitative research methods, extensive fieldwork on the premises of the EP in Brussels and Strasbourg was conducted in September and October 2012, in March and May 2013 as well as in February 2014. This included semi-structured (elite) interviews (e.g. Dexter, 1970; Littig, 2009; Puwar, 1997; Richards, 1996) and observational methods (e.g. Bray, 2008; Bryman, 2012; Flick, 2006). These qualitative techniques were combined with the quantitative analysis of MEP biographies, i.e. their socio-demographic and political features, based on their profiles on the 'MEPs - Section' of the Parliament's website (European Parliament, 2013b). The statistical analysis aims to reveal the 'structural locations and social resources' of MEPs and to link these to (political) actions and strategies (understood as tactics) of individual parliamentarians (e.g. participation and maintenance of Intergroups) as well as to political outcomes (Kauppi, 2005, p. 39). By means of this mixed method approach, the micro-, meso- and macro-levels of the analysis are linked. It is ensured that the institution—the EP—is not detached from the individuals working in it and vice versa. In doing so, an actor-centred and context-sensitive, and hence, more holistic approach to the study of EU affairs is realised in this study (Lynggaard et al., 2015, p. 5). Overall, an interpretive approach to social science research is pursued in this study.

The scope of the study is limited to the MEPs and the 27 officially recognised Intergroups in the 7th EP (2009–2014). With the purpose of exploring the field and achieving breadth and depth, data were generated across the 27 Intergroups and within Intergroups. Thereby, semi-structured elite interviews with MEPs, EP officials and representatives of civil society organisations (CSOs) constitute the main empirical source of this project. In total, 42 semi-structured interviews with MEPs (28), assistants (4), EP officials (4)[15] and representatives of CSOs (6) were conducted (see Appendix B). Interview partners were selected by means of purposive sampling (Bryman, 2012; Mason, 2002). More precisely, the selection of MEPs for the interviews took place on two levels (i.e. the meso-/context and micro-/participant level). Initially, all sitting chairs/co-chairs of the 27 officially recognised Intergroups in the 7th EP were selected to achieve breadth within the sample and to cover the entire population of Intergroup chairs/co-chairs. In total, 17 Intergroup chairs/co- and vice-chairs have been interviewed.[16] In this way, more than half of the entire population of Intergroup is covered in this book.[17] Subsequently, the focus was set on MEPs within four selected Intergroups (e.g. 'Trade Union', 'Urban', 'Welfare and Conservation of Animals'[18] and 'Wine, Fruits and Vegetables, Tradition and Quality Food/Viticulture'[19]). These Intergroups were selected according to a maximum variation sampling strategy (see Teddlie &

Tashakkori, 2009). They vary in their degree of formalisation: from being a very formalised Intergroup with an external bureau, monthly meetings, website, minutes and a large bureau structure (e.g. 'Animal Welfare' Intergroup), to being a less formalised Intergroup with an internal bureau, no monthly meetings, no website, no minutes and a small bureau structure (e.g. 'Viticulture' Intergroup). The four Intergroups vary further with regard to the policy areas that are covered by their themes. Thereby, the decision to deliberately choose an Intergroup from social, environmental, agricultural and regional policy was based on the reasoning to link the book to up to date EP research.[20] Moreover, the literature on MEPs' behaviour in EP committees suggests that MEPs' goals (office, policy and re-election) and their strategies to act may be influenced by the power structure of the EU, i.e. the areas of competence (exclusive, shared and/or no competence) in the respective policy field. For example, MEPs pursuing primarily policy goals may be particularly interested in working in policy fields where the EP enjoys co-legislative powers (see Whitaker, 2011 on EP committees). Similar patterns may apply to their informal engagement in Intergroups. Thereby, MEPs were selected along the criteria of being 'most likely' or 'least likely' to fulfil an expectation in line with the conceptual framework of the study (Flyvbjerg, 2011; Gerring, 2007). Thus, sampling of MEPs within Intergroups was based on the underlying assumption that structural locations and social characteristics condition and constrain MEPs' behaviour and actions with regard to their Intergroup participation. Consequently, 'most likely' cases are those MEPs whose committee membership and previous professional experience/occupation or educational background matched the Intergroup activities or subject.[21]

Interviews were analysed in two steps. It started with thematic indexing of the interview transcripts by means of descriptive and structural coding to set up an inventory of topics covered during the interviews (Miles, Huberman, & Saldaña, 2014). A common dilemma in qualitative research consists of how to deal with prior empirical and theoretical knowledge in the process of data analysis without elapsing into a hypothetico-deductive approach. Following Blumer's (1954) idea of 'sensitizing concepts', Kelle and Kluge (2010) propose to employ a coding scheme in which theoretical concepts are used as heuristic categories that are empirically less contentful, and which are enriched, specified and refined through empirical analysis of the qualitative data. These are complemented with empirically contentful categories in case they match those found in the data. Hence, in the present research project, the sociological concepts (e.g. capital, habitus and field) introduced in the conceptual framework (see Chapter 2) were used as heuristic categories in the coding scheme.

In a second step (after the indexing of themes and topics), only those topics relevant for the exploration of the research question and to which conceptual linkages could be established in an iterative manner were selected for further analysis and interpretation. This step was justified through the problem-driven nature of the research project, as well as the amount of data gathered in the interviews, which made a pragmatic approach to data management and analysis necessary. In this second step, the descriptive codes were merged and subsumed into themes (see Saldaña, 2013 on thematic analysis), and the empirically less contentful heuristic categories were empirically filled, refined and specified. Overall, coding constituted an iterative process in the data analysis and a constant back and forth between data and concepts.[22]

For the quantitative analysis, the sociopolitical characteristics of 77 MEPs were analysed. This included the analysis of socio-demographic features of MEPs (e.g. age, gender, nationality, education and past occupation) as well as of institutional positions of the respective parliamentarians (e.g. posts and positions in EP leadership and official organs). Data selection was conducted for two samples (e.g. for context and for participants, see Bryman, 2012) and took place at two levels (meso- and micro-level). Initially, all chairs and co-chairs of the 27 officially registered Intergroups of the 7th EP, also including those MEPs who resigned during the 7th term and their successors were selected for the statistical analysis to account for MEPs across Intergroups and to achieve breadth within the research project. These added up to 48 MEPs. Subsequently, the most active MEPs (selected participants) from the four Intergroups (selected context) were chosen to analyse biographical data of parliamentarians from within Intergroups with the aim of providing an insight into social characteristics of MEPs within Intergroups and contributing to the depth of the research project. These added up to 29 MEPs (see Appendix A).[23] Given the small-scale sample of 77 MEPs, the data were analysed by means of descriptive statistics (Blaxter, Hughes, & Tight, 2001; Johnson, Reynolds, & Mycoff, 2008; McNabb, 2010).

Drawing on political sociology and a mixed methods approach, this book reveals a link between prior professional occupation, educational background (partially) and Intergroup commitment in the case of the

MEPs in the Intergroups 'Trade Union', 'Urban' and 'Viticulture'. This link points to a practice of MEPs to seek Intergroup assignments where they can draw on previous work experience and have substantial personal interest. Moreover, it shows that it is mainly MEPs with less institutionalised political capital, that is with less valued or no posts in official parliamentary bodies, who join Intergroups. In this way, it is primarily MEPs who are structurally disadvantaged in the field, who engage in Intergroups. These interpretations appear to be consistent with the research conducted by Ringe et al. (2013) arguing that more non-leaders than leaders join Intergroups.

Outline of the Book

In Chapter 2, the conceptual framework of the study is developed. Introducing structural constructivism as theoretical backbone of this study, the EP is subsequently sketched as a transnational political field in this chapter. Within this transnational political field, MEPs are conceptualised as multipositional entrepreneurs who struggle to acquire a variety of social resources, in particular social, informational and political capital. This chapter suggests conceptual specifications and modifications with regard to the concepts of field and capital.

The following Chapter 3 provides a general introduction to Intergroups in the EP. It outlines their development over time, their process of regulation and institutionalisation since the mid-1990s and gives an insight into their diversity in terms of size, objectives, internal organisation and working methods. In line with the theoretical framework of this book that seeks to connect political strategies of actors to their structural locations and social characteristics, Chapter 4 explores the sociopolitical features of those MEPs maintaining and participating in Intergroups. The statistical analysis of MEPs' social configurations and political backgrounds reveals what kind of social resources (e.g. forms of capital) these parliamentarians have at their disposal when engaging in Intergroups, and which positions they occupy in the transnational field. Succeeding the statistical analysis of MEP's biographies, the following Chapters 5–7 establish the main argument of the book. They build on one another as they demonstrate initially what kind of capital is accumulated to show further, how different forms of capital are converted and mobilised for the cause of the Intergroup. Chapter 5 argues for a conceptualisation of Intergroups as bridging social capital, i.e. as outward-looking, heterogeneous social groupings that resemble professional ties of acquaintance. It examines the membership in and composition of Intergroups, looks at the durability and regularity with which social interactions are practised by MEPs in Intergroups and discusses the notion of trust as an important component of social capital. Subsequently, Chapter 6 demonstrates how MEPs through Intergroups acquire informational capital. The chapter offers an innovative conceptual modification of the Bourdieusian concept of informational capital that is composed of expert, organisational and political knowledge. In this way, the chapter provides a more comprehensive and holistic conceptualisation of not only information but knowledge going beyond the terms of policy information and political information used in theories of legislative organisation. Based on the conceptualisation of Intergroups as bridging social capital and informational capital, Chapter 7 is dedicated to the conversion and mobilisation of the acquired social resources. It shows how MEPs use social and informational capital to gain political capital, i.e. increased visibility and reputation. Moreover, it demonstrates how MEPs mobilise political capital in combination with their acquired bridging social capital and informational capital to foster opinion-formation in the EP, and to shape the parliamentary agenda and reports in favour of the cause of the Intergroup. The final Chapter 8 reflects upon the empirical and conceptual advances made in this study, provides an outlook to the future of Intergroups in the EP, and points to avenues for further research.

Notes

1. Hereinafter referred to as 'Council'.
2. In comparison, the 19th German Bundestag (2017–2021) has 709 seats (German Bundestag, 2017). The British House of Commons has 650 seats (United Kingdom Parliament, 2015).
3. For an overview on the EP's empowerment, see Rittberger (2005), Corbett et al. (2016), and Burns (2016).
4. For an extended discussion, see Corbett et al. (2016), Ripoll Servent (2018), Judge & Earnshaw (2008), Rittberger (2005), Mény (2009), and Westlake (1995).
5. For an extended discussion, see Hix & Marsh (2011), Hix et al. (2007), and Hix et al. (1999).
6. For an extended discussion, see Kreppel (2002), McElroy (2006), Neuhold (2001), and Raunio (1997).

7. For an extended discussion, see for instance, research on EU trilogues by Roederer-Rynning & Greenwood (2017), as well as the work by Mühlböck & Rittberger (2015), Naurin & Rasmussen (2011), Priestley (2008), and Wiesner (2018).
8. Among those are: the 'European Constitution' Intergroup, the 'Animal Welfare' Intergroup, 'Health' Intergroup and 'Kangaroo' Group, see Corbett et al. (2007, pp. 188–190) and Dutoit (2001, pp. 66–75).
9. For an interesting discussion on the conceptual relationship between behaviour, action and practice, see Adler & Pouliot (2011).
10. One of the pioneers of anthropological studies on EU institutions is Abélès (1992) with his study on the European Parliament and European Commission. Another example is the study by Ross (1995) on the cabinet of former European Commission president Jacques Delors. For an overview, see Adler-Nissen (2016).
11. There are exceptional cases of MEPs serving in two committees or none, see Corbett et al. (2011, p. 146ff).
12. For the sake of completeness, it has to be noted that the EP is constituted by additional formal organs (e.g. parliamentary delegations) and different political bodies (e.g. the Conference of Presidents and the Bureau) which are responsible for the (legislative) organisation of the Parliament. For an insight into the parliamentary delegations and EP political bodies, see Corbett et al. (2016) and Judge and Earnshaw (2008).
13. For an interesting discussion on the comparability and compatibility of network theory and the Bourdieusian field approach, see Bernhard (2010) and Madsen (2002).
14. The study by Ringe et al. (2013) covers the following Intergroups: Sky and Space, Ageing and Intergenerational Solidarity, New Media, Public Services, Tibet and Social Economy as well as Extreme Poverty and Human Rights.
15. This includes EP quaestors, staff of political groups and EP officials (e.g. committee secretariats).
16. For the final data analysis, 13 out of 17 interviews were considered.
17. The following Intergroups are covered in this research: Welfare and Conservation of Animals, Wine, Fruits and Vegetables, Tradition and Quality Food/Viticulture, Trade Union, Urban, Western Sahara, Tibet, Disability, Baltic-Europe, Social Economy, SME "Small and Medium-Sized Enterprise", Ageing and Intergenerational Solidarity, Climate Change, Biodiversity and Sustainable Development, Extreme Poverty and Human Rights.
18. Hereinafter referred to as 'Animal Welfare' Intergroup.
19. Hereinafter referred to as 'Viticulture' Intergroup.

20. This is research on EU agricultural policy, see Roederer-Rynning (2015); on EU cohesion policy, see Bache (2015); on EU employment and social policy, see Rhodes (2015) as well as studies on EU environmental policy, see Jordan and Adelle (2013).
21. An example: An MEP who has been a member of the parliamentary committee on Regional Development (REGI), held a local or regional mandate prior to entering the EP (e.g. as mayor) and participates in the 'Urban' Intergroup, was selected as conforming to expectation. By contrast, MEPs who have not been members of REGI, had no local or regional mandate prior to entering the EP and participate in the 'Urban' Intergroup resemble 'least likely' cases.
22. The reliability of the coding process was assessed by fellow researchers in regular intervals, such as in two workshops on the analysis of qualitative data at BIGSSS in June and November 2013, during annual presentations in colloquiums, several conferences (e.g. HEIRS conference 2013 in Sønderborg, Denmark; ECPR conference 2014 in Vienna, Austria; CNRS Summer School 2015 in Moulin d'Andée, France) and through regular discussions with supervisors. Data analysis was supported through the application of the computer-based programme MAXQDA. I would like to thank the Bremen International Graduate School of Social Sciences for the provision of MAXQDA software.
23. The most active members were selected based on their attendance of Intergroup meetings and participation in collective actions on behalf of the Intergroup (e.g., initiation of written declarations). For the Intergroup 'Animal Welfare', those parliamentarians who attended at least, half of the 52 meetings during the 7th term were selected (Intergroup on the Welfare & Conservation of Animals, 2014). In addition, those MEPs whose names frequently appeared in common actions initiated by these MEPs on behalf of the Intergroup (see for instance their written declarations) were also selected. For the Intergroup 'Trade Union', the MEPs who attended at least one-third of the 31 meetings between September 2009 and April 2012 were chosen. For the Intergroups 'Viticulture' and 'Urban', the most active members were identified through interview statements, the personal attendance of Intergroup meetings, as well as through the analysis of photos taken during Intergroup meetings. These are available on the Audiovisual Services website of the EP (European Parliament, 2015b).

References

Abélès, M. (1992). *La vie quotidienne au Parlament européen*. Paris: Hachette.
Adler, E., & Pouliot, V. (2011). *International Practices*. Cambridge: Cambridge University Press.

Adler-Nissen, R. (2009). *The Diplomacy of Opting Out: British and Danish Stigma Management in the European Union* (PhD thesis). Copenhagen: University of Copenhagen.

Adler-Nissen, R. (2015). *Opting Out of the European Union: Diplomacy, Sovereignty and European Integration.* Cambridge: Cambridge University Press.

Adler-Nissen, R. (2016). Towards a Practice Turn in EU Studies: The Everyday of European Integration. *Journal of Common Market Studies, 54*(1), 87–103.

Andeweg, R. (1995). The Reshaping of National Party Systems. In J. Hayward (Ed.), *The Crisis of Representation in Europe* (pp. 58–78). London: Frank Cass.

Bache, I. (2015). Cohesion Policy: A New Direction for New Times. In H. Wallace, M. A. Pollack, & A. R. Young (Eds.), *Policy-Making in the European Union* (7th ed., pp. 243–262). Oxford: Oxford University Press.

Bale, T., & Taggart, P. (2006). *First-Timers Yes, Virgins No: The Roles and Backgrounds of New Members of the European Parliament* (SEI Working Paper No. 89), 1–30.

Bardi, L. (1992). Transnational Party Federations in the European Community. In R. S. Katz & P. Mair (Eds.), *Party Organizations: A Data Handbook on Party Organizations in Western Democracies, 1960–90* (pp. 931–973). London: Sage.

Beauvallet, W., Lepaux, V., & Michon, S. (2013). Who Are the MEPs? A Statistical Analysis of the Backgrounds of Members of European Parliament (2004–2014) and of Their Transformations. *Études Européennes*, 1–12.

Beauvallet, W., & Michon, S. (2010). Professionalization and Socialization of the Members of the European Parliament. *French Politics, 8*(2), 145–165.

Benedetto, G. (2005). Rapporteurs as Legislative Entrepreneurs: The Dynamics of the Codecision Procedure in Europe's Parliament. *Journal of European Public Policy, 12*(1), 67–88.

Bernhard, S. (2010). Netzwerkanalyse und Feldtheorie: Grundriss einer Integration im Rahmen von Bourdieus Sozialtheorie. In C. Stegbauer (Ed.), *Netzwerkanalyse und Netzwerktheorie: Ein neues Paradigma in den Sozialwissenschaften* (pp. 121–130). Wiesbaden: VS Verlag für Sozialwissenschaften.

Blaxter, L., Hughes, C., & Tight, M. (2001). *How to Research* (2nd ed.). Buckingham: Open University Press.

Blumer, H. (1954). What Is Wrong with Social Theory. *American Sociological Review, 18*, 3–10.

Bouwen, P. (2003). A Theoretical and Empirical Study of Corporate Lobbying in the European Parliament. *European Integration Online Papers (EIoP), 7*(11), 1–17. Retrieved from www.eiop.or.at/eiop/texte/2003-011a.htm.

Bowler, S., & Farrell, D. M. (1995). The Organizing of the European Parliament: Committees, Specialization and Co-ordination. *British Journal of Political Science, 25*(02), 219–243.

Bray, Z. (2008). Ethnographic Approaches. In D. Della Porta & M. Keating (Eds.), *Approaches and Methodologies in the Social Sciences: A Pluralist Perspective* (pp. 296–315). Cambridge and New York: Cambridge University Press.

Bryman, A. (2012). *Social Research Methods* (4th ed.). Oxford: Oxford University Press.

Burns, C. J. (2013). The European Parliament. In M. Cini & N. Perez-Solorzano Borragan (Eds.), *European Union Politics* (4th ed., pp. 159–171). Oxford: Oxford University Press.

Burns, C. J. (2016). The European Parliament. In M. Cini & N. Perez-Solorzano Borragan (Eds.), *European Union Politics* (5th ed., pp. 155–166). Oxford: Oxford University Press.

Busby, A. (2013). *The Everyday Practice and Performance of European Politics: An Ethnography of the European Parliament* (PhD thesis). Sussex: University of Sussex.

Christiansen, T., & Neuhold, C. (Eds.). (2012). *International Handbook on Informal Governance*. Cheltenham, UK and Northampton, MA: Edgar Elgar.

Christiansen, T., & Neuhold, C. (2013). Informal Politics in the EU. *Journal of Common Market Studies, 51*(6), 1196–1206.

Christiansen, T., & Piattoni, S. (2004). *Informal Governance in the European Union*. Northampton, MA: Edward Elgar.

Corbett, R., Jacobs, F., & Neville, D. (2016). *The European Parliament* (9th ed.). London: John Harper Publishing.

Corbett, R., Jacobs, F., & Shackleton, M. (2000). *The European Parliament* (4th ed.). London: John Harper Publishing.

Corbett, R., Jacobs, F., & Shackleton, M. (2007). *The European Parliament* (7th ed.). London: John Harper Publishing.

Corbett, R., Jacobs, F., & Shackleton, M. (2011). *The European Parliament* (8th ed.). London: John Harper Publishing.

Crespo Allen, M. (1996). *Rules on Lobbying and Intergroups in the National Parliaments of the Member States*. Luxembourg: European Parliament.

Crum, B. (2012). The European Parliament as a Driving Force in Informal Institution-Building: The Hard Case of the EP's Relation with the High Representative for the CFSP. In T. Christiansen & C. Neuhold (Eds.), *International Handbook on Informal Governance* (pp. 354–373). Cheltenham: Edward Elgar.

Daniel, W. T., & Thierse, S. (2017). Individual Determinants for the Selection of Group Coordinators in the European Parliament. *Journal of Common Market Studies, 56*(4), 939–954.

Dexter, L. A. (1970). *Elite and Specialized Interviewing*. Evanston: Northwestern University Press.

Dutoit, L. (2001). *Les Intergroupes au Parlement Européen* (MA thesis). Genève: Institut Européen de l' Université de Genève.

Dutoit, L. (2009). *Parlement Européen et Société Civile: Vers de Nouveaux Aménagements Institutionnels*. Louvain-la-Neuve: Bruylant-Academia.

European Parliament. (2013a). *About Parliament: Organisation and Work—Intergroups*. Retrieved 24 January 2013, from http://www.europarl.europa.eu/about-parliament/en/00c9d93c87/Intergroups.html.

European Parliament. (2013b). *MEPs*. Retrieved 16 December 2013, from http://www.europarl.europa.eu/meps/en/map.html.

European Parliament. (2015a). *About Parliament: Organisation and Rules—Multilingualism*. Retrieved 1 July 2015, from http://www.europarl.europa.eu/aboutparliament/en/20150201PVL00013/Multilingualism.

European Parliament. (2015b). *Audiovisual Services for Media*. Retrieved 20 November 2015, from http://audiovisual.europarl.europa.eu/.

European Parliament. (2017). *About Parliament—Organisation and Rules*. Retrieved 22 November 2017, from www.europarl.europa.eu/aboutparliament/en/20150201PVL00010/Organisation-and-rules.

European Parliament. (2018). *About Parliament: Powers and Procedures—Legislative Powers*. Retrieved 4 May 2018, from http://www.europarl.europa.eu/aboutparliament/en/20150201PVL00004/Powers-and-procedures.

Farrell, H., & Héritier, A. (2003). Formal and Informal Institutions Under Codecision: Continuous Constitution-Building in Europe. *Governance, 16*(4), 577–600.

Favell, A., & Guiraudon, V. (2011). *Sociology of the European Union*. Basingstoke: Palgrave Macmillan.

Flick, U. (2006). *An Introduction to Qualitative Research* (3rd ed.). London: Sage.

Fligstein, N. (2008). *Euroclash: The EU, European Identity and the Future of Europe*. Oxford: Oxford University Press.

Flyvbjerg, B. (2011). Case Study. In N. K. Denzin & Y. S. Lincoln (Eds.), *The Sage Handbook of Qualitative Research* (pp. 301–316). Thousand Oaks, CA: Sage.

Franklin, M. N., & Scarrow, S. (1999). Making Europeans? The Socializing Power of the European Parliament. In R. S. Katz & B. Wessels (Eds.), *The European Parliament, National Parliaments, and European Integration* (pp. 45–60). Oxford: Oxford University Press.

Georgakakis, D., & Rowell, J. (Eds.). (2013). *Field of Eurocracy: The Mapping EU Actors and Professionals*. Basingstoke: Palgrave Macmillan.

Georgakakis, D., & Weisbein, J. (2010). From Above and from Below: A Political Sociology of European Actors. *Comparative European Politics, 8*(1), 93–109.

Gerring, J. (2007). *Case Study Research: Principles and Practices.* New York: Cambridge University Press.

Greenwood, J. (2003). *Interest Representation in the European Union.* Basingstoke: Palgrave Macmillan.

Greenwood, J. (2007). *Interest Representation in the European Union* (2nd ed.). Basingstoke: Palgrave Macmillan.

Häge, F. M., & Kaeding, M. (2007). Reconsidering the European Parliament's Legislative Influence: Formal vs. Informal Procedures. *Journal of European Integration, 29*(3), 341–361.

Héritier, A. (2012). Formal and Informal Institutions in the EU's Legislative Process. In T. Christiansen & C. Neuhold (Eds.), *International Handbook on Informal Governance* (pp. 335–353). Cheltenham: Edward Elgar.

Hix, S. (2008). Towards a Partisan Theory of EU Politics. *Journal of European Public Policy, 15*(8), 1254–1265.

Hix, S., & Høyland, B. (2013). Empowerment of the European Parliament. *Annual Review of Political Science, 16,* 171–189.

Hix, S., Kreppel, A., & Noury, A. G. (2003). The Party System in the European Parliament: Collusive or Competitive? *Journal of Common Market Studies, 41*(2), 309–331.

Hix, S., & Lord, C. (1997). *Political Parties in the European Union.* New York: St. Martin's Press.

Hix, S., & Marsh, M. (2011). Second-Order Effects Plus Pan-European Political Swings: An Analysis of European Parliament Elections Across Time. *Electoral Studies, 30*(1), 4–15.

Hix, S., Noury, A. G., & Roland, G. (2007). *Democratic Politics in the European Parliament.* Cambridge: Cambridge University Press.

Hix, S., Raunio, T., & Roger, S. (1999). *An Institutional Theory of Behaviour in the European Parliament.* Paper Presented at the Joint Sessions of the European Consortium for Political Research.

Hix, S., Raunio, T., & Scully, R. (2003). Fifty Years On: Research on the European Parliament. *Journal of Common Market Studies, 41*(2), 191–202.

Hobolt, S. B. (2014). A Vote for the President? The Role of Spitzenkandidaten in the 2014 European Parliament Elections. *Journal of European Public Policy, 21*(10), 1528–1540.

Hurka, S., Kaeding, M., & Obholzer, L. (2015). Learning on the Job? EU Enlargement and the Assignment of (Shadow) Rapporteurships in the European Parliament. *Journal of Common Market Studies, 53*(6), 1230–1247.

Intergroup on the Welfare & Conservation of Animals. (2014). *Intergroup Attendance September 2009—March 2014.* Retrieved 01 August 2014, from http://www.animalwelfareintergroup.eu/wp-content/uploads/2011/08/3-Intergroup-attendance-September-2009-March-2014.pdf.

Jacobs, F., & Corbett, R. (1990). *The European Parliament*. Harlow: Longman Current Affairs.
Jacobs, F., Corbett, R., & Shackleton, M. (1992). *The European Parliament* (2nd ed.). Harlow: Longman Current Affairs.
Jacobs, F., Corbett, R., & Shackleton, M. (1995). *The European Parliament* (3rd ed.). London: Cartermill.
Jenson, J., & Mérand, F. (2010). Sociology, Institutionalism and the European Union. *Comparative European Politics, 8*(1), 74–92.
Johnson, R. B., Onwuegbuzie, A. J., & Turner, L. A. (2007). Toward a Definition of Mixed Methods Research. *Journal of Mixed Methods Research, 1*(2), 112–133.
Johnson, J. B., Reynolds, H. T., & Mycoff, J. D. (2008). *Political Science Research Methods* (6th ed.). Washington, DC: CQ Press.
Jordan, A., & Adelle, C. (Eds.). (2013). *Environmental Policy in the EU: Actors, Institutions and Processes* (3rd ed.). London and New York: Routledge.
Judge, D., & Earnshaw, D. (2008). *The European Parliament* (2nd ed.). Basingstoke: Palgrave Macmillan.
Kaeding, M. (2004). Rapporteurship Allocation in the European Parliament: Information or Distribution? *European Union Politics, 5*(3), 353–371.
Kaeding, M. (2005). The World of Committee Reports: Rapporteurship Assignment in the European Parliament. *The Journal of Legislative Studies, 11*(1), 82–104.
Kaeding, M., & Obholzer, L. (2012). Pulling the Strings: Party Group Coordinators in the European Parliament. *EIPAScope, 1,* 13–18.
Katz, R. S. (1999). Role Orientations in Parliaments. In R. S. Katz & B. Wessels (Eds.), *The European Parliament, National Parliaments, and European Integration* (pp. 61–85). Oxford: Oxford University Press.
Kauppi, N. (2003). Bourdieu's Political Sociology and the Politics of European Integration. *Theory and Society, 32*(5/6), 775–789.
Kauppi, N. (2005). *Democracy, Social Resources and Political Power in the European Union*. Manchester: Manchester University Press.
Kauppi, N. (2010). The Political Ontology of European Integration. *Comparative European Politics, 8,* 19–36.
Kauppi, N. (2011). EU Politics. In A. Favell & V. Guiraudon (Eds.), *Sociology of the European Union* (pp. 150–171). Basingstoke: Palgrave Macmillan.
Kauppi, N. (Ed.). (2013). *A Political Sociology of Transnational Europe*. Colchester: ECPR Press.
Kauppi, N. (2018). *Toward a Reflexive Political Sociology of the European Union: Fields, Intellectuals and Politicians*. Cham: Palgrave Macmillan.
Kelle, U., & Kluge, S. (2010). *Vom Einzelfall zum Typus: Fallvergleich und Fallkontrastierung in der Qualitativen Sozialforschung*. Wiesbaden: VS Verlag für Sozialwissenschaften.

Kleine, M. (2013). *Informal Governance in the European Union: How Governments Make International Organizations Work*. Ithaca, NY: Cornell University Press.

Kohler-Koch, B. (1997). Organized Interests in the EC and the European Parliament. *European Integration Online Papers (EIoP), 1*(9), 1–27.

Kreppel, A. (2002). *The European Parliament and Supranational Party System: A Study in Institutional Development*. Cambridge: Cambridge University Press.

Kreppel, A., & Hix, S. (2003). From "Grand Coalition" to Left-Right Confrontation: Explaining the Shifting Structure of Party Competition in the European Parliament. *Comparative Political Studies, 36*(1/2), 75–96.

Kreppel, A., & Tsebelis, G. (1999). Coalition Formation in the European Parliament. *Comparative Political Studies, 32*(8), 933–966.

Landorff, L. (2010). *The Role and Function of Intergroups in the European Parliament: A Study on the Intergroup for Traditional National Minorities, Constitutional Regions and Regional Languages in the 6th Parliamentary Term (2004–2009)* (Unpublished MA thesis). Aarhus: University of Aarhus.

Lindberg, B. (2008). Are Political Parties Controlling Legislative Decision-Making in the European Parliament? The Case of the Services Directive. *Journal of European Public Policy, 15*(8), 1184–1204.

Lindberg, B., Rasmussen, A., & Warntjen, A. (2008). Party Politics as Usual? The Role of Political Parties in EU Legislative Decision-Making. *Journal of European Public Policy, 15*(8), 1107–1126.

Littig, B. (2009). Interviewing the Elite—Interviewing Experts: Is There a Difference? In A. Bogner, B. Littig, & W. Menz (Eds.), *Interviewing Experts* (pp. 98–113). Basingstoke: Palgrave Macmillan.

Lynggaard, K., Manners, I., & Löfgren, K. (2015). *Research Methods in European Union Studies*. Basingstoke: Palgrave Macmillan.

Madsen, M. R. (2002). Legal 'Field' or Legal 'Network'? A Bourdieusian Critique of Manuel Castells 'Network Society' *Retfærd. Nordisk Juridisk Tidsskrift, 4*, 4–18.

Mamadouh, V. D., & Raunio, T. (2003). The Committee System: Powers, Appointments and Report Allocation. *Journal of Common Market Studies, 41*(2), 333–351.

Marks, G. (1996). An Actor-Centered Approach to Multi-level Governance. *Regional and Federal Studies, 6*(2), 20–40.

Mason, J. (2002). *Qualitative Researching* (2nd ed.). London: Sage.

McElroy, G. (2006). Committee Representation in the European Parliament. *European Union Politics, 7*(1), 5–29.

McElroy, G. (2007). Legislative Politics as Normal? Voting Behaviour and Beyond in the European Parliament. *European Union Politics, 8*(3), 433–448.

McNabb, D. E. (2010). *Research Methods for Political Science: Quantitative and Qualitative Approaches* (2nd ed.). Armonk, NY: M.E. Sharpe.

Mény, Y. (2009). *Building Parliament: 50 Years of European Parliament History 1958–2008*. Luxembourg: Office for Official Publications of the European Communities.

Mérand, F. (2011). EU Policies. In A. Favell & V. Guiraudon (Eds.), *The Sociology of European Union* (pp. 172–192). Basingstoke: Palgrave Macmillan.

Miles, M. B., Huberman, A. M., & Saldaña, J. (2014). *Qualitative Data Analysis: A Methods Sourcebook* (3rd ed.). Thousand Oaks, CA: Sage.

Mühlböck, M., & Rittberger, B. (2015). The Council, the European Parliament, and the Paradox of Inter-institutional Cooperation. *European Integration Online Papers (EIoP), 19*(1), 1–20.

Mundell, I. (2010, October 13). An Ethnographic Perspective. *European Voice*. Retrieved from www.europeanvoice.com/article/imported/an-ethnographic-perspective-/69166.aspx.

Naurin, D., & Rasmussen, A. (2011). New External Rules, New Internal Games: How the EU Institutions Respond When Inter-institutional Rules Change. *West European Politics, 34*(1), 1–17.

Nedergaard, P., & Jensen, M. D. (2014). The Anatomy of Intergroups: Network Governance in the Political Engine Room of the European Parliament. *Policy Studies*, 1–19.

Neuhold, C. (2001). The 'Legislative Backbone' Keeping the Institution Upright? The Role of European Parliament Committees in the EU Policy-Making Process. *European Integration Online Papers (EIoP), 5*(10), 1–29.

Priestley, J. (2008). *Six Battles That Shaped Europe's Parliament*. London: John Harper Publishing.

Puwar, N. (1997). Reflections on Interviewing Women MPs. *Sociological Research Online, 2*(1).

Raunio, T. (1997). *The European Perspective: Transnational Party Groups in the 1989–1994 European Parliament*. Aldershot: Ashgate.

Reh, C., Héritier, A., Bressanelli, E., & Koop, C. (2011). The Informal Politics of Legislation: Explaining Secluded Decision Making in the European Union. *Comparative Political Studies, 46*(9), 1112–1142.

Rhodes, M. (2015). Employment Policy Between Efficacy and Experimentation. In H. Wallace, M. A. Pollack, & A. R. Young (Eds.), *Policy-Making in the European Union* (7th ed., pp. 293–318). Oxford: Oxford University Press.

Richards, D. (1996). Elite Interviewing: Approaches and Pitfalls. *Politics, 16*(3), 199–204.

Ringe, N. (2010). *Who Decides, and How? Preferences, Uncertainty, and Policy Choice in the European Parliament*. Oxford: Oxford University Press.

Ringe, N., Victor, J. N., & Carman, C. J. (2013). *Bridging the Information Gap: Legislative Member Organizations as Social Networks in the United States and the European Union*. Ann Arbor: University of Michigan Press.

Ripoll Servent, A. (2015). *Institutional and Policy Change in the European Parliament: Deciding on Freedom, Security and Justice*. Basingstoke: Palgrave Macmillan.

Ripoll Servent, A. (2018). *The European Parliament*. Basingstoke: Palgrave Macmillan.

Rittberger, B. (2005). *Building Europe's Parliament: Democratic Representation Beyond the Nation-State*. Oxford: Oxford University Press.

Roederer-Rynning, C. (2015). The Common Agricultural Policy: The Fortress Challenged. In H. Wallace, M. A. Pollack, & A. R. Young (Eds.), *Policy-Making in the European Union* (7th ed., pp. 196–219). Oxford: Oxford University Press.

Roederer-Rynning, C., & Greenwood, J. (2017). The European Parliament as a Developing Legislature: Coming of Age in Trilogues? *Journal of European Public Policy, 24*(5), 735–754.

Ross, G. (1995). *Jacques Delors and European Integration*. New York: Oxford University Press.

Sabbati, G. (2014). *European Parliament: Facts and Figures* (No. PE 542.150). Brussels: European Parliamentary Research Service.

Saldaña, J. (2013). *The Coding Manual for Qualitative Researchers* (2nd ed.). Los Angeles: Sage.

Scully, R. (2005). *Becoming Europeans? Attitudes, Behaviour, and Socialization in the European Parliament* (Repr. ed.). Oxford: Oxford University Press.

Scully, R., & Farrell, D. M. (2003). MEPs as Representatives: Individual and Institutional Roles. *Journal of Common Market Studies, 41*(2), 269–288.

Settembri, P., & Neuhold, C. (2009). Achieving Consensus Through Committees: Does the European Parliament Manage? *Journal of Common Market Studies, 47*(1), 127–151.

Teddlie, C., & Tashakkori, A. (2009). *Foundations of Mixed Methods Research: Integrating Quantitative and Qualitative Approaches in the Social and Behavioral Sciences*. Los Angeles: Sage.

United Kingdom Parliament. (2015). *MPs, Lords & Offices*. Retrieved 23 December 2015, from www.parliament.uk/mps-lords-and-offices/mps/.

Westlake, M. (1995). *A Modern Guide to the European Parliament* (Repr. ed.). London: Pinter.

Westlake, M. (2011). The European Parliament's Committees: National Party Influence and Legislative Empowerment. *The Journal of Legislative Studies, 17*(4), 559–560.

Whitaker, R. (2001). Party Control in a Committee-Based Legislature? The Case of the European Parliament. *The Journal of Legislative Studies, 7*(4), 63–88.

Whitaker, R. (2011). *The European Parliament's Committees: National Party Influence and Legislative Empowerment*. London: Routledge.

Wiesner, C. (2018). The Micro-Politics of Parliamentary Powers: European Parliament Strategies for Expanding Its Influence in the EU Institutional System. *Journal of European Integration, 40*(4), 375–391.

Yordanova, N. (2009). The Rationale Behind Committee Assignment in the European Parliament: Distributive, Informational and Partisan Perspectives. *European Union Politics, 10*(2), 253–280.

Yordanova, N. (2011). Inter-institutional Rules and Division of Power in the European Parliament: Allocation of Consultation and Co-decision Reports. *West European Politics, 34*(1), 97–121.

Yordanova, N. (2013). *Organising the European Parliament: The Role of Committees and their Legislative Influence.* Colchester: ECPR Press.

Yoshinaka, A., McElroy, G., & Bowler, S. (2010). The Appointment of Rapporteurs in the European Parliament. *Legislative Studies Quarterly, 35*(4), 457–486.

Zimmermann, A., & Favell, A. (2011). Governmentality, Political Field or Public Sphere? Theoretical Alternatives in the Political Sociology of the EU. *European Journal of Social Theory, 14*(4), 489–515.

CHAPTER 2

Opening up Institutional Black Boxes: The European Parliament from a Sociological Perspective

Sociological approaches and explanations were once 'at the heart of studies of European regional integration' (Favell & Guiraudon, 2009, p. 551). Ernst Haas (1958) and Karl Deutsch et al. (1957), as the founders of European integration studies, stressed the role of societal groups, e.g. of interest groups and elites, in supranational cooperation. Recalling Milward's (1997) argument about the social basis of the European integration process, it appears that European integration 'is largely a socially driven process' (Adler-Nissen, 2009, p. 15). Despite these sociological beginnings of explaining European integration, the picture we have today of the European Union (EU), its institutions and the integration process is predominately shaped by political scientists (Ross, 2011). Supported by a few economists and lawyers, they provide us with an image of the EU as a distant, opaque and cumbersome bureaucracy. The portray of the EU as a hollow complex of institutions in which decisions are made over people's head, without accounting for people's real life, nurtures the enduring discussion of the EU's democratic deficit. The increasing complexity of EU politics and the argument that the EU 'does not do anything by itself' (Kauppi, 2011, p. 150) require a rethinking in terms of how to study the EU, its institutions and the integration process. It is people, who as everyday political agents, make the EU happen. To counter a manifestation of the democratic deficit and a further alienation of the EU from its citizen and vice versa, scholars need to open up the EU's institutional black boxes. Research on EU institutions needs to shed light

L. Landorff, *Inside European Parliament Politics*,
Palgrave Studies in European Political Sociology,
https://doi.org/10.1007/978-3-030-04206-6_2

on those people and groups who practices EU politics on a daily basis, on the professions of political actors (e.g. Members of the European Parliament [MEPs]) to de-mystify EU politics and to reveal potential practices that may (re-)produce the democratic deficit. In line with this reasoning, this book is inspired by the latest revival of sociological approaches in EU studies. For an overview, see Favell and Guiraudon (2011), Kauppi (2013, 2018), Rowell and Mangenot (2010).[1] Consistent with these works, the upcoming conceptual framework is informed by a 'distinctive form of political sociology' that is represented by scholars of the Strasbourg school (Favell & Guiraudon, 2009, p. 565; Kauppi, 2011). Representatives of the Strasbourg school draw on the work of the French sociologist Pierre Bourdieu and apply his main theoretical concepts, i.e. field, capital and habitus, to analyse the European integration process. In particular, they focus on specific social groups such as MEPs (e.g. Beauvallet & Michon, 2008, 2010, 2013; Kauppi, 2005, 2011) or European civil servants (e.g. Georgakakis, 2017; Georgakakis & de Lasalle, 2010) and their role in the integration process. For an overview, see Kauppi (2011). Following the Bourdieusian way of thinking politics, these works seek to connect political strategies of actors to their structural location and social characteristics (e.g. education and gender) in order to analyse 'broader processes such as the construction of a transnational political field' (Kauppi, 2003, p. 782). Drawing on French political sociology, valuable contributions of the application and adaptation of field, capital and habitus to the transnational level also emerge from German sociology, see Bernhard and Schmidt-Wellenburg (2012) or Büttner and Mau (2014) as well as from Danish academia, see for instance, the work by Adler-Nissen (2011, 2012, 2015) on the British and Danish opt-outs from EU cooperation or Madsen (2002, 2006) on the internationalisation of law.

Inspired by these second-wave Bourdieusian scholars in EU studies, this chapter develops a political sociological framework for the study of MEPs' practices in European Parliament (EP) Intergroups using the three inter-related concepts of field, capital and habitus. Inter-related means here that these concepts cannot be defined in isolation (Bourdieu & Wacquant, 1992). In the context of this book, they are employed as scholastic devices, as analytical concepts which are, however, temporary constructs shaped 'for and by empirical work' (Wacquant in Jenkins, 1992, p. 67). They are used as heuristics—as thinking tools by which the object of study is mentally constructed by the researcher (Kauppi, 2011). Given that these three concepts have been originally developed within the context of the French nation state, working in the same theoretical vein as Bourdieu always includes the challenge of adapting these 'often ambiguous or underspecified' concepts to the supranational context of EU politics (Adler-Nissen, 2009, p. 87; Kauppi, 2005).

Taking into account the literature on the EP's internal organisations, previous research on informal groupings in (US) legislatures as well as institutional theories of political behaviour, this chapter advances conceptual specifications and modifications with regard to the concepts of field and capital. These adaptations are empirically demonstrated in the upcoming Chapters 5–7. This present chapter proceeds as follows. Initially, structural constructivism as the theoretical backbone of this study is introduced. On this basis, the EP is sketched as a transnational political field in which MEPs are conceptualised as multipositional entrepreneurs who struggle for a variety of different social resources. Taking into account the consensus-style of EU decision-making, this chapter advocates a field approach to the EP and the EU at large that encompasses both conflict and cooperation as its elements. This makes it distinct from the antagonist take inherent in the Bourdieusian field approach. Finally, the chapter introduces the different forms of capital, i.e. social resources, to which agents in the transnational political field have access to, and struggle for. In this context, it is argued that next to political capital, as the specific form of capital in the political field, MEPs also strive for the accumulation of social and informational capital via their Intergroup membership. In this way, the developed conceptual framework includes additional forms of capital and suggests modifications of the respective concepts.

Structural Constructivism

Based on the premise that social reality is constructed through the dialectical relationship between structure and agency, structural constructivism informs the theoretical background of this interdisciplinary study (Kauppi, 2005). In the epistemological spirit of Berger and Luckmann (1967), Anthony Giddens (1979), and Bourdieu and Wacquant (1992), it is assumed that individuals and structures shape each other in a dialectical fashion. The former is determined and constrained by the latter, which in turn is a product of the interactions between individuals.

With reference to Weber (1922), structural constructivists account for reality as being constructed by agents who 'struggle to accumulate political resources and increase their own power' (Kauppi, 2005, p. 39). In this struggle, the agents are 'constrained and empowered by structures that are material and symbolic' (Kauppi, 2005, p. 39). Thereby, structures are understood as sets of power relationships (Kauppi, 2005). This goes beyond constructivist accounts which conceive of 'structures as regularities in social interaction' (i.e. as purely symbolic and linguistic) (Christiansen, Jørgensen, & Wiener, 1999; Kauppi, 2005, p. 47). In this context, power is understood as 'the ability of an agent to realise his or her will even against the will of others' (Kauppi, 2011, p. 152).

Pursuing political sociology as an interdisciplinary and interpretative approach based on structural constructivism has several advantages, above all:

A Bourdieu-inspired approach offers an alternative to objective structuralism 'without relapsing into subjectivism' (Bourdieu, 1990, p. 61). Bourdieu's epistemology provides a combination of both objectivism and subjectivism, where 'the importance of social relations and hierarchies' is demonstrated (see Adler-Nissen, 2008, p. 668). Both individuals and structures are 'meaningful components of the social world' (Mason, 2002, p. 17). By introducing the concept of habitus, Bourdieu provides an answer to the question of how social structure and individual agency can be merged (Maton, 2008).

Through the combination of theory and empirical research, the structural constructivist approach offers an analysis of organisational strategies of European political players that emphasises the interaction between agency and structure in 'a much more empirically specifiable' way than structurationist theory (Favell, 2006, p. 127). Using the inter-related concepts field, habitus and capital makes it possible to study the 'messy middle ground' where 'structure and agency intersect' and where the real action takes place (see Checkel, 1999, pp. 557–558). This account is neither provided by 'rational choice, postmodernism nor by large parts of constructivism, which occupy the endpoints in the structure-agency debate' (Checkel, 1999, p. 558).

In addition, the usage of terms such as field or capital/resources as analytical and critical thinking tools allows us to take a dynamic, transnational perspective on EU institutions and politics that transcends 'European national specificities, narrow political agendas and the ideology of the European Union', as these terms can be applied in 'any other area of research and any national context' (Kauppi, 2011, pp. 158, 170). This allows us 'to develop a less state-centric approach' and to 'see beyond the nation state and detect transnational or regional trends at work' (Favell & Guiraudon, 2011, p. 13; Kauppi, 2011, p. 158).

Moreover, in comparison with social constructivist accounts and sociological institutionalism, agency is much more explored. Social characteristics and the multipositionalities of agents are taken into account. This is of utmost importance in the case of the MEP who acts simultaneously in multiple political and social spheres, trying to fulfil demands from voters, from colleagues in the EP, in national, regional and local parties, from interest groups or his/her own ambitions as parliamentarian, which may not always be compatible (Katz, 1999).

A Structural Constructivist Approach to EU Politics

A Bourdieusian-inspired structural constructivist perspective perceives European integration as a process of 'supranational political stratification' (Kauppi, 2005, p. 42). In this process, 'certain interests have been favoured at the expense of others, i.e. business at the expense of labour, consumers at the expense of citizens, elites at the expense of general populace' (Kauppi, 2005, p. 42). European integration is perceived as a series of power struggles over the 'definition of Europe', institutional structures, over 'ideas of the political order', economic policies and political careers (Kauppi, 2005, pp. 41–42, 43). Power relations are central in the structural constructivist endeavour to grasp European integration. Thereby, structuralist constructivists are interested in distribution issues, asking: 'who gets what, when and how during' the European integration process? (Kauppi, 2005, p. 47) They are interested in the mechanisms through which individuals and groups institute structured power relations, how political agents mobilise certain resources and regularise certain interactions to (re-)produce and change the EU's political order (Kauppi, 2005, p. 47).

Field

To explain European integration from a structural constructivist perspective, EU politics is analysed as social action that takes place in relation to historically evolving fields of power (see Kauppi, 2005). A field denotes a relational and structural entity or a network, that is 'a configuration of objective relations between positions' (Bourdieu & Wacquant, 1992, p. 97). It is a 'structured system of social positions' which are occupied either by individuals or institutions (Jenkins, 1992; 2002, pp. 84–85). Within fields, individuals or groups struggle over specific resources 'and access to them' (Jenkins, 1992; 2002, pp. 84–85). The positions of individuals or institutions in the field are defined 'by their present and potential situation' in the power structure and in relation to other agents in the field in the form of dominance or subordination or equivalence (Bourdieu & Wacquant, 1992, p. 97). Hence, to think in terms of a field means to 'think relationally' (Bourdieu & Wacquant, 1992, p. 96).

As a relatively autonomously structured space, each field has its own distinct logic and rules which provide for competent action in line with these rules (Adler-Nissen, 2009; Bourdieu & Wacquant, 1992). Every field is 'orientated towards the struggle for particular combinations of capital', the dominant forms of capital establishing the 'hierarchy of the field are crucial to drawing borders around each field' (Adler-Nissen, 2009, p. 88). Hence, the limits of a field are situated at the point where the struggle for 'a particular mix of relevant capital' eases (Adler-Nissen, 2009, p. 88; Bourdieu & Wacquant, 1992, p. 100). Capital is conceptualised as the 'resources which count as valid in order to achieve' power and status within the field (Adler-Nissen, 2009, p. 113). Thereby, every field is characterised by the unequal distribution of resources with some groups or individuals having many valued resources while others do not possess any form of valued capital (Adler-Nissen, 2015). The main resources in the political field have been defined as political, economic (e.g. money) and cultural capital (e.g. educational qualifications) (see Bourdieu, 1986, 1991; Kauppi, 2005). A more detailed discussion of the concept of (political) capital follows below. Accordingly, the boundaries of each field are always shifting and 'can only be determined by an empirical investigation' (Bourdieu & Wacquant, 1992, p. 100).

As mentioned in the beginning of this chapter, the concepts of field, capital and habitus have been developed in the realm of the French nation state. Bourdieu himself never studied the EU. With regard to the applicability of his thinking tools to the supranational level, his outline of field has been criticised for not including qualitative differences between different types of fields. That is, for analysing the political field like any other field despite its specific properties, such as elections, that distinguishes it, for example, from the literary field (for an in-depth discussion, see Kauppi, 2003, 2005). The ambiguity and conceptual complexity of the concept of field are reflected in its various interpretations (see Crum & Fossum, 2009, 2012; Fligstein, 2008; Fligstein & McAdam, 2012; Kauppi, 2005).

Applying the field concept to EU politics, Kauppi (2005, p. 41) conceptualises the EU as 'a more or less structured multipolar political field where supranational, intergovernmental, national and regional, public, semi-public, private institutions share power'. In this multipolar political field 'different actors define themselves in relation to others, and struggle over dominance and influence over each other' (Favell & Guiraudon, 2011, p. 21). As such a multipolar emerging political field, the EU constitutes a field of forces that is the outcome of an on-going struggle between various groups competing over the institutional structure of the EU, 'ideas of the political order', forms of EU public policy and political careers (Kauppi, 2005, pp. 41–42). In doing so, structural constructivism provides the formal framework for the study of political behaviour where 'individuals and groups act in a structured environment' and display a goal-oriented behaviour to accumulate political capital (Kauppi, 2005, p. 48). In this context, agents are guided by their habitus in their actions.

Habitus

Habitus can be 'individual, collective and societal' (Wilken, 2006, p. 44). At individual level, habitus is the 'product of history'; it is accumulated experiences (Bourdieu & Wacquant, 1992, p. 136). It is 'socially and historically constituted categories of perception and appreciation' that agents develop through their socialisation (Bourdieu & Wacquant, 1992, p. 138). These dispositions provide the basis for practices, and they allow agents to 'do certain things' (Jenkins, 1992; 2002, p. 78). Consequently, the concept of habitus 'helps us to understand why some actors perceive and seize some opportunities whereas other actors do not' in the field (Swartz, 2013, p. 24). As 'a way of being', of acting, thinking and feeling, habitus is also subject to change (Bourdieu, 1977, p. 214). The dispositions become subject to modification when the explanations of our 'habitus no longer make sense [...] or when agents use their [...] feel for the rules of the game as a means' to further and improve their own position and capital in the field (Webb, Schirato, & Danaher, 2002, p. 41). Habitus bears some resemblance to the notion of the logic of appropriateness used from the institutionalist's perspective to account for agents' behaviour (March & Olsen, 1989, 2009). In contrast, habitus reserves room for improvisation as agents may manipulate 'common understandings in their favour' (for an interesting argument, see Adler-Nissen, 2009, p. 95ff). As the socially constituted principle of perception and apprehension, habitus may differ between actors and between contexts since 'what is understood as natural, self-evident or even logical behaviour' may be quite different from agent to agent (Crum & Fossum, 2009, p. 262). Thus, structural constructivists assume that agents may share the same internal habitus based on shared structural locations or certain shared experiences (Kauppi, 2005). At collective or field level, habitus is perceived as an 'internalised set of principles of action, preference, and evaluation that regulates' the accumulation of resources (Kauppi, 2005, p. 46). Hence, the access, value and accumulation of these forms of capital are regulated and controlled for by the dominant habitus of the field, here understood as 'specific, internalised culture' (Kauppi, 2005, p. 46). Through this set of principles, roles are assigned to MEPs and 'guidelines for legitimate behaviour' are provided which define what is (not) acceptable within the field (Kauppi, 2005, p. 46). In line with the dialectical relationship between institutions and agents, there is no empowerment of the individual without structural constraints and vice versa. Recalling again our knowledge on the EP's internal organisation, the access to resources is primarily regulated through the political groups in the EP and the specific, internalised culture of the EP recorded in the EP's Rules of Procedure. It is reflected in the practice of grouping MEPs in transnational political groups according to political affinities and not according to nationalities or territories, the specialisation processes taking place within the EP parliamentary committees while the political groups control and coordinate committee assignments as well as report allocation (see Bowler & Farrell, 1995; Kaeding, 2004, 2005; Yordanova, 2009, 2011).

While Kauppi (2005) stays rather close to Bourdieu's original antagonistic notion of field, conceptualising the EU as a more or less homogenous, multipolar and multileveled emerging political field, Fligstein (2008) departs from Bourdieu with his notion of Europe-wide social fields and focuses more on entrepreneurship than domination. In this way, less attention is paid to the 'internal dynamics of fields, and how are they changing in terms of hierarchy, capital and domination' (Favell, 2008, p. 500). Crum and Fossum (2009, 2012) offer an excellent example of how to use the concept of field to theorise representative democracy in the EU. Drawing on Powell and DiMaggio (1991) and Bourdieu (1989), they introduce the notion of a Multilevel Parliamentary Field by which the different parliamentary bodies of the EU are 'depicted as an organisational field, that is, a set of institutions that, in the aggregate, constitute a recognised area of institutional life' (2012, p. 98). However, Crum and Fossum (2009, 2012) stay at the institutional level and do not zoom in on the very individual and his/her practices of parliamentary democracy at the EU level. Their focus is exclusively on parliaments and formal institutions. As Crum and Fossum (2009, p. 268) acknowledge themselves, they leave out 'non-parliamentary channels' such as civil society, interest groups and Intergroups as such as an alternative or complement to electoral representation. In response to these shortcomings, this study uses the concept of field to 'go beyond the fragmented vision of European institutional fields' and to conceptualise the EP as a transnational field that has permeable boundaries with many (national or transnational) neighbouring fields (Georgakakis & Weisbein, 2010, p. 98; Vauchez, 2011).

The European Parliament as a Transnational Political Field

The EP as a transnational political field shall be understood as a relational and structural entity where nothing 'has meaning except relationally' (Bourdieu, 1991, p. 185). It is constructed as a more or less hierarchical, structured parliamentary space in which various individuals and (social) groups struggle over dominance and influence over each other (Favell & Guiraudon, 2011, p. 21). As outlined in the literature, the EP operates as a transnational body 'in a system of multilevel governance', the EU (Judge & Earnshaw, 2008, p. 24). It is part of an institutional triangle consisting of the European Commission and the Council, which distinguishes it from other legislative institutions (Judge & Earnshaw, 2008). Hence, it cannot be understood without reference to the EU as a whole and the unique characteristics that mark it out from any other international organisation in the world (Corbett, Jacobs, & Shackleton, 2007, p. 2).

Accordingly, the EP is a transnational field with many overlaps with neighbouring fields; the EP is embedded within the overarching 'superfield' (Kauppi, 2011, p. 154). Thus, the EU is conceptualised here as an overall power structure: as an emerging, 'multileveled and polycentric evolving political field' that consists of a variety of smaller, interdependent fields, such as institutional fields and national political fields (Kauppi, 2005, p. 22; 2011, p. 154). Intergroups are an excellent example of the overlap of transnational settings. As shown in the upcoming analysis, their meetings are attended by MEPs, representatives of other EU institutions, civil society and EU citizens coming from all the neighbouring fields of the EP. Hence, as a parliamentary space, the EP is deeply interwoven with the overall EU power structure. It is embedded within a wider network of objective relations between different positions that are occupied by the European Commission, the Council, national governments and parliaments, as well as public and private institutions at national, regional and local level. Acknowledging the ambiguity and complexity of the concept of field, this study argues that the concept is particularly suitable for capturing both the specific features of the EP and informal practices of MEPs in Intergroups, for the following reasons:

Initially, the concept of field, being a heuristic and shaped by empirical research, helps to capture the fluid and dynamic nature of the EP and the EU at large. As touched upon in Chapter 1, in comparison with national parliaments, the EP is a rather young parliament that is despite strong (national) party control, still a weakly structured institution (Bale & Taggart, 2006; Kauppi, 2005). The EP is always in change with a high personnel turnover from one parliamentary term to another. In the 7th EP, more than half of the 736 MEPs elected to be parliamentarians in 2009 were entirely new (Corbett et al., 2016). In doing so, turnover in membership is 'certainly higher than in most national parliaments' (Nugent, 2010, p. 199). This has an impact on the organisation and composition of political groups and parliamentary committees in every legislative term. Moreover, the EP records a constant amendment of its rules of procedure, i.e. its internal operational and organisational rules that lay down the objective guidelines for the legitimate behaviour for MEPs (European Parliament, 2009, 2018). In addition, the particular parliamentary style of the EP with no government emerging from EP elections, no fixed opposition, no single political group holding an outright majority requires that coalitions have to be formed on every single issue and 'vary from one issue to another' (Corbett et al., 2016, p. 11). Finally, the continuous increase in powers of the EP in the course of successive Treaty reforms and its rise 'from a toothless consultation chamber to a powerful legislative institution' proves once again its dynamic character (Hix & Høyland, 2013, p. 185).

Given the weak structuration of the EP as an institution, the concept of field and the idea of subfields help to capture the internal fragmentation and differentiation of the EP.[2] Bourdieu and Wacquant (1992, p. 104) argued that a field does not have parts but consists of subfields which have their 'own logic, rules and regularities', and their own specific capital at stake. Merging Vauchez's (2011) interpretation of a transnational field consisting of emerged and settled elements with the idea of subfields appears to be a fruitful approach. It allows us to conceptualise the EP as a transnational, fragmented field consisting of emergent and settled subfields. These subfields represent those settled and emergent subunits into which the EP is internally divided. For the purpose of this study, the formalised and highly institutionalised official organs of the EP, such as the parliamentary committees, are conceptualised as settled subfields of the EP with clear boundaries (because membership is limited and controlled by the political groups) and their own internal logic. In contrast, voluntary informal groupings, such as Intergroups, are conceptualised as emerging, dynamic, less institutionalised and formalised subfields of the transnational field with blurry and fuzzy boundaries that are not officially codified.

Finally yet importantly, the concept of field and its relational underpinning help to capture the various and constant power struggles in which the EP and MEPs are involved. The Bourdieusian analysis of politics stresses conflict and domination (Bourdieu, 1991, p. 171ff). In this way, it neglects actors 'who themselves might see their own actions in terms of the purest benevolent or professional motives' (Favell, 2006, p. 127). Moreover, an antagonistic take on politics neglects that MEPs' actions and their work are characterised by both conflict and cooperation. In response to this shortcoming, this study argues for a field concept that accounts for the subtle tension between conflict and cooperation that is inherent in EU politics. For one thing, the prevalence of 'consensus-style decision-making at EU level' entails a constant need and necessity for cooperation and compromise among individual MEPs across heterogeneous political groups to establish a common and collective EP position vis-à-vis other EU institutions, such as the European Commission, the Council and national parliaments (Corbett et al., 2016, p. 12). Collective actions vis-à-vis the EU as an overarching 'superfield' are only possible through the coordination of individual parliamentarians based on a reached consensus and compromise among those agents. In addition to these external power struggles, the EP is shaped by internal battles and an unequal distribution of political capital. This is because some parliamentarians possess a lot of valued capital, i.e. those in the EP Leadership positions as Beauvallet and

Michon (2010) show, while others such as backbenchers and followers possess less. There is an internal struggle for posts and positions, such as rapporteurships for co-decision reports as Yordanova (2011) shows. Providing for both the political groups and the individual MEPs an opportunity to shape the context of EU legislation, these rapporteurships and posts are highly competitive. In sum, this book advocates an actor-centred field approach to the EP that takes into account that interactions within the transnational field are more characterised by an interplay of coordination and competition and shaped in both a coalitional and hierarchical fashion. The analysis of the EP as a transnational field that has permeable boundaries 'takes seriously the extensive interdependence and overlap of transnational settings' and offers a favourable context for multipositional entrepreneurs, such as MEPs (Vauchez, 2011, p. 342).

The MEP as Multipositional, Political Entrepreneur

Entrepreneurs appear in many different forms and contexts within EU studies, for example as policy entrepreneurs (Kingdon, 2011), institutional entrepreneurs (DiMaggio, 1988), political entrepreneurs (Cohen, 2010; Knudsen, 2010) or legal entrepreneurs (Cohen & Madsen, 2007; Madsen, 2006). Benedetto (2005, p. 68) highlights the role of the rapporteur as a 'legislative entrepreneur' who steers and guides legislative and non-legislative reports through the EP. The rapporteur engages in 'brokering compromises', and depending on his/her ability and skill to create consensus and alliances across divided party lines within the EP and vis-à-vis other EU institutions, has the power to influence the 'content of Parliament's legislative output' (Benedetto, 2005, p. 68). While Benedetto (2005, p. 68) enlightens us on the power of rapporteurs to set the agenda and to 'construct cross-party consensus to secure outcomes', the multipositionality of MEPs in general falls short in his conceptualisation of the 'legislative entrepreneur'.

To conceptualise MEPs as multipositional, political entrepreneurs allows to account for the multiple roles and tasks MEPs have. MEPs do not only perceive themselves as legislators but also as representatives who 'have important responsibilities towards multiple 'constituencies'' (Scully & Farrell, 2003, p. 285). As a result, MEPs enact various roles while exercising their mandate (i.e. as representatives, legislators and members of various social and political groups). They are not just members of the institution, i.e. the EP. MEPs are also members of a variety of intersecting social groups within the transnational field. Next to their affiliation with one of the seven transnational political groups in the 7th EP, they are also members of parliamentary committees and delegations, national political parties, (various) working groups within the EP, and as a matter of fact, of Intergroups. Hence, MEPs occupy several positions at the same time, constituting a reservoir of valuable resources. As multipositional, political entrepreneurs, MEPs are perceived as agents who 'strategically use their position at the crossroads' between various sectors and levels within the transnational field (Vauchez, 2010, p. 110). They mediate 'between different institutional, cultural, and professional settings' and take advantage of being in-between positions (Vauchez, 2010, p. 110 on the Van Gend en Loos doctrine). MEPs are involved in several field struggles at several levels within the EU. As members of the institution, this is the EP, they are and have been constantly involved in external power struggles vis-à-vis the European Commission and the Council (e.g. for enhanced legislative, budgetary and oversight competences). As members of the Parliament, of certain political parties and social groups within the EP, they have been constantly involved in internal power struggles. This is, in struggles over legislative resources that the EP provides to its members (e.g. posts and positions); in a battle for a Statute for MEPs,[3] in struggles over legislation and representation as well as for access to information and knowledge and thus, ultimately for the power to shape and influence the content and scope of EU legislation.

The conceptualisation of the multipositional, political entrepreneur complements the concept of social skill (see Fligstein, 1997; Fligstein & McAdam, 2012). Here, social skill is understood as the 'skill to mobilise others either to help them to build a political coalition able to organise the field or to use their superior resources to produce hierarchies' (Fligstein & McAdam, 2012, p. 17). Drawing on Corbett et al. (2016, p. 11) arguing that an effective MEP is 'someone who is good at explaining, persuading and negotiating', this addition of the concept by the cognitive dimension is useful. In this way, it also differs from the notion of the institutional entrepreneur originally coined by DiMaggio (1988, p. 15) which puts resource mobilisation at the front and calls institutional entrepreneurs 'organised actors with sufficient resources' who view institutional change or the emergence of (new) institutions as an opportunity 'to realize interests that they highly value'. In the context of this study, social skill is perceived as a component of habitus.

As previously outlined, habitus helps us to realise why some agents seize some opportunities whereas other agents do not (Swartz, 2013). Hence, the notion of habitus is useful for understanding why some MEPs maintain and participate in Intergroups while others do not. The 'habitus of the politician depends on a special training' (Bourdieu, 1991, p. 176). This training includes the entire apprenticeship to acquire the specific kinds of knowledge which are further produced and accumulated by the political work of the professional (Bourdieu, 1991). The upcoming Chapter 4 on the sociopolitical characteristics will therefore shed light on the professional experience and previous occupation of those MEPs who engage in Intergroups. In this way, the chapter delivers an insight into the forms and volumes of capital these MEPs possess, and subsequently into the positions, they take within the transnational field.

Institutional theory of political behaviour suggests that MEPs' behaviour is 'influenced primarily by three different sorts of career goals', namely re-election, policy and office (Hix, Raunio, & Roger, 1999, p. 12). Thereby, re-election is presented as the main goal of MEPs, while policy and office goals are perceived as strategies to accomplish this goal. It is further assumed that legislators do not 'pursue only one goal and one goal alone' but that 'at different points in time, in response to different stimuli', politicians are 'faced with different strategic choices, [and] may favour one set of goals over others' (Hix et al., 1999, p. 13). One shortcoming of the institutional framework on MEPs' behaviour by Hix et al. (1999) is that it simply assumes that MEPs are interested in pursuing a career in the EP. The works of Scarrow (1997, p. 259) and Kauppi (2005, 2011) have shown that MEPs may use the EP as a 'stepping stone for gaining national parliamentary office'. Scarrow (1997) previously identified three career patterns: First, those MEPs using the EP to gain an office in national politics; second, the 'European Careerists' who display long-term and 'primary commitment to their European jobs' (1997, p. 259); and third, the group of parliamentarians who plan to stay in the EP only briefly. Scarrow (1997, p. 259) refers to them as the 'Political

Deadend'. Likewise, studies on American legislatures (see Fenno, 1995) refer to a career beyond the House and to personal gains as aims of legislators. As a result, in contrast to Bourdieu's original notion of strategic agents, however, it is assumed that not all agents succeed in accumulating status and therefore rather resign themselves to subordinate status, which results in the difference between those MEPs in top parliamentary positions and those in rank-and-file positions (Kauppi, 2005). Recalling Corbett, Jacobs, and Shackleton (2011) instancing personal, constituency and national concerns for MEPs' activities in Intergroups in combination with the structural constructivist framework of this study and insights from institutional theory of political behaviour, MEPs are perceived as strategic agents who display goal-oriented behaviour. That is, MEPs show behaviour that is aimed at accumulating status and power in the transnational field. Their Intergroup activities are further conceptualised as a strategy[4] and thus, 'as more or less accurate and more or less intentional plan of practices' adopted by individual actors to achieve a particular political goal, and suggested by the habitus as a 'feel for the game' pursued by individuals and groups to accumulate and mobilise various forms of capital (Bourdieu & Wacquant, 1992, p. 128; Wodak, 2009, p. 40).

Forms of Capital in the European Parliament

As previously noted, each field has its specific capitals. The main resources in the political field have been previously defined as political, economic and cultural capital (see Bourdieu, 1991; Kauppi, 2005). The mapping of cultural and economic capital as the main resources in the political field next to political capital was primarily based on the observation of who participates in politics—who is granted access to the national (French) political field (e.g. those with 'leisure time and cultural capital') (see Bourdieu, 1991, p. 172). The present study is less concerned with the forms of capital needed to access the EP as a transnational field, as MEPs are already part of it, but more interested in the valued resources they acquire and mobilise in and through Intergroups to exert influence. It is suggested to focus primarily on political capital as the specific resource of the political field. In addition, it is proposed to include two additional types of capital, i.e. social capital and informational capital, in the conceptual framework. Previous research on the

EP's internal organisations shows that the EP is primarily shaped by the informational rationale of legislative organisation (Krehbiel, 1992; Yordanova, 2009) and that 'information is a highly valued good in legislative politics' (Ringe, Victor, & Carman, 2013, p. 25). Moreover, studies on informal legislative organisations, such as the caucuses in the US Congress, point to three principal functions that these informal groupings perform for legislators. First, they serve 'to signal their policy preferences and priorities to their colleagues and constituents' (Victor & Ringe, 2009, p. 745). Second, they 'serve as venues for the exchange of information within the legislature' (Victor & Ringe, 2009, p. 745). Third, they 'allow for the coordination of legislative action outside the formal party and committee structure' (see also Ainsworth & Akins, 1997; Fiellin, 1962; Hammond, 1998; Victor & Ringe, 2009, p. 745). Hence, social and informational capital are understood as valuable resources within the EP, both in their own right and as being convertible into political capital. Consequently, these three types of capital are presented in the following sections.

Political Capital in the European Parliament

Political capital appears in various forms: as symbolic personal and objectified institutionalised political capital that is acquired individually or by delegation (Bourdieu, 1991). As symbolic personal capital, it is credit and refers to political recognition, reputation, prestige and the fact of being known as a parliamentarian, which is of utmost importance in the EP (i.e. not being marginalised among 736 MEPs in order to pursue one's own aims and interests) and which vanishes with the individual leaving the field (Bourdieu, 1991; Kauppi, 2005). It is the product of slow accumulation over time or 'of action in a situation of institutional void and crisis' and disappears with the person (Kauppi, 2005, p. 34). As a form of symbolic capital, political capital includes 'the capacity to mobilise individuals around a common goal' (Kauppi, 2003, p. 778). In doing so, it represents a 'subtype of social capital' which is outlined in the subsequent section (Swartz, 2013, p. 65).

As institutionalised political capital, it is manifested in posts, positions, 'office space or facilities' offered by the EP to its members, as well as the right to speak in the name of the EP (Kauppi, 2011, p. 157). For instance, in contrast to national parliamentarians, MEPs play a decisive role in shaping legislation (Corbett et al., 2016). They do so by occupying certain 'positions of authority' within the parliamentary committees, e.g. those of the chair, party group coordinators and rapporteurs (Mamadouh & Raunio, 2003, p. 339).

Rapporteurs 'largely shape the content of adopted legislative acts' (Yordanova, 2011, p. 98). They draft and amend reports in parliamentary committees, present and defend them in the plenary (Bowler & Farrell, 1995). In the course of a rapporteurship, the respective MEPs gain policy expertise, build the necessary consensus within committees and across party groups for the report and 'negotiate with the Commission and the Council' on the final text (Bowler & Farrell, 1995; Mamadouh & Raunio, 2003, p. 334). In this way, rapporteurs serve as 'the primary intra-institutional agenda-setters and the main parliamentary representatives in the inter-institutional negotiations' with the Commission and the Council (see also Benedetto, 2005; Mamadouh & Raunio, 2003; Neuhold, 2001; Yordanova, 2011, p. 98). Yordanova (2011) reveals a clear competition for report allocation, in particular for co-decision reports in the EP, as rapporteurships provide the opportunity for both political parties and individual MEPs to shape the content of legislative proposals. Hence, these rapporteurships constitute political capital, as they are highly competitive.

Group coordinators are key players in the parliamentary committees. They are the spokesperson of each political group within the parliamentary committee and chosen 'by each party group's members on every committee at the start of each parliamentary term and mid-term, in line with other committee and leadership positions' (Corbett et al., 2011; Kaeding & Obholzer, 2012, p. 14). Group coordinators have a central role in the distribution of rapporteurships, the achievement of consensus within their political groups in the respective committees and the flagging 'of conflictual issues in advance of any vote' (Kaeding & Obholzer, 2012; Settembri & Neuhold, 2009, p. 148).

Committee chairs 'are highly influential positions' and 'appear to be the most attractive' posts within the EP, apart from offices in EP presidency, as they play a decisive role in working out legislative proposals (Mamadouh & Raunio, 2003, p. 339; Neuhold, 2001; Whitaker, 2011, p. 104). They can 'have a powerful role in shaping the agenda of the committee' and in acting as its representative outside the Parliament (Corbett et al., 2011, p. 147).

Consequently, positions as group coordinator, rapporteur and chairman are seen as prestigious, that is, as highly valued institutionalised political capital for MEPs given the importance of EP committees in shaping EU legislation (Corbett et al., 2011; Hix, 1999; Kaeding, 2004, 2005; Kaeding & Obholzer, 2012; Yordanova, 2011). Furthermore, the individual rights attached to the mandate of MEPs, such as tabling amendments to parliamentary reports, asking for a plenary debate, putting down a question to the Parliament or writing letters to the European Commission, are conceived of as institutionalised political capital (Corbett et al., 2016). Finally yet importantly, interpretation and translation facilities constitute important resources that are provided by the EP to its members given the plurality of languages present in the Parliament.

Social Capital in the European Parliament

The term social capital has been coined independently by various scholars in many different contexts throughout the twentieth century, ranging from American social scientists (e.g. Coleman, 1988; Putnam, 2000) to French sociologists (e.g. Bourdieu, 1986) to German economists (e.g. Schlicht, 1984). For a comprehensive overview, see Lin, Cook, and Burt (2001).

A Bourdieusian-inspired adaptation of the concept to the EU level describes social capital as 'relations of trust and durable interpersonal connections and recognition' (Kauppi, 2011, p. 156). As such, social capital is interpreted as a symbolic and intangible resource. Understood as 'inclusion in powerful networks' (Kauppi, 2011, p. 166), the value of social capital 'depends on the size of the network of connections [an actor] can effectively mobilize' as well as 'on the volume of the capital (economic, cultural or symbolic) possessed in his own right by each of those' to whom the actor is connected to in the network (Bourdieu, 1986, p. 251).

In this way, social capital constitutes a more unstable resource that requires from its user 'constant upkeep and usage' to sustain its value (Kauppi, 2011, p. 156). Moreover, social capital is also 'more bound to certain social configuration' (Kauppi, 2011, p. 156). A German parliamentarian may 'have a lot of social capital in Berlin', but this social capital might be less valuable in Brussels (Kauppi, 2011, p. 156).

Applied to the legislative context and to the importance of interpersonal connections in legislatures, Coleman (1988, p. 103) demonstrates in the case of the US Congress that 'a legislator in a position with extra resources (such as the Speaker of the House of Representatives [...]) can, by effective use of resources, build up a set of obligations from other legislators that makes it possible to' pass legislation that would otherwise be blocked. In doing so, the accumulation of obligations, understood as social capital, is also useful in initiating 'an increased level of action on the part of the legislature' (Coleman, 1988, p. 103). Sociological works on the EP show that the possession and control of internal networks (e.g. social capital) constitutes one ingredient for the parliamentarians' institutional credit (e.g. political capital) which is needed to obtain leadership positions within the EP as a political field (Beauvallet & Michon, 2010). Hence, social capital is converted into political capital.

The American political science interpretation of social capital resembles the Bourdieusian-inspired employment of the concept to the degree that it defines social capital as 'connections among individuals' and as social networks that are associated with reciprocity, mutual obligations and trustworthiness (Putnam, 2000, p. 19). Putnam's (2000) interpretation differs, however, from the usage of the concept in French (political) sociology, as he draws a distinction between bridging (or inclusive) and bonding (or exclusive) social capital.

Bonding social capital stands for networks that are 'by choice and necessity, inward looking and tend to reinforce exclusive identities and homogenous groups' (Putnam, 2000, p. 22). 'Ethnic fraternal organizations' are examples of bonding social capital, of closed group ties (Putnam, 2000, p. 22). This type of social capital is useful for strengthening specific reciprocity and organising solidarity (Putnam, 2000). Bridging social capital constitutes networks that are 'outward looking and encompass people across diverse social cleavages' (Putnam, 2000, p. 22). The civil rights movement is an example of bridging social capital (Putnam, 2000). Bridging social capital is useful for establishing links to external assets and 'for information diffusion' (Putnam, 2000, p. 22). As outward-looking, inclusive networks, bridging social capital comes close to 'weak ties' like an acquaintance, while 'strong ties' resemble close and trusted contacts (Carpenter, Esterling, & Lazer, 1998; Granovetter, 1973).

This study argues that the distinction between different types of social capital is very promising for the study of MEPs' engagement in Intergroups for several reasons, above all:

The insights from studies of informal groupings in the US Congress point to Intergroups being 'venues for the exchange of information within the legislature' (Victor & Ringe, 2009, p. 745). Furthermore, given the particular nature of the EP with no predetermined coalitions, as well as the cross-party character of Intergroups, the notion of bridging social capital might be of particular relevance, since in political settings it helps to seek political allies who 'move in different circles from mine' (Putnam, 2000, p. 23).

Initially, 'the value of social capital depends on the size of the network of connections' the actors can effectively mobilise (Bourdieu, 1986, p. 51). In political settings, interpersonal ties regularised in informal groupings are primarily important in terms of channelling and exchanging information on legislation and voting (Caldeira & Patterson, 1987; Fiellin, 1962). Moreover, they provide legislators with access to committees of which they are not members. This access may be used to influence actions of members and the information flow in this committee as Fiellin (1962, p. 80) demonstrated in his explorative study on the New York Democratic Congressmen in the House of Representatives. In other words, bridging social capital is good for creating 'linkage to external assets and for information diffusion' (Putnam, 2000, p. 22). In addition, interpersonal ties provide channels for the formation of coalitions and compromises, may serve as tools for forging socialisation of new members into their legislative roles and the institution or may serve legislators in terms of their career development within or beyond the institution (see Fiellin, 1962; Scarrow, 1997).

Informational Capital in the European Parliament

Informational capital as a concept was originally coined by Bourdieu in connection with his treatise on the state (Bourdieu, 2005; Bourdieu, Wacquant, & Farage, 1994). Conceptualising the state as the 'culmination of a process of concentration of different species of capital', informational capital denotes one of the four different specific types of capital that grants 'the state with a sort of meta-capital to exert power over other forms of capital and their holders' (Bourdieu et al., 1994, p. 4). With informational capital, Bourdieu (1994) refers to statistics, census information, national accounting and surveys on state resources carried out by public authorities, as well as other forms of instruments of knowledge, 'such as weights, measures, maps or land registers' that are characterised by a universal validity (Bourdieu, 2005, p. 12). Through the accumulation and redistribution of information, the state fosters a 'theoretical unification' and imposes common forms of thinking, 'common principles of vision and division' of the social world, and contributes to the construction of national identity (Bourdieu et al., 1994, p. 7).

Munk (2009) and Bernhard (2012, 2015) provide two examples for the application of informational capital beyond the nation state conceptualising it as a transnational resource. Bernhard (2015) shows in the case of EU social policy how the European Commission builds up a statistical infrastructure including social indicators on poverty, social inclusion and exclusion policies. In this way, the EU builds a transnational monopoly of symbolic representation (Bernhard, 2012, p. 212). In his comparative study on student mobility, Munk (2009, p. 5) conceptualises informational capital as academic capital and transnational investment, including 'dimensions of skills and recognised symbolic capital' to demonstrate how students from the upper social classes in Sweden, Denmark and France are more likely to invest in academic qualifications in international educational settings 'than students from other social classes' (2009, p. 5). While Bernhard (2012, 2015) remains close to Bourdieu's original coinage of informational capital focusing on statistics, Munk (2009) chooses an interpretation of the concept that bears a close resemblance to the institutionalised form of cultural capital (e.g. educational qualifications).

The Parliament's internal division of labour, being predominately shaped by the informational rationale of legislative organisation, albeit being controlled by the political groups (see, e.g. Bowler & Farrell, 1995; McElroy, 2006; Yordanova, 2009), and the observed process of professionalisation and specialisation among MEPs (Beauvallet & Michon, 2010; Kauppi, 2011) point to the assumption that informational capital, understood as a statistical infrastructure, does not grasp the reality of MEPs. In a parliament with no overall majority of one political group, with no fixed opposition and with MEPs who have to be 'good at explaining, persuading, and negotiating' (Corbett et al., 2016, p. 11), knowledge about the position and thinking of others and about how to convince them is as necessary as substantial knowledge (including statistical data, numbers and figures) for achieving consensus and creating majorities across heterogeneous political groups. Consequently, this study advocates a refinement of the concept of informational capital. In doing so, it is inspired by the ethnographic work of Wodak (2009) on the everyday life of MEPs. Wodak (2009, p. 26) argues that the distribution of knowledge in organisations (i.e. also in political organisations) 'is [...] a question of hierarchy' of powers and access. Arguing further that 'politics is inherently tied to power struggles', she assumes that these power struggles are linked to 'practices and strategies of inclusion and exclusion, via knowledge management' (2009, p. xiv). With regard to the EP, Wodak (2009, p. 46) shows that MEPs 'playing the political game' draw on three dimensions of knowledge: expert, organisational and political knowledge. These are introduced in the following paragraphs.

Expert knowledge designates 'knowledge of specific agenda' that is necessary for the agents (i.e. MEPs) 'to participate actively in current debates and push ideological agenda [...]' (Wodak, 2009, p. 46). It is reflected in MEPs being specialised in 'specific policy domains' (e.g. in agricultural, regional or social policy) (Wodak, 2009, p. 46). In doing so, Wodak's notion of expert knowledge includes what is understood by policy information, policy-oriented, substantive information in informational theories of legislatures.

Organisational knowledge designates 'shared knowledge about preceding events and debates, rules and routines, and about the positions and opinions of specific MEPs' or political groups (Wodak, 2009, p. 46). In terms of the EP, knowing about positions of different actors within the transnational field is of utmost importance. Thereby, it concerns not only the positions of MEPs and political groups, but also the positions of civil society organisations (CSOs) and their representatives, as well as representatives of other EU institutions given the transnational and overlapping character of the EP as a political field with its permeable boundaries. In doing so, it includes the term political information used by theorists of informational theory of legislatures designating 'strategic information about policy positions of other decision-makers' (Ringe et al., 2013, p. 4).

Political knowledge designates the 'know-how' of how to convince, advise and persuade others (outsiders) of one's opinion, how to debate, argue and struggle 'to win in motions', how to form alliances, prepare and influence decision-making (Wodak, 2009, p. 46). This political knowledge presumes knowledge of strategies and tactics, of positions and ideologies (Wodak, 2009). One needs to know the strong and weak points of colleagues; thus, 'one has to know the 'rules of the game'' (Wodak, 2009, p. 46). In doing so, political knowledge, understood as the 'know-how' of how to persuade others and forge alliances, is also linked to the habitus of the individual (i.e. the MEP), understood as the 'structuring mechanism that operates from within agents' (Bourdieu & Wacquant, 1992, p. 18). Chapter 6 of this book discusses each of these three dimensions in the context of MEPs engagement in Intergroups. In this way, the conceptual modification of Bourdieu's original coinage of informational capital is demonstrated.

Conclusion

This chapter developed the conceptual framework of the study. Inspired by a fairly new research agenda in European Studies, calling for a return of sociological approaches in the study of EU politics and institutions, this project advances a political sociological perspective to the EP.

Informed by structural constructivism and inspired by recent applications of the Bourdieusian concepts field, capital and habitus in European integration studies, the EP is analysed as a social organisation. It is conceptualised as a transnational political field in which agents (individuals and groups) guided by their habitus struggle for specific resources (i.e. forms of capital) to exert influence.

Within this conceptual framework, MEPs are conceptualised as multi-positional, political entrepreneurs. As such, they are perceived as strategic agents who display goal-oriented behaviour (i.e. behaviour that is aimed at accumulating status and power in the transnational field). Their engagement in Intergroups is conceptualised as part of their strategic behaviour and thus, as part of their parliamentary practices.

While political capital has been previously coined as the specific resource of the political field for which agents compete for, this conceptual framework proposes to include two additional forms of capital in the analysis. Drawing on the literature on legislative organisation and informal groupings in legislatures, it suggests the inclusion of informational and social capital in the conceptual framework.

Notes

1. See also Georgakakis & Weisbein (2010) and Zimmermann & Favell (2011).
2. See also Büttner and Mau (2014) on EU professionalisation as a transnational field.

3. See Priestley (2008).
4. 'Strategy generally refers to a (more or less accurate and more or less intentional) plan of practices [...] adopted to achieve a particular social, political, psychological or linguistic goal' (Wodak, 2009, p. 40).

References

Adler-Nissen, R. (2008). The Diplomacy of Opting Out: A Bourdieudian Approach to National Integration Strategies. *Journal of Common Market Studies, 46*(3), 663–684.

Adler-Nissen, R. (2009). *The Diplomacy of Opting Out: British and Danish Stigma Management in the European Union* (PhD thesis). Copenhagen: University of Copenhagen.

Adler-Nissen, R. (2011). On a Field Trip with Bourdieu. *International Political Sociology, 5*(3), 327–330.

Adler-Nissen, R. (Ed.). (2012). *Bourdieu in International Relations Rethinking Key Concepts in IR*. Abingdon: Routledge.

Adler-Nissen, R. (2015). *Opting Out of the European Union: Diplomacy, Sovereignty and European Integration.* Cambridge: Cambridge University Press.

Ainsworth, S. H., & Akins, F. (1997). The Informational Role of Caucuses in the US Congress. *American Politics Quarterly, 25*(4), 407.

Bale, T., & Taggart, P. (2006). *First-Timers Yes, Virgins No: The Roles and Backgrounds of New Members of the European Parliament* (SEI Working Paper No. 89), 1–30.

Beauvallet, W., & Michon, S. (2008). *Women in the European Parliament: Effects of the Voting System, Strategies and Political Resources. The Case of the French Delegation* (GSPE Working Papers), 1–20.

Beauvallet, W., & Michon, S. (2010). Professionalization and Socialization of the Members of the European Parliament. *French Politics, 8*(2), 145–165.

Beauvallet, W., & Michon, S. (2013). MEPs: Towards a Specialization of European Political Work? In J. Rowell & D. Georgakakis (Eds.), *The Field of Eurocracy: Mapping EU Actors and Professionals* (pp. 16–34). Houndmills, Basingstoke, Hampshire, and New York, NY: Palgrave Macmillan.

Benedetto, G. (2005). Rapporteurs as Legislative Entrepreneurs: The Dynamics of the Codecision Procedure in Europe's Parliament. *Journal of European Public Policy, 12*(1), 67–88.

Berger, P., & Luckmann, T. (1967). *The Social Construction of Reality.* Allan Lane: The Penguin Press.

Bernhard, S. (2012). Informationelles Kapital als Transnationale Ressource. In S. Bernhard & C. Schmidt-Wellenburg (Eds.), *Feldanalyse als Forschungsprogramm 2: Gegenstandsbezogene Theoriebildung* (pp. 195–216). Wiesbaden: VS Verlag für Sozialwissenschaften.

Bernhard, S. (2015). Informational Capital: How It Is Developed and Used by CSOs and EU Institutions. In H. Johansson & S. Kalm (Eds.), *EU Civil Society. Patterns of Cooperation, Competition and Conflict* (pp. 43–60). Basingstoke: Palgrave Macmillan.

Bernhard, S., & Schmidt-Wellenburg, C. (Eds.). (2012). *Feldanalyse als Forschungsprogramm 2: Gegenstandsbezogene Theoriebildung*. Wiesbaden: Springer VS Verlag für Sozialwissenschaften.

Bourdieu, P. (1977). Structures, Habitus, Power: Basis for a Theory of Symbolic Power. In P. Bourdieu (Ed.), *Outline of a Theory of Practice* (pp. 159–198). Cambridge: Cambridge University Press.

Bourdieu, P. (1986). The Forms of Capital. In J. G. Richardson (Ed.), *Handbook of Theory and Research for the Sociology of Education* (pp. 1–16). London: Greenwood Press.

Bourdieu, P. (1989). Social Space and Symbolic Power. *Sociological Theory, 7*(1), 14–25.

Bourdieu, P. (1990). From Rules to Strategies. In P. Bourdieu (Ed.), *In Other Words* (pp. 59–75). London: Polity Press.

Bourdieu, P. (1991). *Language & Symbolic Power*. Cambridge: Polity Press in Association with Blackwell Publishers.

Bourdieu, P. (2005). *The Social Structures of the Economy*. Oxford: Polity Press.

Bourdieu, P., & Wacquant, L. J. D. (Eds.). (1992). *An Invitation to Reflexive Sociology* (1st ed.). Chicago: University of Chicago Press.

Bourdieu, P., Wacquant, L. J. D., & Farage, S. (1994). Rethinking the State: Genesis and Structure of the Bureaucratic Field. *Sociological Theory, 12*(1), 1–18.

Bowler, S., & Farrell, D. M. (1995). The Organizing of the European Parliament: Committees, Specialization and Co-ordination. *British Journal of Political Science, 25*(2), 219–243.

Büttner, S. M., & Mau, S. (2014). EU-Professionalismus als Transnationales Feld. *Berliner Journal für Soziologie, 24*(2), 141–167.

Caldeira, G. A., & Patterson, S. C. (1987). Political Friendship in the Legislature. *The Journal of Politics, 49*(4), 953–975.

Carpenter, D. P., Esterling, K. M., & Lazer, D. M. J. (1998). The Strength of Weak Ties in Lobbying Networks: Evidence from Health-Care Politics in the United States. *Journal of Theoretical Politics, 10*(4), 417–444.

Checkel, J. (1999). Social Construction and Integration. *Journal of European Public Policy, 6*(4), 545–560.

Christiansen, T., Jørgensen, K. E., & Wiener, A. (1999). The Social Construction of Europe. *Journal of European Public Policy, 6*(4), 528–544.

Cohen, A. (2010). Legal Professionals or Political Entrepreneurs? Constitution Making as a Process of Social Construction and Political Mobilization. *International Political Sociology, 4*(2), 107–123.

Cohen, A., & Madsen, M. R. (2007). Cold War Law: Legal Entrepreneurs and the Genesis of a European Legal Field (1945–65). In V. Gessner & D. Nelken (Eds.), *European Ways of Law* (pp. 175–201). Oxford: Hart.

Coleman, J. S. (1988). Social Capital in the Creation of Human Capital. *American Journal of Sociology, 94*(S1), 95–120.

Corbett, R., Jacobs, F., & Neville, D. (2016). *The European Parliament* (9th ed.). London: John Harper Publishing.

Corbett, R., Jacobs, F., & Shackleton, M. (2007). *The European Parliament* (7th ed.). London: John Harper Publishing.

Corbett, R., Jacobs, F., & Shackleton, M. (2011). *The European Parliament* (8th ed.). London: John Harper Publishing.

Crum, B., & Fossum, J. E. (2009). The Multilevel Parliamentary Field: A Framework for Theorizing Representative Democracy in the EU. *European Political Science Review, 1*(2), 249–271.

Crum, B., & Fossum, J. E. (2012). A Democratic Backbone for International Organisations: The Multilevel Parliamentary Field. In T. Evas, U. Liebert, & C. Lord (Eds.), *Multilayered Representation Across the European Union in Dialogue* (pp. 91–105). Baden-Baden: NOMOS Verlagsgesellschaft.

Deutsch, K. W., Burell, S. A., Kann, R. A., Lee, J. Jr., Lichtermann, M., Lindgren, R. E., Loewenheim, F. L., & Van Wagenen, R. W. (1957). *Political Community in the North-Atlantic Area: International Organization in the Light of Historical Experience*. Princeton: Princeton University Press.

DiMaggio, P. J. (1988). Interest and Agency in Institutional Theory. In L. G. Zucker (Ed.), *Institutional Patterns and Organizations: Culture and Environment* (pp. 3–21). Cambridge, MA: Ballinger Publishing House.

European Parliament. (2009). *Rules of Procedure: 7th Parliamentary Term December 2009*. European Parliament.

European Parliament. (2018). *About Parliament: Organisation and Rules—Rules of Procedure*. Retrieved 16 April 2018, from http://www.europarl.europa.eu/aboutparliament/en/20150201PVL00010/Organisation-and-rules.

Favell, A. (2006). The Sociology of EU Politics. In K. E. Joergensen, M. A. Pollack, & B. Rosamond (Eds.), *Sage Handbook of European Union Politics* (pp. 122–137). London: Sage.

Favell, A. (2008). Euroclash: Towards a Sociology of the European Union. *European Journal of Sociology/Archives Européennes de Sociologie, 49*(3), 495–501.

Favell, A., & Guiraudon, V. (2009). The Sociology of the European Union: An Agenda. *European Union Politics, 10*(4), 550–576.

Favell, A., & Guiraudon, V. (2011). *Sociology of the European Union*. Basingstoke: Palgrave Macmillan.

Fenno, R. F. (1995). *Congressmen in Committees*. University of California, Berkeley: Institute for Governmental Studies Press.

Fiellin, A. (1962). The Functions of Informal Groups in Legislative Institutions. *The Journal of Politics, 24*(1), 72–91.

Fligstein, N. (1997). Social Skill and Institutional Theory. *American Behavioral Scientist, 40*(4), 397–405.

Fligstein, N. (2008). *Euroclash: The EU, European Identity, and the Future of Europe*. Oxford: Oxford University Press.

Fligstein, N., & McAdam, D. (2012). *A Theory of Fields* Oxford: Oxford University Press.

Georgakakis, D. (2017). *European Civil Service in (Times of) Crisis: A Political Sociology of the Changing Power of Eurocrats* (1st ed.). Cham: Palgrave Macmillan.

Georgakakis, D., & de Lasalle, M. (2010). Making Top Civil Servants: Europeaness as an Identity and Resource. In J. Rowell & M. Mangenot (Eds.), *A Political Sociology of the European Union: Reassessing Constructivism* (pp. 25–45). Manchester: Manchester University Press.

Georgakakis, D., & Weisbein, J. (2010). From Above and From Below: A Political Sociology of European Actors. *Comparative European Politics, 8*(1), 93–109.

Giddens, A. (1979). *Central Problems in Social Theory*. London: Macmillan Press.

Granovetter, M. S. (1973). The Strengths of Weak Ties. *American Journal of Sociology, 78*(6), 1360–1380.

Haas, E. B. (1958). *The Uniting of Europe: Political, Social and Economic Forces, 1950–1957*. Stanford: Stanford University Press.

Hammond, S. W. (1998). *Congressional Caucuses in National Policy Making*. Baltimore: Johns Hopkins University Press.

Hix, S. (1999). *The Political System of the European Union*. New York: St. Martin's Press.

Hix, S., & Høyland, B. (2013). Empowerment of the European Parliament. *Annual Review of Political Science, 16*, 171–189.

Hix, S., Raunio, T., & Roger, S. (1999). *An Institutional Theory of Behaviour in the European Parliament*. Paper Presented at the Joint Sessions of the European Consortium for Political Research.

Jenkins, R. (1992). *Pierre Bourdieu*. London: Routledge.

Jenkins, R. (2002). *Pierre Bourdieu* (Rev. ed.). London: Routledge.

Judge, D., & Earnshaw, D. (2008). *The European Parliament* (2nd ed.). Basingstoke: Palgrave Macmillan.

Kaeding, M. (2004). Rapporteurship Allocation in the European Parliament: Information or Distribution? *European Union Politics, 5*(3), 353–371.

Kaeding, M. (2005). The World of Committee Reports: Rapporteurship Assignment in the European Parliament. *The Journal of Legislative Studies, 11*(1), 82–104.

Kaeding, M., & Obholzer, L. (2012). Pulling the Strings: Party Group Coordinators in the European Parliament. *EIPAScope, 1*, 13–18.
Katz, R. S. (1999). Role Orientations in Parliaments. In R. S. Katz & B. Wessels (Eds.), *The European Parliament, National Parliaments, and European Integration* (pp. 61–85). Oxford: Oxford University Press.
Kauppi, N. (2003). Bourdieu's Political Sociology and the Politics of European Integration. *Theory and Society, 32*(5/6), 775–789.
Kauppi, N. (2005). *Democracy, Social Resources and Political Power in the European Union*. Manchester: Manchester University Press.
Kauppi, N. (2011). EU Politics. In A. Favell & V. Guiraudon (Eds.), *Sociology of the European Union* (pp. 150–171). Basingstoke: Palgrave Macmillan.
Kauppi, N. (Ed.). (2013). *A Political Sociology of Transnational Europe*. Colchester: ECPR Press.
Kauppi, N. (2018). *Toward a Reflexive Political Sociology of the European Union: Fields, Intellectuals and Politicians*. Cham: Palgrave Macmillan.
Kingdon, J. W. (2011). *Agendas, Alternatives, and Public Policies* (Updated 2nd ed.). Boston: Longman.
Knudsen, A.-C. L. (2010). Shaping the Common Agricultural Policy: Networks and Political Entrepreneurship in the European Commission. In W. Kaiser, B. Leucht, & M. Gehler (Eds.), *Transnational Networks in Regional Integration Governing Europe 1945–83* (pp. 129–151). Basingstoke: Palgrave Macmillan.
Krehbiel, K. (1992). *Information and Legislative Organization*. Ann Arbor: University of Michigan Press.
Lin, N., Cook, K. S., & Burt, R. S. (2001). *Social Capital: Theory and Research*. New York: Aldine de Gruyter.
Madsen, M. R. (2002). Legal 'Field' or Legal 'Network'? A Bourdieusian Critique of Manuel Castells' Network Society. *Retfærd Nordisk Juridisk Tidsskrift, 4*, 4–18.
Madsen, M. R. (2006). Transnational Fields: Elements of a Reflexive Sociology of the Internationalisation of Law. *Retfærd. Nordisk Juridisk Tidsskrift, 29*(3/114), 34–41.
Mamadouh, V. D., & Raunio, T. (2003). The Committee System: Powers, Appointments and Report allocation. *Journal of Common Market Studies, 41*(2), 333–351.
March, J. G., & Olsen, J. P. (1989). *Rediscovering Institutions*. New York: Free Press.
March, J. G., & Olsen, J. P. (2009). *The Logic of Appropriateness* (ARENA Working Papers, [WP 04/09]), 1–28.
Mason, J. (2002). *Qualitative Researching* (2nd ed.). London: Sage.
Maton, K. (2008). Habitus. In M. Grenfell (Ed.), *Pierre Bourdieu Key Concepts* (pp. 49–65). Stocksfield: Acumen Publishing Limited.

McElroy, G. (2006). Committee Representation in the European Parliament. *European Union Politics, 7*(1), 5–29.

Milward, A. S. (1997). The Social Bases of Monetary Union. In P. Gowan & P. Anderson (Eds.), *The Question of Europe* (pp. 149–161). London: Verso.

Munk, M. D. (2009). Transnational Investments in Informational Capital. *Acta Sociologica, 52*(1), 5–32.

Neuhold, C. (2001). The 'Legislative Backbone' Keeping the Institution Upright? The Role of European Parliament Committees in the EU Policy-Making Process. *European Integration Online Papers (EioP), 5*(10), 1–29.

Nugent, N. (2010). *The Government and Politics of the European Union* (7th ed.). Basingstoke: Palgrave Macmillan.

Powell, W. W., & DiMaggio, P. J. (1991). *The New Institutionalism in Organizational Analysis*. Chicago: University of Chicago.

Priestley, J. (2008). *Six Battles That Shaped Europe's Parliament*. London: John Harper Publishing.

Putnam, R. D. (2000). *Bowling Alone: The Collapse and Revival of American Community*. New York: Simon & Schuster.

Ringe, N., Victor, J. N., & Carman, C. J. (2013). *Bridging the Information Gap: Legislative Member Organizations as Social Networks in the United States and the European Union*. Ann Arbor: University of Michigan Press.

Ross, G. (2011). Postscript. In A. Favell & V. Guiraudon (Eds.), *Sociology of the European Union* (pp. 215–224). Basingstoke: Palgrave Macmillan.

Rowell, J., & Mangenot, M. (2010). *A Political Sociology of the European Union: Reassessing Constructivism*. Manchester: Manchester University Press.

Scarrow, S. E. (1997). Political Career Paths and the European Parliament. *Legislative Studies Quarterly, 22*(2), 253–263.

Schlicht, E. (1984). Cognitive Dissonance in Economics. In H. Todt (Ed.), *Normengeleitetes Verhalten in den Sozialwissenschaften* (pp. 61–81). Berlin: Duncker & Humblot.

Scully, R., & Farrell, D. M. (2003). MEPs as Representatives: Individual and Institutional Roles. *Journal of Common Market Studies, 41*(2), 269–288.

Settembri, P., & Neuhold, C. (2009). Achieving Consensus Through Committees: Does the European Parliament Manage? *Journal of Common Market Studies, 47*(1), 127–151.

Swartz, D. (2013). *Symbolic Power, Politics, and Intellectuals: The Political Sociology of Pierre Bourdieu*. Chicago: University of Chicago Press.

Vauchez, A. (2010). The Making of the European Union's Constitutional Foundations: The Brokering Role of Legal Entrepreneurs and Networks. In W. Kaiser, B. Leucht, & M. Gehler (Eds.), *Transnational Networks in Regional Integration Governing Europe 1945–83* (pp. 108–128). Basingstoke: Palgrave Macmillan.

Vauchez, A. (2011). Interstitial Power in Fields of Limited Statehood: Introducing a "Weak Field" Approach to the Study of Transnational Settings. *International Political Sociology, 5*(3), 340–345.

Victor, J. N., & Ringe, N. (2009). The Social Utility of Informal Institutions: Caucuses as Networks in the 110th U.S. House of Representatives. *American Politics Research, 37*(5), 742–766.

Webb, J., Schirato, T., & Danaher, G. (2002). *Understanding Bourdieu* (Repr. ed.). London: Sage.

Weber, M. (1922). *Gesammelte Aufsätze zur Religionssoziologie I.* Tübingen: J.C.B. Mohr.

Whitaker, R. (2011). *The European Parliament's Committees: National Party Influence and Legislative Empowerment.* London: Routledge.

Wilken, L. (2006). *Pierre Bourdieu.* Roskilde Universitetsforlag.

Wodak, R. (2009). *The Discourse of Politics in Action: Politics as Usual.* New York: Palgrave Macmillan.

Yordanova, N. (2009). The Rationale Behind Committee Assignment in the European Parliament: Distributive, Informational and Partisan Perspectives. *European Union Politics, 10*(2), 253–280.

Yordanova, N. (2011). Inter-institutional Rules and Division of Power in the European Parliament: Allocation of Consultation and Co-decision Reports. *West European Politics, 34*(1), 97–121.

Zimmermann, A., & Favell, A. (2011). Governmentality, Political Field or Public Sphere? Theoretical Alternatives in the Political Sociology of the EU. *European Journal of Social Theory, 14*(4), 489–515.

CHAPTER 3

Intergroups in the European Parliament: Institutionalisation and Regulation

A sociological view on the European Parliament (EP) focuses on the individuals and social groups who make up the institution. It looks at their interactions and seeks to link the cultural as well as social variables of these collectives to their practice of politics. In this context, institutionalisation is a key sociological concept. Understood as the 'establishment of customs, practices and patterns of interactions' (Kauppi, 2011, p. 154), it constitutes a useful conceptual bracket to analyse the practices of Members of the European Parliament (MEPs) in Intergroups, and the construction of organisational procedures beyond the official EP structure over time. This chapter constitutes a general introduction to Intergroups in the EP. It looks at the development of Intergroups over time, sheds light on the process of regulation and institutionalisation during the mid-1990s, and gives an insight into the diverse organisational features of Intergroups.

Intergroups over Time

Intergroups are not a phenomenon of the 7th EP. By contrast, they have existed since the first direct elections of the EP in 1979. Among the first Intergroups were the Kangaroo Group and the Crocodile Club (Jacobs, Corbett, & Shackleton, 1992). The former started out as 'an informal group of friends' (Kangaroo Group, 2014) around the British MEP Basil de Ferranti in 1979, who promoted the development of the Single Market (Jacobs et al., 1992). The latter was

L. Landorff, *Inside European Parliament Politics*,
Palgrave Studies in European Political Sociology,
https://doi.org/10.1007/978-3-030-04206-6_3

established by Altiero Spinelli 'together with other Federalist-minded MEPs' in 1980 (European Commission, 2014). Both Intergroups, or rather their spin-offs, have been active until today. The Spinelli Group counts more than 110 MEPs as their supporters (Spinelli Group, 2016). Next to these 'well-known' Intergroups, a handful of other Intergroups were founded in the first term of the directly elected Parliament. Among these were the Intergroup of 'Local and Regional Representatives', the 'Trade Union' Intergroup, the 'Disability' and 'Extreme Poverty and Human Rights' Intergroups, both founded in 1980; and the Intergroups on 'Minority Languages and Culture' and on 'Animal Welfare', both created in 1983.

Throughout the last seven legislatures, the popularity and number of Intergroups among MEPs rose steadily (Fig. 3.1). For the second parliamentary term (1984–1989), over 50 Intergroups are documented (Jacobs et al., 1992). A similar number is recorded after the elections in 1989 (Jacobs et al., 1992).

As Fig. 3.1 outlines, by the end of the 4th EP (1994–1999), '58 Intergroups were registered with the EP Secretary-General' (Corbett, Jacobs, & Shackleton, 2011, p. 208). For the subsequent 5th EP (1999–2004) around 80 Intergroups were active, of which 24 were officially recognised by the EP (European Parliament, 2005). The distinction between officially recognised and not officially recognised Intergroups is the result of the decision made by the Conference of Presidents in

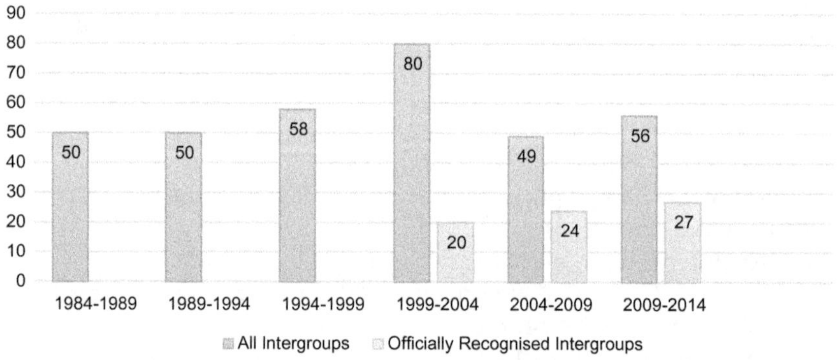

Fig. 3.1 EP Intergroups over time: From the 2nd to the 7th EP (1984–2014) (*Source* Author's own figure based on Jacobs et al. [1992, 1995], Corbett et al. [2000, 2005, 2007, 2011] and European Parliament [2002, 2003, 2005, 2016])

1995/1999 to establish rules on the creation and official status of Intergroups in the EP (Corbett, Jacobs, & Neville, 2016). The set-up of these rules is discussed in more detail below.

Institutionalisation and Regulation

As long as Intergroups have existed in the EP, MEPs have been demanding official recognition for their respective Intergroups. Minutes of EP Bureau meetings[1] obtained for this study document the successive requests by MEPs in the 1980s and early 1990s. Among these were requests for official recognition, for the conversion into a special delegation which would then have its own secretariat[2] and for administrative facilities for the Intergroups 'Cultural and Linguistic Minorities' (Europäisches Parlament—Erweitertes Präsidium, 1986, 1988, 1990a, 1990c), 'Local and Regional Representatives' (Europäisches Parlament—Erweitertes Präsidium, 1990d, 1991a, 1991b, 1991c, 1991d) and the 'Federalist' Intergroup (Europäisches Parlament—Erweitertes Präsidium, 1987a, 1987b). All of these requests for official recognition were linked to requests for administrative support (e.g. to the provision of rooms and translation facilities) needed for the functioning and activities of the Intergroup. Here again the particularity of the EP as a multilingual legislature plays into the functioning of an Intergroup. To speak in terms of capital, these requests concerned collective political resources that the EP can offer to its members (e.g. office space and facilities) (see Kauppi, 2011). The EP Bureau rejected all of these requests on two grounds: first, it pointed to the political groups and their responsibility for the organisational matters of Intergroups (Europäisches Parlament—Erweitertes Präsidium, 1988, 1990b, 1991d). Second, it pointed to 'unavoidable conflicts of responsibility' that would occur with the creation of a competing structure to the parliamentary committee on Regional Development in the case of a conversion of the 'Local and Regional Representatives' Intergroup into a special delegation (Europäisches Parlament—Erweitertes Präsidium, 1990b, 1991d).[3]

The concern on the emergence of a competing structure to the parliamentary committees appears again in 1995 in the context of the decision made by the Conference of Presidents on Intergroups, and the subsequent introduction of rules governing their establishment in 1999 (Corbett et al., 2016). A number of reservations were addressed to Klaus Hänsch, president of the EP at the time, with the rising numbers of Intergroups in the early and mid-1990s, displayed in Fig. 3.1. The president of the Group of the European Liberal, Democrat and Reform Party (ELDR) Gijs M. de Vries issued concerns that several Intergroups would benefit from financial and/or organisational support from private companies or pressure groups (de Vries, 1995). Together with his colleague Gerhard Schmid, they further raised concerns that some Intergroups would be mistaken by outsiders as official bodies of the EP (de Vries, 1995; Schmid, 1994). Finally, the Scottish MEP Jack Stewart-Clark, EP vice-president at the time, argued that a certain number of 'réunions périphérique' (e.g. Intergroups) could harm the efficiency of the EP (Stewart-Clark, 1994).

To elaborate in depth on these concerns is beyond the scope of this book whose focus is on MEPs and their practices in Intergroups. What is, however, important in this context is that MEPs' engagement in Intergroups is a controversial topic among MEPs, and that MEPs in EP leadership positions (e.g. EP vice-presidents and chairs of political groups) have fostered the regulation of Intergroups. This indicates different positions on how the EP should organise itself and on how MEPs should carry out their mandate, which makes research on MEPs' reasoning to engage in Intergroups even more interesting and important.

Because of these concerns, the Conference of Presidents adopted a first agreement on Intergroups in 1995 (Corbett et al., 2016). This agreement stated that Intergroups are not official EP organs, have no official status, cannot express the Parliament's opinion and cannot use its name or logo or 'any other denominations that could lead to confusion with official organs of the EP' (Corbett et al., 2011, p. 210). With this, Intergroups as groups were deprived of collective, institutionalised political capital that the EP has to offer. In addition, rules on 'the provision of technical facilities for Intergroups' through the political groups were introduced and further detailed in 1999 (Corbett et al., 2011, p. 210; European Parliament, 2012).

With the set-up of rules governing the establishment of Intergroups, gaining official recognition as an Intergroup required MEPs to submit an annual declaration of financial interests, precise statements of the Intergroup's objectives as well as at least three political groups which support the official recognition of the respective Intergroup with their signature (European Parliament, 2012). In turn, these political groups are then responsible for the provision of meeting rooms, of translation and interpretation facilities for the respective Intergroup. In addition, meeting times and locations of Intergroups were assigned to the part-time EP sessions in Strasbourg, France, initially on Wednesday afternoons, Thursdays and Fridays in 1999 (European Parliament, 1999; Jacobs et al., 1995). From February 2008 onwards, they were assigned to Thursdays only (European Parliament, 2008). This restriction has been subject to major criticism by MEPs.[4] One the one hand, MEPs show understanding that there cannot be an unlimited number of Intergroups given that the EP's physical capacities (in terms of rooms, buildings, translation and interpretation facilities) are limited.[5] Hence, there is an immanent competition for physical, collective resources within the Parliament. On the other hand, MEPs perceive in particular the restriction of meeting times to Thursdays during the Strasbourg session as 'ridiculous'[6] and 'unnecessarily restrictive'.[7] Some claim that these rules were 'designed to kill Intergroups'[8] or rather 'to cause maximum difficulty for the Intergroups'.[9] MEPs criticise that Intergroup meetings collide with meetings of official organs taking place on Thursday mornings or afternoons, such as coordinator meetings[10] or urgent debates on human rights topics.[11] Moreover, MEPs argue that 'everybody leaves after lunch on a Thursday in Strasbourg to go home because it takes twelve hours for most people to get from Strasbourg to anywhere'.[12] As a result, it is very difficult to have many MEPs attending Intergroup meetings on Thursdays in Strasbourg. A phenomenon that Intergroups share with the committee meetings that take place on Thursday afternoon in Brussels (Corbett et al., 2016). The disagreement on the place and timing of Intergroup meetings has to be related to the particularity of the parliamentary timetable. Parliamentary business follows a strict monthly schedule with a plenary week in Strasbourg, followed by two committee weeks and a 'Group Week' in Brussels (Corbett et al., 2016). In addition, MEPs have to make time to travel between Strasbourg, Brussels and their constituency. This cycle of activities does not leave much scope for extra sittings. Time is a scarce resource to compete for in the EP. With regard to Intergroups, MEPs point to 'other powerful formal structures in the Parliament', such as the Conference of Committee Chairs and the Conference of Presidents, 'where the real regulatory power [...] in the sense of regulating the work of the Parliament lies',[13] and attribute this restriction to a 'jealously amongst the Conference of Presidents that the Intergroups are taking on too much power [...] and having too much influence'.[14] These observations point to an internal struggle between various social groups in the Parliament, between those in the EP leadership, i.e. the Conference of Presidents, that are perceived as 'bureaucrats'[15] by MEPs and those parliamentarians engaging in Intergroups. It is a struggle on who regulates the work of the EP, who determines on what MEPs work on, speak about and when they do it. It is a battle for institutionalised resources in the EP on the one hand. It is a battle about who defines whose interests and rights are favoured by MEPs and the EP at the expense of others on the other hand. Attempts by MEPs to counteract these rules have been without success.[16] MEPs argue that they 'have to accept the decisions that are made by these bodies'.[17] By contrast, field research conducted for this book has also shown that parliamentarians have ended up 'working around the rules'.[18] This means they have found means to circumvent these institutional rules by, for example, conducting meetings in Brussels. Chapter 5 will discuss this aspect in more depth again.

As just mentioned, the recognition of an Intergroup requires the support of at least three political groups. Thereby, the number of signatures each political group has for supporting Intergroups is determined at the beginning of each parliamentary term in accordance with an agreement concluded by the political groups (European Parliament, 2012). For the parliamentary term 2009–2014, the signature allocation scheme looked as displayed in Table 3.1. From this, it shows that signatures are allocated proportionally with the biggest political groups receiving the most signatures, while it is noticeable that the EPP and S&D group receive the same amount of signatures despite their different group size.

The procedures within the political groups on which Intergroups should be supported vary. Hence, there is no common practice across the transnational political groups in the EP on how to determine those Intergroups that should be supported by the respective political group. In one political group, all requests of MEPs for an Intergroup are first collected. The bureau of the political group (e.g. including among others the chair, the vice-chairs and treasurers) subsequently sets up a 'priority

Table 3.1 Signature Scheme for the Establishment of Intergroups in the 7th EP (2009–2014)

EPP	*S&D*	*ALDE*	*GREENS/EFA*	*ECR*	*GUE/NGL*	*EFD*
21	21	10	8	8	6	5

Source European Parliament (2012)

list',[19] selecting those suggestions for Intergroups that best reflect the political priorities of the political group. This 'priority list' serves as the basis for the negotiations with the other political groups. In another political group, all members are asked to compile a 'list of a limited number of Intergroups which they wanted to support individually'.[20] On the basis of this list, a ranking is established listing those Intergroups which have been asked most by the members to be supported in descending order as 'the first Intergroup, the second, the third, the fourth, the fifth [...]'.[21] Again also in this political group, it is important that the list 'politically reflect[s] the priorities of the group'.[22] In this context, the task is to reach a combination, which reflects the 'specific interest of the members but which takes into account the general priorities of the group'.[23] In yet another political group, an open list, in which any item for an Intergroup can be proposed by the members of the political group, is established first. Then a ranking is established by MEPs attaching 10 points to their 1st priority Intergroup and one point to their 10th priority Intergroup.[24] Equipped with their priority lists, the representatives of the political groups (e.g. in one case, the Deputy Secretary General of the political group, in another the Secretary General), 'enter into negotiations'[25] with the different political groups in the EP. During these negotiations, the different group representatives make their bids for their prioritised Intergroups on the basis of the number of available signatures at their disposal (e.g. the EPP has 21 signatures to be allocated to Intergroups while the Greens/EFA have eight signatures).[26] As 'you will never find a group supporting [...] all of your requests' and vice versa, the representatives of the political groups 'have to start negotiating and see what you are ready to [...] trade off [and] what is really something that you cannot trade off' as one representative of a political group described the process.[27]

With this practice of negotiating and bidding for Intergroups, the political groups apply similar procedures as observed in the context of the allocation of rapporteurships (Kaeding, 2004). The distribution of rapporteurships is not regulated by 'the standing orders of the EP' but through an 'auction-like system based primarily on the rule of proportionality' where the political groups 'receive a quote of points according to their size' and make their bids (Kaeding, 2004, p. 354). Thus, in terms of institutionalisation, there is a replication of practices on the side of the political groups.

Similar to the process of committee assignment that is controlled by party groups in the EP (Bowler & Farrell, 1995; Corbett et al., 2016; McElroy, 2006), the process of recognition of Intergroups, their regulation and formalisation is a process under the control and scrutiny of the political groups in the EP. While individual members come up with suggestions for Intergroups, and may join as many Intergroups as they like, the final selection and recognition of Intergroups as officially registered occurs under the control of the political groups and in correspondence with their political priorities.

Given that the signature scheme is based primarily on the rule of proportionality, the overall majority ratios in the EP are reproduced in the official recognition of Intergroups, with the largest political groups having the most signatures to push for their prioritised Intergroups. Given that those political groups which support an Intergroup also provide the chairs,[28] this results in the EPP group providing the majority of Intergroup chairs in the 7th EP, as outlined in the following Chapter 4.

Next to the reproduction of already existing hierarchies in the EP (e.g. in terms of majority ratios and political preferences of political groups), these rules have several results:

First, they put Intergroups into an intermediate position within the Parliament. They are not officially recognised as official EP organs by the political groups. Their members are, however, official members of the EP and conduct their meetings on the premises of the EP. Corbett et al. (2011, p. 187) argue that this makes them 'almost semi-official'.

Second, Intergroups are limited to 27 in number in the 7th EP (2009–2014) as result of the signature allocation scheme set up by the political groups. MEPs have to (re-)apply for official recognition of their Intergroup at every new parliamentary term. Hence, being official recognised for one term does not secure official recognition for the subsequent term. This causes a competition within the political groups and among MEPs for which Intergroups should be supported by the group.[29]

Third, next to the officially recognised Intergroups, there are then a number of non-registered Intergroups. It is up for debate whether to call these non-registered groups also Intergroups as Corbett et al. (2011) do. Interviewed MEPs defined only those groups as Intergroups which are established according to the rules of the EP, and which are limited in time (e.g. to the parliamentary term), while the others (i.e. the non-registered ones) are perceived of as think tanks, which claim for instance a membership fee and are not limited in time.[30]

Fourth, while there are formal rules on the establishment of Intergroups, a number of interviewed MEPs described the processes and procedures within Intergroups as informal.[31] In fact, the Intergroup 'Animal Welfare' is the only Intergroup among the 27 that has written rules of procedure guiding the Intergroup's activities, such as the election of chairs (Intergroup on the Welfare & Conservation of Animals, 2013).

Thus, the next section looks into the internal organisation and working methods of Intergroups, providing an insight into the degree of formality and institutionalisation (e.g. set-up of practices) within Intergroups.

Internal Organisation of Intergroups

For the 7th EP (2009–2014), on which this study focuses, 27 received official recognition as EP Intergroup while around 29 unregistered Intergroups were active (Corbett et al., 2011, p. 211). Appendix A provides an overview of these 27 officially recognised Intergroups.

As Appendix A shows, Intergroups differ substantially in their content, goals, membership, internal organisation and visibility. In the 7th Parliament, listed members of Intergroups ranged from 12 MEPs ('Extreme Poverty and Human Rights') to 126 MEPs ('Climate Change, Biodiversity and Sustainable Development') (European Parliament, 2013). Among those are long-standing Intergroups, such as the aforementioned Intergroups 'Trade Union', 'Animal Welfare' and 'Disability' as well as Intergroup novices, which just started to work in the 7th legislature (e.g. Intergroups 'Water', 'Youth Issues' or 'Mountains, Islands and Sparsely Populated Regions').

In terms of content, Intergroups cover a wide range of themes and objectives (see Appendix A). There are several Intergroups dedicated to social groups, such as older and young people as well as minorities. There are a number of Intergroups dealing with rather functional, sector-related topics, such as the Intergroups on 'Viticulture' or 'Sky and Space'. There are a few Intergroups concentrating on certain regions and a handful of Intergroups focusing on issues related to the common good, such as human rights (see Intergroups 'Anti-Racism and Diversity' or 'Tibet'), climate change (see Intergroup 'Climate Change, Biodiversity and Sustainable Development') and culture (see Intergroup 'Ways of Saint James/Caminos de Santiago'). In terms of representation, two broad groups within Intergroups can be identified: one group deals with interests of the common good (e.g. including environmental and social interests) and universal values (e.g. human rights), and another group deals with particular interests of certain sectors, industries and regions. These two groups appear evenly distributed among the officially recognised Intergroups.

Some Intergroups meet on a monthly basis, have a website and issue newsletters, such as the Intergroups 'Water' and 'Urban' (EP Water Group, 2014; Urban Intergroup at the European Parliament, 2014). Others meet only on ad hoc basis, on demand and publish hardly anything on their activities (e.g. Intergroups 'New Media' or 'Ways of Saint James/ Caminos de Santiago'). Overall, 14 out of the 27 officially registered Intergroups convened meetings on a monthly basis or met every other month. This constitutes the most frequent interaction pattern among MEPs in Intergroups. The remaining Intergroups held up to four meetings a year.

With regard to their internal organisation, a common feature of all Intergroups is their division into a 'Bureau' and 'Members'. The 'Bureau' constitutes the core of the Intergroup. It consists of a chair and vice-chairs. Some Intergroups, such as the Intergroup 'Animal Welfare', have also 'honorary presidents' (Intergroup on the Welfare & Conservation of Animals, 2014). The members of the 'Bureau' provide the steering of the Intergroup. They set up the agenda for the Intergroup, organise its meetings and liaise with external partners.[32] The vice-presidents are from the different political groups, which support the Intergroup in the official recognition, and in most cases from different committees.[33] Thereby, the cross-party and cross-committee character of the Intergroup is also reflected in the 'Bureau'. Being composed of a chair, vice-presidents and members, Intergroups resemble the organisational set-up of the EP parliamentary committees. Thus, in terms of institutionalisation there is again a replication of organisational patterns that already exist at the official formal level. The individual composition and size of the Bureau vary from small ones containing 2–4 MEP, such as in the Intergroups 'Viticulture' and 'Traditional Minorities, National Communities and Languages', to big ones comprising 20 MEPs, such as in the Intergroup 'Animal Welfare'. In doing so, an Intergroup can offer up to 20 posts (e.g. institutionalised political capital) as vice-presidents to MEPs.

With regard to the four Intergroups under scrutiny, there are two long-standing Intergroups and a fairly new one. The 'Trade Union' Intergroup started out in 1979 as a loose cooperation of trade union-friendly MEPs.[34] The 'Animal Welfare' Intergroup was established in 1983 (Intergroup on the Welfare & Conservation of Animals, 2014).

By contrast, the 'Urban' Intergroup was set up in 2005 with the beginning of the 6th EP (2004–2009). The 'Trade Union', 'Animal Welfare' and 'Urban' Intergroups organise monthly meetings and thus regularise monthly interactions among MEPs, between MEPs and, for example, civil society representatives. In comparison with the overall population of Intergroups, this frequency of meetings is the most common one, with eight of the 27 officially recognised Intergroups meeting on a monthly basis. The four Intergroups vary as well with regard to their members (see Table 3.2): the Intergroup 'Trade Union' counted 20 MEPs as their members, the Intergroup 'Viticulture' counted 95 MEPs, the 'Urban' had 61 members while 44 MEPs have subscribed to the Intergroup 'Animal Welfare' in the 7th EP (European Parliament, 2013). In view of the 27 officially recognised Intergroups, these four Intergroups cover both the higher and lower end of the official membership figures. These features will be discussed in more detail throughout the upcoming chapters.

Table 3.2 Features of Four Intergroups

'Trade Union' – Established in 1979 – Chair in 7th EP: Alejandro Cercas (S&D) and Elisabeth Morin-Chartier (EPP) – Official recognition as Intergroup: 2005 – Enrolled MEPs in 7th EP: 20 – Monthly meetings in Brussels, Belgium – Website/Newsletter: No – Secretariat: S&D and EPP Group	**'Urban'** – Established in 2005 – Chair in 7th EP: Jan Olbrycht (EPP) – Official recognition as Intergroup: 2005 – Enrolled MEPs in 7th EP: 61 – Monthly meetings in Strasbourg, France – Website/Newsletter: Yes/Yes – Secretariat: Internal (office of MEP Olbrycht)
'Viticulture' – Established in 1993/1994 – Chair in 7th EP: Astrid Lulling (EPP) (since 1999) – Official recognition as Intergroup: 2000 – Enrolled MEPs in 7th EP: 95 – Meetings every 2nd month in Strasbourg, France – Website/Newsletter: No – Secretariat: Internal (office of MEP Lulling)	**'Animal Welfare'** – Established in 1983 – Chairs in 7th EP: Caroline Lucas (Greens/EFA), Carl Schlyter (Greens/EFA), Dan Jørgensen (S&D), and Pavel Poc (S&D) – Official recognition as Intergroup: 2000 – Enrolled MEPs in 7th EP: 44 – Monthly meetings in Strasbourg, France – Website/Newsletter: Yes/No – Secretariat: External (Eurogroup for Animals since 1983)

Source Author's own table based on European Parliament (2002, 2003, 2005, 2016), Intergroup on the Welfare & Conservation of Animals (2014), and Urban Intergroup at the European Parliament (2014); Interviews MEPs 1, 13; CSO 1, 2, 6

External Secretariats

A little more than one third of the officially recognised Intergroups operated with an external organisation as their secretariat (e.g. Intergroups 'Social Economy', 'Water' or 'Disability'). The remaining Intergroups were organised by the office of the MEP chairing the Intergroup (e.g. Intergroups 'Urban', 'Baltic-Europe' or 'Traditional Minorities, National Communities and Languages'). Previous research suggests that Intergroups play 'a central role in the way its members interact with certain civil society organisations' (Greenwood, 2011; Mény, 2009, p. 97). For an in-depth insight into civil society engagement in Intergroups, see Landorff (Accepted/In press). As outlined in Table 3.3, 11 out of the 27 officially recognised Intergroups of the 7th EP worked with a civil society organisation as their external secretariat. These are primarily European associations representing citizens' interests, i.e. social, environmental and human rights interests.

Table 3.3 Intergroups and their External Secretariats (2009–2014)

Intergroup	*Civil Society Organisation*
1. Ageing and Intergenerational Solidarity	AGE Platform Europe
2. Climate Change, Biodiversity and Sustainable Development	European Bureau for Conservation and Development (EBCD) and International Union for Conservation of Nature (IUCN)
3. Disability	European Disability Forum (EDF)
4. Extreme Poverty and Human Rights	ATD Fourth World
5. Seas and Coastal Areas	Conference of Peripheral Maritime Regions (CPMR)
6. Social Economy	Social Economy Europe
7. Sustainable Hunting, Biodiversity, Countryside Activities, and Forestry	European Federation of Associations for Hunting and Conservation of the EU (FACE) and European Landowners' Organisation (ELO)
8. Water	European Federation of National Associations of Water Services (EUREAU)
9. Welfare and Conservation of Animals	Eurogroup for Animals
10. Mountains, Islands and Sparsely Populated Regions	Association Européenne des Élus de Montagne (AEM)
11. Anti-Racism and Diversity	European Network against Racism (ENAR)

Source Individual websites of the Intergroups listed in 'Appendix A'. Missing information on Intergroups 'New Media, Free Software, Open Information Society', 'Family and the Rights of the Child & Bioethics', and 'Sky and Space'

To provide the secretariat for an Intergroup includes a number of quite comprehensive tasks. In the case of the Eurogroup for Animals, that provides the secretariat for the Intergroup 'Animal Welfare', these tasks cover the arrangement of Intergroup meetings and events (including the invitation of guests), the set-up of the Intergroup agenda and the coordination of Intergroup actions (Intergroup on the Welfare & Conservation of Animals, 2013, p. 4). Consequently, the Eurogroup for Animals plays a decisive role in the functioning and management of the Intergroup.

The comparison with other Intergroups, such as the Intergroup 'Climate Change, Biodiversity and Sustainable Development', having an external secretariat discloses similar patterns and tasks (European Bureau for Conservation & Development, 2014 [2012]). However, fieldwork conducted for this book suggests that, with regard to Intergroup activities, the Eurogroup for Animals is presently one of the most organised and active secretariats. The Eurogroup operates as the secretariat of the Intergroup since its creation in 1983, and thus, displays long-term commitment and experience. In addition to the organisation of meetings, the external secretariats provide Intergroups with logistics, such as contacts to external guests and speakers, and visibility, such as a website and posters inside the EP buildings announcing Intergroup events.[35] The comparison of Intergroups supported by external secretariats with those organised by the office of an individual parliamentarian (i.e. the Intergroup chair) reveals that the former enjoy a higher visibility than the latter. Consequently, working with an external organisation as a secretariat provides for more visibility of an Intergroup.

Chairmanships

In some Intergroups, the chairmanship rotates after two-and-a-half years. For instance, the Hungarian MEP Kinga Gál and the Finnish MEP Carl Haglund co-chaired the Intergroup 'Traditional Minorities, National Communities and Languages' for the first two-and-a-half years of the 7th EP, the Hungarian MEP Csaba Tabajdi and French MEP François Alfonsi for the second two-and-a-half years (European Parliament, 2013; Gál, Hicks, & Eplényi, 2011). The Spanish MEP Alejandro Cercas led the Intergroup 'Trade Union' for the first two-and-a-half years while the French MEP Elisabeth Morin-Chartier took over for the second half of the parliamentary term. The Intergroup 'Animal Welfare' was chaired initially by the Swedish MEP Carl Schlyter. He was succeeded by the Danish

MEP Dan Jørgensen (Intergroup on the Welfare & Conservation of Animals, 2012). In this way, Intergroups resemble again practices that are regularised in the official structures of the EP, i.e. chairs and vice-chairs of the parliamentary committees having terms of office of two-and-a-half years as well as the EP leadership (Corbett et al., 2016, p. 174). However, the change of leadership is not only due to rotation but also the result of MEPs leaving the Parliament. During the 7th EP, five Intergroup chairs left the Parliament. Among them were the above mentioned Dan Jørgensen and Carl Haglund.[36]

Fieldwork revealed three paths of how to become a chair of an Intergroup. These findings should be perceived as an indication, but not yet as general trends because further systematic research covering all Intergroup chairs over time is required. However, three patterns emerged from the interviews:

First, MEPs may be approached by external organisations (e.g. those civil society organisations which either provide the secretariat or have regular contact with the Intergroup) with the request to chair the Intergroup. These MEPs may be approached because of their position in certain committees, their seniority and the reputation they had built up as long-serving MEP, or their previous professional occupation. These characteristics are not mutually exclusive, as for instance reputation goes along with being involved in a certain policy area and thus, in a parliamentary committee for successive terms. In addition, previously acquired interpersonal relations, e.g. social capital, may also play a role. For instance, incoming chairs were acquainted with CSO representatives prior their EP mandate and have been approached by the latter with the request to take up the post.

Second, MEPs themselves may express the interest to chair an Intergroup and are subsequently elected by acclamation.[37] Another interesting observation made in this context is that MEPs may need to have personal political capital, in other words, a reputation, a name and the trust of their transnational political group (e.g. the EPP, S&D group, Greens/EFA and so forth) in the first place to become an Intergroup chair. Newly elected MEPs needed first to become known to colleagues and to receive the trust of their respective political group, by occupying several posts in official parliamentary structures, in order to be considered as a candidate for a chairmanship of an Intergroup.

Third, the group coordinators of the two biggest political groups in a certain committee may become chair of an Intergroup.[38] This practice applies so far only to the Intergroup 'Trade Union'. Here the group coordinators of the EPP and S&D in the committee on Employment and Social Affairs (EMPL), e.g. the Spanish MEP Alejandro Cercas and the French MEP Elisabeth Morin-Chartier, are 'automatically the chairs of the Intergroup'.[39] In this way, the two transnational political groups (EPP and S&D) ensure the control on the steering of the Intergroup. Moreover, this case shows that occupying a certain position in the transnational field, a position of authority (e.g. the position of a group coordinator in a parliamentary committee) can be a prerequisite for obtaining a position as Intergroup chair.

In sum, the findings indicate that to take up a post as an Intergroup chair requires either a position in a committee that matches the interest of the external organisation engaged in the Intergroup or as group coordinator (i.e. institutionalised political capital), or seniority and (professional) reputation and experience (i.e. personal political capital) in the Parliament that is valued by the transnational political group.

Conclusion

This chapter provided a descriptive introduction to the topic of Intergroups in the EP. It expanded upon the numerical development of Intergroups in the EP over time, their institutionalisation within the Parliament, as well as their organisational structures. The chapter showed that Intergroups as an organisational arrangement, as cross-party groupings beyond the official parliamentary structures, existed since the first direct elections of the EP in 1979. Thus, they have always been a part of the parliamentary practices of MEPs. Thereby, Intergroups represent two broad groups. One is related to the interests of a common good. The other one is related to particular interests of certain industries, sectors and regions. The discussion on the regulation of Intergroups in the mid-1990s revealed that Intergroups are a contentious issue between MEPs and the Parliament's leadership bodies. The regulation is the expression of an internal struggle between various groups in the Parliament on how MEPs shall exercise their mandate, and over the physical resources that the EP as an institution provides to its members to conduct parliamentary business. The analysis of Intergroups' internal structures showed further a replication of organisational practices that are already in place at the official EP structures. Consisting of a bureau (chair and vice-chairs) and members, Intergroups resemble existing parliamentary structures (e.g. those of the parliamentary committees). Moreover, the process of official recognition of Intergroups displays strong similarities with the practices observed in the context of the allocation of parliamentary reports. It is controlled by the political groups in the EP, and based on proportionality. This means that the largest political groups receive the highest number of signatures to support an Intergroup in its official recognition. In this way, the established majority ratios are reproduced. In sum, analysing the institutionalisation of Intergroups over time has revealed a reproduction of already existing practices and therewith, a reproduction of established majority ratios and organisational hierarchies.

Notes

1. Obtained from the European Parliament: Archive and Documentation Centre (CARDOC)—Historical Archives of the EP—Luxembourg, Luxembourg via e-mail on 16–19 March 2010.
2. The request was made with regard to the Intergroup 'Local and Regional Representatives'.
3. See Minutes of EP Bureau meetings on 5 May 1990 (PE 142.086/PRÄS) and 29 April 1991 (PE 151.564/PRÄS); original quote: '[…] angesichts der unvermeidlichen Kompetenzstreitigkeiten, die bei der Schaffung einer mit dem Ausschuß für Regionalpolitik konkurrierenden Struktur auftreten würden, [spricht sich das erweiterte Präsidium] gegen die Umwandlung der interfraktionellen Arbeitsgruppe in eine offizielle und besondere Delegation […]', p. 10.
4. See Interviews MEPs 3, 4, 8, 10, 13, 15, 20, 21.
5. See Interviews MEPs 4, 6, 8, 9, 15, 16, 17.
6. See Interview MEP 13.
7. See Interview MEP 8.
8. See Interview MEP 13.
9. See Interview MEP 3.
10. See Interview MEP 8.
11. See Interview MEP 10.
12. See Interviews MEP 3; see also MEPs 8, 10.
13. See Interview MEP 13.
14. See Interview MEP 3, for a similar insight MEP 21.
15. See Interviews MEP 20; see also MEP 4.
16. See Interviews MEPs 13, 8, 10.
17. See Interview MEP 13.
18. See Interview MEP 8.

19. See Interview PG 1.
20. See Interview PG 2.
21. See Interview PG 2.
22. See Interview PG 2.
23. See Interview PG 2.
24. See Interview political group in Landorff (2010).
25. See Interview PG 1.
26. See Interviews PG 1 and 2.
27. See Interview PG 1.
28. See, e.g., Interview MEP 1.
29. See Interviews MEPs 3, 18.
30. See Interview MEP 5.
31. See Interviews MEPs 1, 2, 9, 10, 11, 13, 14, 15, 19, 20, 21; CSO 1, 3, 4.
32. See Interviews MEPs 1, 2, 5, 13; CSO 1, 2, 5.
33. See Interviews MEPs 1, 5.
34. See Interview CSO 2.
35. See, e.g., Intergroups 'Animal Welfare', 'Climate Change, Biodiversity and Sustainable Development' and 'Water' observed during fieldwork in the EP in September and October 2012, March and May 2013.
36. See also the Spanish MEP Iñigo Méndez de Vigo, chair of the Intergroup 'Extreme Poverty and Human Rights'; the French MEP Damian Abad, founder and chair of the Intergroup 'Youth Issues'; and the Italian MEP Mario Mauro, former co-chair of the Intergroup 'Social Economy'.
37. See Interviews CSO 1, 6.
38. See Interview PG 1.
39. See Interview PG 1.

References

Bowler, S., & Farrell, D. M. (1995). The Organizing of the European Parliament: Committees, Specialization and Co-ordination. *British Journal of Political Science, 25*(02), 219–243.

Corbett, R., Jacobs, F., & Shackleton, M. (2000). *The European Parliament* (4th ed.). London: John Harper Publishing.

Corbett, R., Jacobs, F., & Shackleton, M. (2005). *The European Parliament* (6th ed.). London: John Harper Publishing.

Corbett, R., Jacobs, F., & Shackleton, M. (2007). *The European Parliament* (7th ed.). London: John Harper Publishing.

Corbett, R., Jacobs, F., & Neville, D. (2016). *The European Parliament* (9th ed.). London: John Harper Publishing.

Corbett, R., Jacobs, F., & Shackleton, M. (2011). *The European Parliament* (8th ed.). London: John Harper Publishing.

de Vries, G. (1995). *Concerns: Intergroups* (Letter by Gijs M. de Vries, President of the Group of the European Liberal, Democrat and Reform Party, to the President of the European Parliament, 26 January 1995 PE 186.957/BUR ed.). Brussels: Group of the European Liberal, Democrat and Reform Party.

EP Water Group. (2014 [2013]). *EP Water Group*. Retrieved 4 April 2014, from http://epwatergroup.eu/.

Europäisches Parlament—Erweitertes Präsidium. (1986). *Protokoll der Sitzung vom 18. Februar 1986*. Luxembourg: European Parliament Archive and Documentation Centre (CARDOC).

Europäisches Parlament—Erweitertes Präsidium. (1987a). *Protokoll zur Sitzung vom 7. April 1987*. Luxembourg: European Parliament Archive and Documentation Centre (CARDOC).

Europäisches Parlament—Erweitertes Präsidium. (1987b). *Protokoll zur Sitzung vom 30. April 1987*. Luxembourg: European Parliament Archive and Documentation Centre (CARDOC).

Europäisches Parlament—Erweitertes Präsidium. (1988). *Protokoll zur Sitzung vom 25. April 1988*. Luxembourg: European Parliament Archive and Documentation Centre (CARDOC).

Europäisches Parlament—Erweitertes Präsidium. (1990a). *Protokoll zur Sitzung vom 3. April 1990*. Luxembourg: European Parliament Archive and Documentation Centre (CARDOC).

Europäisches Parlament—Erweitertes Präsidium. (1990b). *Protokoll zur Sitzung vom 5. Mai 1990*. Luxembourg: European Parliament Archive and Documentation Centre (CARDOC).

Europäisches Parlament—Erweitertes Präsidium. (1990c). *Protokoll zur Sitzung vom 13./14. März 1990*. Luxembourg: European Parliament Archive and Documentation Centre (CARDOC).

Europäisches Parlament—Erweitertes Präsidium. (1990d). *Protokoll zur Sitzung vom 21. November 1990*. Luxembourg: European Parliament Archive and Documentation Centre (CARDOC).

Europäisches Parlament—Erweitertes Präsidium. (1991a). *Protokoll zur Sitzung vom 4. April 1991*. Luxembourg: European Parliament Archive and Documentation Centre (CARDOC).

Europäisches Parlament—Erweitertes Präsidium. (1991b). *Protokoll zur Sitzung vom 19. Februar 1991*. Luxembourg: European Parliament Archive and Documentation Centre (CARDOC).

Europäisches Parlament—Erweitertes Präsidium. (1991c). *Protokoll zur Sitzung vom 20. März 1991*. Luxembourg: European Parliament Archive and Documentation Centre (CARDOC).

Europäisches Parlament—Erweitertes Präsidium. (1991d). *Protokoll zur Sitzung vom 29. April 1991*. Luxembourg: European Parliament Archive and Documentation Centre (CARDOC).

European Bureau for Conservation & Development. (2014 [2012]). *EP Intergroup CCBSD: General Information*. Retrieved 8 March 2012, 13 June 2014, from http://www.ebcd.org/en/EP_Intergroup_CCBSD/.

European Commission. (2014, June 3). Altiero Spinelli: An Unrelenting Federalist. *The Founding Fathers of the EU*. Retrieved 3 June 2014, from http://europa.eu/about-eu/eu-history/founding-fathers/pdf/altiero_spinelli_en.pdf.

European Parliament. (1999). *Rules Governing the Establishment of Intergroups* (No. PE282.037/BUR/DEF, NT\386429EN.doc). Brussels: European Parliament: Conference of Presidents.

European Parliament. (2002). *Activities: 12/A-2002—Bulletin*. Brussels: European Parliament: Directorate for the Planning of Parliamentary Business.

European Parliament. (2003). *Activities: 03/A-2003—Bulletin*. Brussels: European Parliament: Directorate for the Planning of Parliamentary Business.

European Parliament. (2005). *Activities: 08/A-2005—Bulletin*. Brussels: European Parliament: Directorate for the Planning of Parliamentary Business.

European Parliament. (2008). *One-Minute Speeches on Matters of Political Importance: Thomas Mann* (No. P6_CRE(2008)05-19(19)). Strasbourg: European Parliament.

European Parliament. (2012). *Rules Governing the Establishment of Intergroups: Decision of the Conference of Presidents of 16 December 1999, Consolidated and Amended on 3 May 2004, 14 February 2008 and 12 April 2012*. Brussels: European Parliament: Conference of Presidents.

European Parliament. (2013). *About Parliament: Organisation and Work—Intergroups*. Retrieved 24 January 2013, from http://www.europarl.europa.eu/aboutparliament/en/00c9d93c87/Intergroups.html.

European Parliament. (2016). *About Parliament: Organisation and Rules—Intergroups*. Retrieved 5 April 2016, from http://www.europarl.europa.eu/aboutparliament/en/20150201PVL00010/Organisation-and-rules.

Gál, K., Hicks, D., & Eplényi, K. (2011). *Traditional Minorities, National Communities and Languages: The Issues Raised in the European Parliament Intergroup, 2009–2011*. Brussels and Budapest: Kinga Gál.

Greenwood, J. (2011). *Interest Representation in the European Union* (3rd ed.). Basingstoke: Palgrave Macmillan.

Intergroup on the Welfare & Conservation of Animals. (2012). *Press Release: New President Takes Helm at Intergroup on the Welfare & Conservation of Animals*. Brussels: Intergroup on the Welfare & Conservation of Animals.

Intergroup on the Welfare & Conservation of Animals. (2013). *Rules of Procedure*. Retrieved 31 May 2014, from http://www.animalwelfareintergroup.eu/wp-content/uploads/2013/01/Rules-of-procedure-final-11-01-2013.pdf.

Intergroup on the Welfare & Conservation of Animals. (2014). *About Us: Members*. Retrieved 27 November 2014, from http://www.animalwelfare-intergroup.eu/about-us/members/.

Jacobs, F., Corbett, R., & Shackleton, M. (1992). *The European Parliament* (2nd ed.). Harlow: Longman Current Affairs.

Jacobs, F., Corbett, R., & Shackleton, M. (1995). *The European Parliament* (3rd ed.). London: Cartermill Publishing.

Kaeding, M. (2004). Rapporteurship Allocation in the European Parliament: Information or Distribution? *European Union Politics, 5*(3), 353–371.

Kangaroo Group, T. (2014). *Who We Are: Origin*. Retrieved 3 June 2014, from http://www.kangaroogroup.eu/E/032_origin_D.lasso.

Kauppi, N. (2011). EU Politics. In A. Favell & V. Guiraudon (Eds.), *Sociology of the European Union* (pp. 150–171). Basingstoke: Palgrave Macmillan.

Landorff, L. (2010). *The Role and Function of Intergroups in the European Parliament: A Study on the Intergroup for Traditional National Minorities, Constitutional Regions and Regional Languages in the 6th Parliamentary Term (2004–2009)* (Unpublished MA thesis). University of Aarhus, Aarhus.

Landorff, L. (Accepted/In press). Intergroups as Alternative Venues in the European Parliament: Lessons for Civil Society. In U. Liebert & A. Jenichen (Eds.), *Europeanisation and Renationalisation: Learning from Crises for Innovation and Development*. Leverkusen: Barbara Budrich Publishers.

McElroy, G. (2006). Committee Representation in the European Parliament. *European Union Politics, 7*(1), 5–29.

Mény, Y. (2009). *Building Parliament: 50 Years of European Parliament History 1958–2008*. Luxembourg: Office for Official Publications of the European Communities.

Schmid, G. (1994). *Le Fonctionnement des Intergroups* (Letter by Gerhard Schmid to Klaus Hänsch, President of the European Parliament 26 October 1994 PE 184.528/BUR ed.). Brussels: European Parliament.

Spinelli Group, T. (2016). *MEP Spinelli Group*. Retrieved 10 January 2016, from http://www.spinelligroup.eu/mep-spinelli-group.

Stewart-Clark, S. J. (1994). *Concernant les Intergroups* (Letter by Sir Jack Stewart-Clark, Vice-President of the European Parliament, to Klaus Hänsch, President of the European Parliament 20 July 1994 PE 182.405/BUR ed.). Brussels: European Parliament.

Urban Intergroup at the European Parliament. (2014). *Urban Intergroup at the European Parliament*. Retrieved 30 July 2014, from http://urban-intergroup.eu.

CHAPTER 4

Who Are the MEPs Making up Intergroups? A Sociopolitical Analysis

Who are the Members of the European Parliament (MEPs) that establish, maintain and participate in Intergroups? Is it MEPs in top parliamentary positions or rank-and-file parliamentarians? Is it political novices or experienced politicians? Is it MEPs at the beginning or end of their political career who engage voluntarily in Intergroups?

The present chapter addresses all of these questions by analysing the socio-demographic features and political trajectories of those MEPs maintaining and participating in Intergroups.[1] In this way, the chapter takes up the argument that MEPs' individual choices and activities, such as in Intergroups, might not necessarily institutionally set, but influenced by their social characteristics and the person, given the European Parliament's weakly codified institutional structures and dynamic nature (see Kauppi, 2005, 2011). It further links to the theoretical framework of this study, and the related aim to connect political strategies of MEPs to their structural locations and social characteristics to analyse EP politics. The exploration of MEPs' social configurations and political backgrounds will show what kind of social resources (e.g. forms of capital) MEPs have at their disposal when engaging in Intergroups, and thus what positions they occupy within the transnational field.

The importance of social origin (e.g. education, gender, class) on the behaviour and priorities of MEPs has been previously demonstrated within political science by works of Norris (1999), Norris and Franklin (1997), and Wessels (1997). These studies have shown that age matters

L. Landorff, *Inside European Parliament Politics*,
Palgrave Studies in European Political Sociology,
https://doi.org/10.1007/978-3-030-04206-6_4

in terms of younger generations bringing 'distinctive values and priorities to public life' or that an early entry into parliamentary life may facilitate 'life-time service, stronger institutional socialization, and internal promotion within' the legislature (Norris, 1999, p. 97). In the light of the Parliament's long-term reputation as 'retirement home' (Hix, 1999, p. 75), these arguments put another complexion on the EP and prompt further discussions. Moreover, gender plays an important role when it comes to the promotion of 'equal opportunity policies' (Norris & Franklin, 1997, p. 208). Latest sociological works on the European Parliament highlight gender as a political resource of French MEPs (see Beauvallet & Michon, 2008; Kauppi, 2005). Furthermore, research on the EP's internal organisation has shown that less experienced and 'less well-known backbenchers' are often disadvantaged in their first EP term when it comes to committee assignments (Corbett, Jacobs, & Shackleton, 2011, p. 146). Additionally, occupational and interest group ties, however, 'matter as well for' MEPs' committee assignments, for instance with regard to the distribution of rapporteurships (see also Kaeding, 2004 on the ENVI committee; McElroy, 2006, p. 17; Yordanova, 2011). Consequently, nationality and interest group associations as well as previous occupation, education and seniority are valuable resources for obtaining key positions within the Parliament.

With regard to the political trajectories of legislators engaging in informal groupings, studies on informal institutions within the US Congress, i.e. on legislative caucuses, provide some initial, though inconclusive, points of reference. Previous studies argue that it is primarily structurally disadvantaged legislators, i.e. members without any formal leadership positions, policy outliers or junior representatives, who use these informal institutions as an alternative place to exert legislative influence (see Ainsworth & Akins, 1997; Hammond, 1998). Recent works, however, demonstrate the opposite. According to Victor and Ringe (2009, p. 762), it is senior members, legislative leaders and 'electorally safe' representatives who make use of these informal institutions to coordinate legislative activities and to disseminate information. In view of these mixed findings, it is highly relevant to gain new insights into the sociopolitical characteristics of MEPs engaging in EP Intergroups, and to contribute from a comparative perspective to the discussion on who is using informal arrangements in legislative settings.

The mapping of the sociopolitical characteristics focuses on the following indicators: age, gender, nationality, education, previous professional occupation as well as prior political/parliamentary experience. In addition, the positions these MEPs occupy within EP official organs (e.g. political groups, parliamentary committees and EP leadership bodies[2]) are mapped to explore whether it is primarily MEPs in top parliamentary positions or rank-and-file parliamentarians. In this context, the link between MEPs engagement in Intergroups and seniority is analysed, as well. In total, the sociopolitical characteristics of 77 MEPs (48 Intergroups chairs/co-chairs and 29 MEPs across four Intergroups) are analysed in this chapter.

The European Parliament as a Social Organisation

The EP qualifies as a unique entity along several lines. It is not only the 'only transnational directly elected representative' chamber in the world (Judge & Earnshaw, 2008, p. 148), a multilingual parliament with 24 official languages operating from three different locations but also a social organisation that is characterised by a high turnover of its personnel with every parliamentary term. Throughout its history as a directly elected chamber, just about 50% or less of the MEPs were re-elected parliamentarians.

As shown in Table 4.1, more than half of the 736 MEPs[3] elected to be parliamentarians in the 7th EP in 2009 were entirely new (Corbett, Jacobs, & Neville, 2016). In doing so, turnover in membership is 'certainly higher than in most national parliaments' (Nugent, 2010, p. 199). In comparison, the re-election ratio for the German Bundestag between 1994 and 2013 levelled out at between 70% and 80%, with 20% of the MPs in the 18th Bundestag (2013–2017) being newcomers to the German Bundestag (Deutscher Bundestag, 2014). This observation

Table 4.1 Proportion of Re-elected MEPs to the EP (1984–2014)

Parliamentary term	*Re-elected MEPs in %*
1984–	N/A
1989–	51.4
1994–	42.5
1999–	45.7
2004–	54
2009–	49.6
2014–	51. 5

Source Corbett et al. (2016, pp. 52–53) and Sabbati (2014)

already points to the temporal properties of the EP and its members, where around half of the elected parliamentarians are newcomers who have to become acquainted with the Parliament's structures and working rhythm, and thus with the Parliament's habitus in the first place. Hence, in comparison with national parliaments, the EP as a social organisation lacks continuity in its membership. This has implications for its legislative organisation and functioning (e.g. for the continuous availability of legislative expertise in the EP), as well as for the regularisation of durable interpersonal relationships, i.e. the development and mobilisation of social capital, as the following chapter will show.

For a long time, the Parliament has been ill-reputed as either a 'training ground for national politics or 'retirement home' at the end of a national career' (Hix, 1999, p. 75). Given its marginal position within the institutional set-up between the European Commission and the Council of the European Union, the EP has in the past attracted a number of political novices as well as female and regional politicians 'whose socio-political profiles placed them at slight disadvantage in national political fields' (Beauvallet, Lepaux, & Michon, 2013, p. 23; Kauppi, 2005). Studies conducted in the 1990s on the social representation in the EP documented that the Parliament, 'in common with most legislatures, draws disproportionately from the better-educated, more affluent, middle-aged, and male sections of society', in particular from the caste of jurists and academics (Hix & Lord, 1997; Norris & Franklin, 1997, p. 185).

Recent sociological studies show, however, that the EP has developed from a home of 'end-of-career' politicians 'towards an area of political professionalization for a predominately middle-aged, intellectual, partly internationalized and feminized elite' where MEPs' professional backgrounds tend to match those of the political personnel in general (Beauvallet & Michon, 2010, p. 148; Best & Cotta, 2000). With regard to age, the MEPs in the 7th EP were on 'average 51.2 years old at the time of their election', which stands at odds with the previously addressed image of the EP as a retirement home (Beauvallet et al., 2013, p. 10). With this average entry age, MEPs do not diverge from professional politicians in national parliaments; however 'they are slightly younger than many national' parliamentarians, as for instance French MPs (see Beauvallet et al., 2013, p. 10). Speaking about gender equality, the share of female MEPs has doubled since the 1st EP to 35% in the 7th EP, constituting 258 out of 736 MEPs (see Corbett et al., 2011).

With more than one-third of the overall population, the EP has a higher share of female politicians than national parliaments, which show an 'average of 24% share of female parliamentarians' (Corbett et al., 2011, p. 53). Hence, the EP is becoming an 'increasingly feminized institution'; gender equality, however, has still not been achieved (Beauvallet et al., 2013, p. 11). In terms of nationality, 27 different member states were represented among the 736 MEPs of the incoming 7th EP, with the German national delegation providing the largest national group with 99 MEPs, followed by France, Italy and the UK with 72 delegates each (European Parliament, 2015). Malta provided the smallest national group with five national delegates (European Parliament, 2015). With regard to education, MEPs displayed high levels of educational attainment over time, which points to the high volumes of cultural capital (e.g. educational qualifications) they bring into the Parliament. In the 7th EP, 'seven out of ten MEPs had received a higher education' and nearly one-fourth of the 736 MEPs had a Ph.D. (Beauvallet et al., 2013, p. 7). Thereby, MEPs are most frequently trained in the humanities (26.5%) and law (23.5%) (Beauvallet et al., 2013, p. 7). By contrast, graduates from political science constituted only 10% of the overall MEP population (Beauvallet et al., 2013). Ergo the tradition of jurists and academics representing European Union (EU) citizens in the EP continues and is reproduced over time. With reference to professional backgrounds and original occupations, the 7th EP assembled a potpourri of professionals comprising of former prime ministers and presidents as well as former members of other EU institutions. Examples are the former Belgian prime minister Guy Verhofstadt, chair of the Group of the Alliance of Liberals and Democrats for Europe (ALDE) since 2009 or the Polish MEP Danuta Hübner who served as European Commissioner for Regional Development before entering the EP in 2009 (Corbett et al., 2011, 2016; EPP Group in the European Parliament, 2013). Moreover, we see 'celebrated judges and magistrates, […] anti-mafia campaigners, […] trade union leaders, […] former diplomats, academics […], doctors, engineers and scientists […] media personalities, journalists and former TV stars' (Corbett et al., 2011, pp. 57, 59). However, nowadays MEPs have less previous experience at national parliamentary or governmental level than their colleagues from the first parliamentary terms in the 1980s (Beauvallet & Michon, 2013). Only around one-third of the 7th term MEPs possessed previous national parliamentary experience as compared with 45% in the 1st EP (see Corbett et al., 2011, p. 54ff.).

By contrast, many MEPs entering the EP in the 1990s and 2000s just entered 'the political profession through' the Parliament (Beauvallet et al., 2013, p. 5). As stated at the beginning of this chapter, the EP has attracted in the past a number of regional politicians from the national political fields. This trend is still reflected in the 7th EP with nearly half of the MEPs holding a local mandate prior to their European mandate (Beauvallet et al., 2013). Hence, experienced regional and local politicians account for at least half of the EP as a social organisation.

Knowing this, how does the picture look when we zoom in on the MEPs maintaining and participating in Intergroups? Do these MEPs share the socio-demographic and political features of the overall EP population or are they in any way particular? The following section investigates these questions based on the same social indicators outlined above. The statistical analysis focuses on both Intergroup chairs across the entire population of Intergroups in the 7th EP as well as on the most active MEPs in the four selected Intergroups.

Socio-Demographic Features of MEPs in Intergroups

With regard to age, more than half of the Intergroup chairs were under the age of 50 when entering the EP (26 out of 48 chairs and co-chairs) and thus, were younger than the average MEP with an entry age of 51.2 years (Beauvallet et al., 2013, p. 10). This indicates that it is predominately parliamentarians at the beginning or middle of their political career who chair Intergroups. In view of the four chosen Intergroups and their most active members, the picture is almost balanced between MEPs starting their EP career under or above the age of fifty. In no case was there a parliamentarian who started his or her EP career above the age of 65 (see Table 4.2).

With regard to gender, the dominance of male over female MEPs is reproduced in the distribution of Intergroup chairs and co-chairs at the two-thirds and one-third ratio respectively, anchored within the overall EP population (see Table 4.3). Zooming in on the four Intergroups, however, shows that female MEPs outweigh their male colleagues in the Intergroups 'Viticulture' and 'Animal Welfare', while we see a balanced ratio of female and male parliamentarians in the Intergroup 'Urban'. For the Intergroup 'Trade Union', male MEPs outweigh their female colleagues. Hence, established gender hierarchies are reversed inside Intergroups while they are maintained in terms of chairmanships. With

Table 4.2 Age and Intergroups

Age[a] (when entering the EP)	*Chairs/ Co-chairs (N=48)*	*Viticulture (N=10)[b]*	*Trade Union (N=7)[c]*	*Urban (N=12)[d]*	*Animal Welfare (N=9)[e]*
Under 35	9	–	2	1	3
35–49	17	6	1	5	2
50–65	20	4	4	6	4
Above 65	2	–	–	–	–
N/A	–	–	–	–	–
Total	48	10	7	12	9

[a]Reference date is in each case the start of the mandate (e.g. 1st of July 2009 for the 7th term). Age classes are taken from Beauvallet et al. (2013, p. 10) for reasons of comparison
[b]Includes chair
[c]Includes chair
[d]Includes chair
[e]Includes chair

Table 4.3 Gender and Intergroups

Gender	*Chairs/Co-chairs (N=48)*	*Viticulture (N=10)*	*Trade Union (N=7)*	*Urban (N=12)*	*Animal Welfare (N=9)*
Male	29	4	5	6	4
Female	19	6	2	6	5
Total	48	10	7	12	8

the limitation that only four Intergroups were studied in depth, this finding supports previous research arguing that more female than male MEPs join Intergroups (Ringe, Victor, & Carman, 2013).

In combination with nationality, it shows that French female MEPs take the lead in presenting chairs of Intergroups. Five out 48 chairs and co-chairs were taken by French female MEPs. These are MEP Sylvie Goulard, Intergroup 'Extreme Poverty and Human Rights', MEP Corinne Lépage, Intergroup 'Seas and Coastal Areas', MEP Elisabeth Morin-Chartier, Intergroup 'Trade Union', MEP Françoise Castex, Intergroup 'Public Services' and MEP Véronique Houillon Mathieu, Intergroup 'Sustainable Hunting, Biodiversity, Countryside Activities and Forests' (European Parliament, 2013a). For an interesting discussion on the career trajectories and strategies of French female MEPs in the EP, see Kauppi (2005) as well as Beauvallet and Michon (2008). Overall, 17 nationalities out of 27 member states are represented among the chairs and co-chairs. French MEPs take the lead with eight posts, followed by British MEPs with six and by Spanish and Austrian representatives with five posts each. Ireland, Portugal, Slovenia, Romania, Greece, Malta, Latvia, Lithuania, Bulgaria and Cyprus were not represented among the Intergroup chairs and co-chairs (European Parliament, 2013a). Hence, it shows that it is predominately MEPs from the 'old' member states than from the 'new' member states (i.e. those who joined the EU in 2004, 2007/8) providing a chair for an Intergroup. Compared to the overall population of the 7th EP, where German parliamentarians constituted the largest national group with 99 MEPs (European Parliament, 2015) followed by France, Italy and the UK (72 MEPs each), it is notable that German MEPs feature only with two Intergroup chairs, i.e. with MEP Thomas Mann ('Tibet') and MEP Norbert Neuser ('Western Sahara') (European Parliament, 2013a). By contrast, Austrian MEPs, ranking mid-range within the overall population, feature more frequently with five posts. Hence, in terms of nationality it shows that it is not necessarily the largest national delegations that have the most Intergroup chairs. It is furthermore interesting to note that with French and British MEPs taking the lead as Intergroup chairs and co-chairs, we see parliamentarians whose national parliamentary systems include similar phenomena to Intergroups (e.g. all-party groups in the UK, working and study groups in the French Senate) (Corbett et al., 2011; Crespo Allen, 1996). This aspect constitutes an interesting avenue for future research (see also Chapter 8).

With regard to the individual Intergroups, it is rather the diversity of member states that prevails than the dominance of one nationality, with one exception. In the Intergroup 'Viticulture', it is predominately French (female) MEPs providing five parliamentarians followed by two MEPs from Italy and Luxembourg each, and one from Germany. In addition, a strong link to regional representation became apparent among those most active parliamentarians. Six out of ten come from or represent a vine-growing region, such as the French MEPs Morin-Chartier, Nathalie Griesbeck and Françoise Grossetête or their Italian colleagues Herbert Dorfmann and Giancarlo Scottà.[4] Similar to the Intergroup 'Viticulture', there is a slight surplus of three French female MEPs in the 'Urban' Intergroup with the MEPs Karima Delli, Marie Thérèse Sanchez-Schmid and Sophie Auconie. Overall, mostly MEPs from nine different member states interact in the 'Urban' Intergroup.[5] Another particularity, which was also stated as a success of the Intergroup, emerged with regard to the Intergroup 'Animal

Welfare'. Starting out in the early 1980s as an initiative of mainly British MEPs, the Intergroup is 'now […] very multinational'[6] as it is mostly parliamentarians from Germany, Denmark, Sweden, Romania, Italy and Poland among the most active MEPs. While 25 British MEPs have been listed as members of the Intergroup, none of these attended at least half of the 52 meetings organised in the 7th parliamentary term (Intergroup on the Welfare & Conservation of Animals, 2014). In sum, however, Intergroups are rather characterised by a diversity of member states than the dominance of one member state. The aspect of cross-country membership in Intergroups is picked up again in Chapter 5 when discussing the composition of the four Intergroups in more depth.

In terms of educational attainment, Intergroup chairs and co-chairs reflect the overall pattern of high levels of education found among the entire population of MEPs in the 6th and 7th term,[7] with 40 out of 42 holding a university degree and one-sixth of them holding a doctoral degree (see Table 4.4).

With regard to the most active members of the four Intergroups, educational backgrounds become more mixed. While in the Intergroups 'Trade Union' and 'Viticulture' the spectrum ranges from Ph.D.-holders to high school graduates, all most active MEPs of the 'Urban' Intergroup[8] have a university degree, and four out of eleven hold a Ph.D. In the 'Animal Welfare' Intergroup, six out of nine MEPs hold a university degree,[9] see Table 4.4.

In the light of academic disciplines, Intergroup chairs, co-chairs and members reflect the patterns anchored in the overall population. MEPs are predominately trained in the humanities, followed at some distance

Table 4.4 Education and Intergroups

Education	*Chairs/ Co-chairs (N= 48)*	*Viticulture (N= 10)*	*Trade Union (N= 7)*	*Urban (N= 12)*	*Animal Welfare (N= 9)*
High school graduate or under	2	3	2	–	1
University degree lower than Ph.D.	32	5	4	7	6
Ph.D.	8	1	1	4	–
N/A	6[a]	1	–	1	2
Total	48	10	7	12	9

[a]See MEPs Michael Cashman, Eider Gardiazábal Rubial, Kartika Tamara Liotard, Elisabeth Lynne, Véronique Mathieu Houillon and Marietje Schaake

by training in law. However, the first tentative linkages emerge between Intergroup activities and educational background, pointing to the cultural capital these parliamentarians acquired prior to entering the EP. Examples are the MEPs Dorfmann, Michel Dantin and Christa Klass from the Intergroup 'Viticulture': all have been trained in agriculture or agricultural science. In the Intergroup 'Urban', the Dutch MEP Lambert van Nistelrooij stands out as having been trained in geography and social geography. An even stronger link is revealed between Intergroup activities and the previous professional experience of MEPs.

Looking at the four Intergroups, the following patterns emerge. In the Intergroup 'Urban',[10] it is experienced local, regional politicians, and urban-related professionals with some European work experience. Examples are the Polish MEP and chair of the Intergroup Jan Olbrycht, and his colleagues the Czech MEP Oldřich Vlasák, the Dutch MEP van Nistelrooij, the German MEP Joachim Zeller as well as the Spanish MEP Sanchez-Schmid who all were mayors or deputy mayors prior to their EP mandate. Moreover, the MEPs Olbrycht, Vlasák and van Nistelrooij have previous European work experiences with the Council of European Municipalities and Region (CEMR), Committee of the Regions (CoR) and Assembly of European Regions (AER).

In the Intergroup 'Trade Union', it is MEPs with a strong trade union affinity as (former) members or leading figures in the trade union sector in their national fields[11] who also gained European work experience prior to entering the EP. Examples include the Austrian MEP Evelyn Regner as head of the Austrian Trade Union Federation Europe Office in Brussels from 1999 to 2008 or the Luxembourgish MEP Georges Bach as official negotiator for the railways section of the European Transport Workers' Federation (ETF) from 2002 to 2009.

It is predominately parliamentarians with an agricultural and vintners background in the Intergroup 'Viticulture', such as the Italian MEP Dorfmann, former Secretary General of the Assembly of European Wine Regions (AREV) (2005–2008) and holding a Ph.D. degree in agrarian science. Another example is the German MEP Klass who worked on a family-owned vineyard prior to entering the EP in 1994 and serves as a Bureau member of the farmers and vintners association Nassau (Rhineland-Palatinate) since 1990. Likewise, the French MEP Dantin was trained as an agricultural technician and was previously employed as an adviser to several French ministers of agriculture, among them Michel Barnier from 2007 to 2009. For the remaining most active MEPs in the

Intergroup 'Viticulture', a link between prior occupation and Intergroup activities could not be established as they are teachers (e.g. MEP Morin-Chartier) and lawyers (e.g. MEPs Grossetête and Griesbeck). In their case, a strong link between regional representation and Intergroup commitment has been detected as previously discussed under the aspect of nationality.

For the most active members of the Intergroup 'Animal Welfare', a straight link between previous profession and activities in the Intergroup is not immediately visible. The parliamentarians have diverse professional backgrounds ranging from former lecturers and researchers, to lawyers and judges, to farmers and environmental officers. This finding confirms an interview statement that animal welfare and protection denotes a rather universal topic for which various social groups with diverse political and professional backgrounds may engage.[12]

Finally, in terms of previous experience at national parliamentary and/or governmental level, it is a blend of experienced politicians and political novices among the Intergroup chairs and co-chairs. However, those MEPs with previous political mandates prevail over those without any prior political experience. More than half of the respective MEPs held a post in national, regional or local politics (see Table 4.5). Twelve MEPs have been members of national parliaments, e.g. Astrid Lulling 'Viticulture', Othmar Karas 'Small and Medium-Sized Enterprise' or Alejandro Cercas 'Trade Union'. Five MEPs have previous experience at the ministry level in their national fields, e.g. Marc Tarabella 'Social Economy', Corinne Lépage 'Seas and Coastal Areas' or Cristina Gutiérrez-Cortines 'Urban' and 'Ageing and Intergenerational Solidarity'. Two of these were also members of national parliaments, e.g. the Hungarian MEP Csaba Sándor Tabajdi and the Czech MEP Milan Cabrnoch. Ten MEPs held a local mandate[13] (e.g. as regional or departmental councillor, mayor, municipal councillor) prior their EP mandate. Among them are for instance the MEPs Jan Olbrycht 'Urban', Pavel Poc 'Animal Welfare', Thomas Mann 'Tibet' or François Alfonsi 'Traditional Minorities, National Communities and Languages'. In contrast to those experienced politicians, there is a group of 20 MEPs without prior national, regional or local mandates chairing an Intergroup in the 7th EP. These are, however, not necessarily politically inexperienced.

Some of these MEPs have worked as political or policy advisors for regional or national governmental authorities as well as for European institutions. Examples of this group are the British MEP Caroline

Table 4.5 Previous Parliamentary/Governmental Experience and Intergroups

Previous Parliamentary/ Governmental Experience	*Chairs/ Co-chairs (N= 48)*	*Viticulture (N= 10)*	*Trade Union (N= 7)*	*Urban (N= 12)*	*Animal Welfare (N= 9)*
National mandate (Minister and/ or MP)	15	1	2	1	2
Local mandate without MP (Regional or departmental councillor, mayor, municipal councillor)	10	6	3	6	1
Professional of politics	3	1	1	3	3
No previous national and/or local mandate	20	3	2	1	–
N/A	3	1	–	1	3
Total	48	10	7	12	9

Lucas (VoteWatch Europe, 2015a), the Dutch MEP van Nistelrooij, the Spanish MEP Méndez de Vigo (VoteWatch Europe, 2015b) or the French MEP Sylvie Goulard. Some have worked as civil servants and diplomats before they entered the EP, e.g. the Finish MEP Haglund, the Spanish MEP Francisco José Millán Mon and the French MEP Goulard. These parliamentarians are assumed to have obtained substantial political experience before they joined the EP.[14]

Further, some of these MEPs entered the Parliament at a very young age and therefore cannot draw on long-term political experience. Examples of these potential 'professionals of politics', i.e. of MEPs who 'have never (or seldom) been employed in any other field' (Beauvallet et al., 2013, p. 6), are the Danish MEP Dan Jørgensen, chair of the Intergroup 'Animal Welfare' from January 2012 to December 2013 and his Swedish colleague Carl Schlyter, chair of the same Intergroup from May 2010 to January 2012 (Intergroup on the Welfare & Conservation of Animals, 2012, 2013b). Jørgensen joined the EP in 2004 at the age of 29. Schlyter started his EP career as an intern at the age of 28, worked as an advisor for the Greens/EFA Group from 1997 to 2004 before he joined the EP as an MEP in 2004 at the age of 36. The French MEP Damien Abad, chair of the Intergroup 'Youth Issues', is another example. Abad joined the EP in 2009 at the age of 29 and was thereby the youngest French MEP in office (Abad, 2015). Naturally, these MEPs cannot present previous experience at parliamentary or governmental level as the EP is their very first political mandate in general. Interestingly, both Jørgensen and Abad left the EP during the 7th term to take up posts in their respective national fields. Jørgensen became Danish minister for agriculture in 2013 while Abad was elected into the French national assembly in 2012 (Assemblée Nationale, 2018; Intergroup on the Welfare & Conservation of Animals, 2013b). Hence, both cases may also serve as examples of how politicians make use of the EP as a springboard for national political careers.

For only a small group of nine Intergroup chairs and co-chairs, no prior political experience and mandate could be documented on the basis of their EP profiles and personal websites.[15] Consequently, it is primarily experienced politicians among the Intergroup chairs and co-chairs of the 7th EP. In this context, MEPs with prior national parliamentary experience stand out slightly, accounting for more than one-fourth of the Intergroup chairs. They are closely followed by those MEPs who gained their political experiences in local politics.

Within the four Intergroups this trend continues. Predominately professionally experienced politicians (with prior national parliamentary experience, ministerial experience or local mandates) join Intergroups. However, within the Intergroups it is MEPs with local mandates that outweigh those with experience at national level (see Table 4.5). Moreover, there is a handful of MEPs, who have never or rarely work in any other field than politics, and therefore may qualify as professionals of politics. Among those are the British MEP Stephen Hughes ('Trade Union') who works since 1984 in the EP; the British MEP Arlene McCarthy ('Urban') who works since 1994 in the EP as well as the MEPs Karima Delli ('Urban'); Ramona Mănescu ('Urban') and Daciana Octavia Sârbu ('Animal Welfare'). Since the latter three joined the EP at a very young age in 2009 and 2007 respectively, it has to be seen whether they become professionals of politics over time.

Political Positions of MEPs in Intergroups

EP leadership positions, such as the EP presidency, offices in the EP Bureau, political group and committee chairs and vice-chairs, are decided every two-and-a-half years (Corbett et al., 2016). This is at the beginning of each parliamentary term and halfway through. MEPs who aim for office goals within the EP, such as party leadership, committee chairmanship or a senior position in the EP presidency, need to accommodate the interests of those MEPs who control the assignment to these positions (e.g. national delegation leaders or party group leaders) (Hix, Raunio, & Roger, 1999; Mamadouh & Raunio, 2003).

Committee chairs and vice-chairs are shared 'between the national parties within the EP party groups' and among the political groups on a proportional basis by means of the d'Hondt formula[16] (Hix et al., 1999, p. 9; Whitaker, 2011). As a result of this system, the largest group (e.g. the EPP in the 7th EP) gets the 'first choice of committee chair' and thus, MEPs in the larger groups are favoured over those parliamentarians in smaller groups when it comes to the provision of key offices (e.g. committee chairs) (Hix, Kreppel, & Noury, 2003; Whitaker, 2011, p. 34).

In this context, it is even more interesting that seniority, including long-term investment in the EP and its organs, favours access to leadership positions in the EP (Beauvallet & Michon, 2010). By contrast, gender and prior national experience appear to be not significant (Beauvallet & Michon, 2010). EP leadership positions (incl. the EP bureau, the presidency and vice-presidency of parliamentary committees and political groups) 'are governed by actors with a profile of 'professionals of Europe'' (Beauvallet & Michon, 2010, p. 160). These are, for instance, senior officials and former diplomats who are experienced in 'multinational political spaces', who speak several languages and are familiar with the 'subtle games of negotiations and compromise' (Beauvallet & Michon, 2010, pp. 159–160). These leadership positions are, however, more often held by men than women. Hence, gender hierarchies are reproduced within EP leadership positions (Beauvallet & Michon, 2010). While women represented around one-third of the whole 6th EP, only '14% are or have been president of a political group' and only 19% have been committee chairs (Beauvallet & Michon, 2010, p. 158). Hence, the EP has developed into a socialisation environment in which leadership positions can only be obtained by possessing 'a particular form of symbolic internal political capital' that is associated, for instance, with long-term and continuous investment in the EP and 'a large relational network' (Beauvallet & Michon, 2010, p. 161).

Political Groups

Among the population of chairs and co-chairs, six out of the seven established transnational political groups of the 7th EP were represented. Thereby, the largest share of Intergroup chairs and co-chairs came from the EPP-ED Group. The EPP-ED provided 21 MEPs as chairs and co-chairs for 17 Intergroups. These were followed by MEPs from the S&D Group with 12 chairs, the Greens/EFA Group with seven and the Liberals with five parliamentarians as Intergroup chairs and co-chairs (see Table 4.6).

As outlined in Table 4.6, in comparison with the overall seat distribution in the EP, the established majority ratios are reproduced among Intergroup chairs and co-chairs, with the two largest political groups providing the largest shares of Intergroup chairs and co-chairs. What is noticeable, however, is the change of positions between the Liberals and the Greens/EFA Group. The latter is placing more Intergroup chairs than the former despite less seats in the overall Parliament.

One reason for this distribution can be found in the procedure for official recognition of Intergroups as outlined in Chapter 3. In the course of this process, each political group proportionately receives a certain amount of signatures that it can distribute to support the official recognition of an Intergroup. The political group that supports an Intergroup with its signature usually also places the Intergroup chair(s). For the 7th EP (2009–2014) the EPP-ED and S&D received 21 signatures each to support the official recognition of an Intergroup. The Liberals received 10 signatures, while the Greens/EFA and the ECR received eight signatures each, followed by the GUE/NGL with six signatures and the EFD with five signatures. Since the largest political groups are allocated the most signatures, the chances of EPP-ED and

Table 4.6 Transnational Political Groups and Intergroups

Political Groups	*EP Total*	*Chairs/ Co-chairs (N=48)*	*Viticulture (N=10)*	*Trade Union (N=7)*	*Urban (N=12)*	*Animal Welfare (N=9)*
EPP-ED	265	21	7	2	6	1
S&D	184	12	–	5	2	2
Greens/EFA	55	7	1	–	2	1
ALDE	84	5	1	–	1	3
GUE/NGL	35	1	–	–	–	–
ECR	54	2	–	–	1	1
EFD	32	–	1	–	–	1
Non-Attached	27	–	–	–	–	–
Total	736	48	10	7	12	9

S&D members to obtain an Intergroup chair are higher. In this context, belonging to one of these political groups is interpreted as a valuable asset for MEPs: this is institutionalised political capital vested in membership in the largest transnational groups in the EP.

A brief look back to the 6th EP (2004–2009) reveals that the Christian Democrats (EPP-ED) also provided the majority of Intergroup chairs, i.e. 11 out of 24 Intergroup chairs, closely followed by the Socialists with 10 chairs (European Parliament, 2005). In comparison with the 7th term, however, only four political groups set Intergroup chairs. These were the Christian Democrats, the Socialists, the Liberals and the Greens/EFA Group (European Parliament, 2005). Hence, it is noticeable that small groups on the very right, such as the European Conservatives and Reformists (ECR), and on the very left, such as the GUE/NGL, set Intergroup chairs in the 7th EP as well. For the ECR, the Scottish MEP Struan Stevenson chaired the Intergroup on 'Climate Change' while his Czech colleague Cabrnoch co-chaired the Intergroup 'Ageing and Intergenerational Solidarity' (European Parliament, 2013a). For the GUE/NGL, Dutch MEP Kartika Tamara Liotard held the post as co-chair of the Intergroup 'Ageing and Intergenerational Solidarity' (European Parliament, 2013a).

With regard to the four individual Intergroups, the prevalence of members from the European People's Party (EPP-ED) continues in the 'Urban' and 'Viticulture' Intergroup, where half of the most active parliamentarians are EPP-ED members. In contrast, Liberals and Socialists constitute the largest groups in the Intergroups 'Animal Welfare' and 'Trade Union'. Despite this alleged dominance, which should be treated with caution given the rather small sample, the cross-party character of Intergroups is well displayed as a common feature. In the Intergroup 'Viticulture', it is four out of seven transnational political groups, in the 'Urban' Intergroup five out of seven, and in the Intergroup 'Animal Welfare' six out of seven transnational political groups from which the most active members come from. Thereby, members of the Eurosceptic Europe of Freedom and Democracy Group (EFD) and the European Conservatives and Reformists (ECR) are equally represented with parliamentarians from ALDE and Greens/EFA (see Table 4.6). The 'Trade Union' Intergroup constitutes an exception, as its most active members are only from two political groups: the S&D and EPP-ED Group. This finding is discussed again in more detail in Chapter 5.

EP Leadership Bodies

Looking at the leadership positions in the EP, i.e. presidency and vice-presidency, quaestors, presidency and vice-presidency of political groups, chairs and vice-chairmanships of parliamentary committees, it shows that around one-third of Intergroup chairs and co-chairs hold a leadership position. Among the group of Intergroup chairs and co-chairs, there are one EP vice-president (MEP Karas, Intergroup 'Small and Medium-Sized Enterprise'), one quaestor (MEP Lulling, Intergroup 'Viticulture'), four vice-presidents of political groups (MEPs Lunacek/Greens/EFA Group, Lichtenberger/Greens/EFA Group, Liotard/GUE/NGL Group and Karas/EPP-ED Group) and 11 vice-chairs of parliamentary committees[17] (see Table 4.7). Moreover, it shows that around one-third was without any post at all in the 7th EP. These MEPs qualify as rank-and-file parliamentarians. In addition, there is a group of nine MEPs occupying chairs and vice-chairs of parliamentary delegations.[18] With reference to the literature, these are not accounted for as posts in the EP leadership (Beauvallet & Michon, 2010; Corbett et al., 2016). Likewise, the three heads of national delegations that have been identified among the Intergroup chairs/co-chairs are not included in the discussion.[19]

With roughly one-third of Intergroup chairs and co-chairs holding a position in the EP leadership, one-third holding a formal although not leadership post and one-third holding no posts at all in the 7th EP, this research produces a rather mixed picture concerning the question of whether it is legislative leaders or junior representatives who join Intergroups. Taking into account that it is primarily the second row of EP leadership posts, given the prevalence of vice-chairs or the lack of political groups or committee chairs, it is argued that the majority of Intergroup chairs and co-chairs does not belong to the EP leadership circle. This finding supports Ringe et al. (2013, p. 102) who argue that 'leaders join fewer intergroups than do nonleaders'. The trend of second-row leadership and rank-and-file parliamentarians continues within the four selected Intergroups, namely with a number of committee vice-chairs, and delegation vice-chairs (see Table 4.7). As already indicated, seniority plays a central role when obtaining these positions in the EP leadership bodies (Beauvallet & Michon, 2010). Research in the 6th European Parliament has revealed that, for instance, 'the presidency of a political group is the most seniority-dependent function' (Beauvallet &

Table 4.7 EP Leadership and Intergroups

Posts in EP Leadership	*Chairs/ Co-chairs (N=48)*	*Viticulture (N=10)*	*Trade Union (N=7)*	*Urban (N=12)*	*Animal Welfare (N=9)*
EP Presidency & Vice Presidency	1	–	–	1	–
Quaestor	1	1	–	–	–
Political Group Presidency & Vice Presidency	4	–	1	–	–
Parliamentary Committee Chair & Vice Chairmanship	11	2	2	2	5
Parliamentary Delegations Chair & Vice Chairmanship	9	3	1	–	1
No post	19	3	1	5	1
Total	48	10	7	12	9

Michon, 2010, pp. 154–155). To obtain the chairmanship of a transnational political group, MEPs had served close to four terms in the EP (Beauvallet & Michon, 2010). To become a member of the EP bureau or to obtain the chair of a parliamentary committee, MEPs had to serve close to three mandates (Beauvallet & Michon, 2010).

Seniority

Analysing the position of an Intergroup chair as seniority-dependent function, it shows that the largest group of the Intergroup chairs and co-chairs (22 out of 48) served in their second mandate in the EP (see Table 4.8). One-fourth of the chairs and co-chairs were 'first time' MEPs, while a little more than one-fourth had already served three or more mandates. Hence, the ratio between new and long-serving MEPs is nearly balanced among the Intergroup chairs and co-chairs.

Tracing back the activities of Intergroup chairs and co-chairs to the 6th and 5th EP shows, however, that the large majority of these MEPs picked up an Intergroup chairmanship only after having served at least one mandate in the EP (European Parliament, 2002, 2003, 2005). From this it is concluded that first-time MEPs can become Intergroup chairs; however, it is primarily MEPs in their second mandate who take up the post as chair. As previously discussed in Chapter 3, MEPs may become Intergroup chairs in a number of ways. Initially, civil society organisations that liaise with the Intergroup may approach MEPs with the

Table 4.8 Seniority and Intergroups

Seniority	*Chairs/ Co-chairs (N=48)*	*Viticulture (N=10)*	*Trade Union (N=7)*	*Urban (N=12)*	*Animal Welfare (N=9)*
1 Mandate	12	5	3	6	3
2 Mandates	22	2	2	4	5
3 Mandates	11	–	1	1	1
4 Mandates	1	2		1	–
5 Mandates	2	1	–	–	–
6 Mandates	–	–	1	–	–
7 Mandates	–	–		–	–
Total	48	10	7	12	9

request to preside the Intergroup. Furthermore, MEPs may want to put themselves forward as a candidate for an Intergroup chair. In addition, MEPs may occupy certain 'positions of authority', e.g. the post as group coordinator, in order to become president of an Intergroup (Mamadouh & Raunio, 2003, p. 339).

With regard to the four selected Intergroups and their most active members, the picture looks mixed. In the Intergroups 'Viticulture' and 'Urban', half of the MEPs were first movers to the EP, while two to three MEPs were long-serving parliamentarians.[20] In the Intergroup 'Animal Welfare' it is predominately MEPs in their second mandate, while in the Intergroup 'Trade Union' it is mostly parliamentarians in their first and second mandate with one exception—the British MEP Stephen Hughes. Hughes started as an assistant of the British MEP Roland Boyes in 1979, was elected to the EP in 1984 and served continuously for 30 years as MEP until 2014. Consequently, it is primarily MEPs in their second mandate who chair Intergroups while both first-time MEPs as well as long-term serving parliamentarians are equally present. Hence, in comparison with EP leadership positions, the chairmanship of an Intergroup appears more accessible.

Beyond positions within the EP leadership, additional posts and constellations of posts reoccur among the MEPs engaging in Intergroups. Given the conceptualisation of MEPs as multipositional, political entrepreneurs, these patterns deserve a closer look. Initially, the combination of committee vice-chairs and Intergroup chairs is noticeable. In the Intergroup 'Animal Welfare', the combination of committee vice-chairs and chair or honorary president of the Intergroup appears twice.

For example, MEPs Jørgensen and Schlyter held both posts as ENVI[21] vice-chair and chair of the Intergroup; MEPs Janusz Wojciechowski and Marit Paulsen held both posts as AGRI[22] vice-chair and honorary president of the Intergroup (Intergroup on the Welfare & Conservation of Animals, 2013a). Hence, these MEPs belong to several social groups and occupy multiple positions that could be highly relevant for animal-related topics. The subsequent analysis will show whether MEPs make use of these multiple positions.

In addition, the combination of political group coordinator and Intergroup chair or member figures prominently in the studied sample. Fourteen out of 48 Intergroup chairs and co-chairs, i.e. more than one-fourth were also group coordinators (Corbett et al., 2011, p. 118; Kaeding & Obholzer, 2012, p. 17).[23] Just as a quick reminder, each political group selects a MEP as coordinator in the respective parliamentary committee who acts as its main spokesperson (Corbett et al., 2011). Given the substantial influence of political group coordinators in the allocation of rapporteurships (Kaeding & Obholzer, 2012; Yordanova, 2011), this position is quickly examined in combination with Intergroup chairs and co-chairs. What is noticeable in this regard is the linkage between Intergroup activities and group coordinator activities in a certain committee for a couple of MEPs. Examples are the Spanish MEP Alejandro Cercas (S&D) who is group coordinator in the parliamentary committee on Employment and Social Affairs (EMPL) and chair of the 'Trade Union' Intergroup, or the Austrian MEP Richard Seeber (EPP-ED) who is group coordinator in the parliamentary committee on Environment, Public Health and Food Safety (ENVI) and chair of the Intergroup 'Water'.[24] In these cases, it is MEPs occupying three positions simultaneously (i.e. committee member, group coordinator and Intergroup chair).

With regard to the four selected Intergroups, we see the constellation of political group coordinator, Intergroup chair and member in the Intergroups 'Trade Union' and 'Urban'. For the 'Trade Union' Intergroup, we see two co-chairs: the aforementioned Spanish MEP Cercas as S&D group coordinator in the EMPL committee and his French colleague MEP Morin-Chartier as deputy EPP group coordinator in the EMPL committee. For the Intergroup 'Urban', it stands out that there are three REGI[25] group coordinators from the European Democrats, the Liberals and the ECR among the most active members.[26] Hence, these MEPs occupy positions as committee member, group coordinator and Intergroup member on one and the same topic.

However, this pattern is less distinct in the Intergroups 'Animal Welfare' and 'Viticulture'. For the former, only the ENVI group coordinator Anna Rosbach (ECR) is identified, while for the latter it is DEVE group coordinator Catherine Grèze (Greens/EFA). Again for MEP Grèze, a clear link between the Intergroup 'Viticulture' and the parliamentary committee on Development (DEVE) cannot be established. This multipositionality could provide these MEPs with more valuable resources. The subsequent analysis will show whether this combination of posts is played out by MEPs in order to accumulate and mobilise various forms of capital.

Conclusion

This chapter was dedicated to the socio-demographic and political characteristics of those everyday political agents who make up Intergroups and the EP at large. In doing so, this chapter sought to establish what kind of social resources MEPs have at their disposal when engaging in Intergroups, and thus which positions they occupy within the transnational field. In this way, the sociopolitical analysis provides the groundwork for the upcoming Chapters 5–7 in which the accumulation and mobilisation of additional forms of capital by MEPs through Intergroups are outlined.

Who are the MEPs making up Intergroups? In comparison with the overall population, it is predominately MEPs who are slightly younger when entering the EP, who chair and participate in Intergroups. Moreover, they are mostly at the beginning or middle of their political or professional careers. It is primarily political experienced MEPs and those who do not hold a position in the EP leadership bodies.

At the level of Intergroup chairs, it is primarily male MEPs who share membership in the EPP Group and serve in their second mandate. In terms of gender and majority ratios of political groups in the EP, existing hierarchies are reproduced within the Intergroup leadership. In terms of nationalities, French MEPs provide the largest national group among Intergroup chairs. By contrast, German MEPs constituting the largest national delegation within the EP place only two Intergroup chairs. In general, Intergroup composition is characterised by a diversity of member states, with a prevalence of MEPs from member states prior to the 2004 enlargement among the Intergroup chairs and co-chairs. The generally high levels of education anchored within the overall population of MEPs are also reflected among the Intergroup chairs and co-chairs.

Zooming in on the four selected Intergroups, the socio-demographic features of their most active members become more diverse in terms of seniority, political group membership, nationality and education. Gender hierarchies are partly reversed. Female MEPs outweigh their male colleagues in three of the four Intergroups. In the case of the Intergroups 'Trade Union', 'Urban' and 'Viticulture' a strong link between educational background (partially), previous professional occupation and Intergroup activities was revealed. This points to a connection between the social resources these MEPs have at their disposal and the political strategies they pursue in the EP (e.g. Intergroup activities). These results point further to an interpretation of MEPs seeking Intergroup assignments where they can draw on their previous work experience. In this way, they display a behaviour similar to those legislators who aim for good public policy in their committee work (see Fenno, 1995 on the House of Representatives of the US Congress).

In terms of political positions, it is primarily MEPs in the second row of EP leadership (e.g. holders of vice-posts) or rank-and-file parliamentarians without any other post who obtain Intergroup chairs, co-chairs and participate in Intergroups. Consequently, this book supports previous findings arguing that more rank-and-file parliamentarians join Intergroups than MEPs in EP leadership positions (Ringe et al., 2013). These MEPs are, however, equipped with national or local capital and thus, political experienced. They held posts in national or local politics prior to their mandate in the EP. In this context, former members of national parliaments stand out slightly among the Intergroup chairs and co-chairs, while those MEPs with previous local mandates stand out among the four selected Intergroups. Finally yet importantly, the analysis revealed certain combination of posts and positions in connection with the MEPs' Intergroup commitment. The position of a political group coordinator in combination with an Intergroup membership featured frequently. The subsequent empirical analysis will show to what extent this combination of positions is played out by MEPs within the transnational field.

Notes

1. The quantitative analysis is based on the biographies of members of the 7th European Parliament (2009–2014) available at the Parliament's website 'European Parliament/MEPs' (http://www.europarl.europa.eu/meps/en/map.html). The database has been accessed at several points

in time over the period from 2012 to 2015. The majority of data has been collected in 2013. For five MEPs, CVs could not be obtained through the Parliament's website (European Parliament, 2013b). In these cases, personal websites were consulted to collect biographical information. This applies to the following MEPs in the sample: Damian Abad 'Youth/Jeunesse', Marietje Schaake 'New Media', Kartika Tamara Liotard 'Ageing and Intergenerational Solidarity', Eider Gardiazábal Rubial 'Youth/Jeunesse' and François Alfonsi 'Traditional, National Communities and Languages'. The MEPs Liotard and Gardiazábal Rubial did not have personal websites at the time of data collection.

2. This includes: EP presidency and vice-presidency, quaestors, presidency and vice-presidency of political groups, chairs and vice-chairmanship of parliamentary committees, see Corbett et al. (2016).
3. Reference date is the beginning of the 7th parliamentary term in July 2009. The incoming Parliament had 736 members. The outgoing Parliament had 766 members due to Croatia joining the European Union in 2013, see Corbett et al. (2016).
4. See also the German MEP Christa Klass who is from the Rhineland-Palatinate region.
5. These are Poland, the UK, the Czech Republic, France, the Netherlands, Germany, Portugal, Spain and Romania.
6. See Interview MEP 15.
7. Total population N=42. For six MEPs no information on educational background could be retrieved from their EP profile or their personal website.
8. Statement based on 11 out of 12 selected MEPs. For one MEP, no information on educational background could be retrieved from the EP profile and/or the personal website.
9. Statement based on seven out of nine MEPs. For two MEPs no information on educational background could be retrieved from their EP profile or their personal website (European Parliament, 2013b).
10. See also the German MEP Simon who is trained as a lawyer and has been employed as personal liaison officer to the Principal Mayor of the City of Mannheim from 1996 to 1999. See also the Spanish MEP Gutiérrez-Cortines who worked as a researcher in art and architecture, urban planning and the history of urban development prior to her European parliamentary career.
11. See British MEP Stephen Hughes, Spanish MEP Alejandro Cercas and Czech MEP Richard Falbr.
12. See Interview MEP 2.
13. See classification in Beauvallet et al. (2013).

14. See also the British MEPs Jean Lambert and Claude Moraes. Lambert was a political liaison officer to the Green Group in the EP from 1989 to 1992. Moraes worked as advisor to MPs John Reid and Paul Boateng in the House of Commons from 1987 to 1989.
15. See MEPs Michael Cashman, Heinz K. Becker, Ádám Kosá, Jean-Marie Cavada, Véronique Mathieu Houillon, Richard Seeber, Mario Mauro, Kinga Gál and Emine Bozkurt.
16. The d'Hondt method is 'a system of proportional representation and [committee] seat allocation' used in the European Parliament (Hix et al., 2003, p. 320). Accordingly, political groups 'choose posts in an order determined by the size of the group' (Corbett et al., 2011, p. 147). As a result, the larger groups are favoured over smaller groups.
17. These are the following MEPs: Carl Schlyter, Thomas Mann, Kinga Gál, Struan Stevenson, Françoise Castex, Dan Jørgensen, Eider Gardiazábal Rubial, Carl Haglund, Elisabeth Morin-Chartier, Sonik Boguslaw and Jan Olbrycht.
18. These are the following MEPs: Emine Bozkurt, Milan Cabrnoch, Michael Cashman, Jean Lambert, Struan Stevenson, Margarete Auken, Véronique Mathieu Houillon, Jan Olbrycht and Claude Moraes.
19. These are the following MEPs: Anna Záborská, Csaba Tabajdi and Tunne Kelam.
20. For Intergroup 'Viticulture': MEPs Lulling (since 1989), Klass (since 1994) and Grossetête (since 1994). For Intergroup 'Urban': MEPs McCarthy (since 1994) and Gutiérrez-Cortines (since 1999).
21. Committee on Environment, Public Health and Food Safety.
22. Committee on Agriculture and Rural Development.
23. These are the following MEPs: François Alfonsi, Margarete Auken, Milan Cabrnoch, Alejandro Cercas, Sylvie Goulard, Jean Lambert, Ulrike Lunacek, Claude Moraes, Lambert van Nistelrooij, Eva Lichtenberger, Iñigo Méndez de Vigo and Richard Seeber.
24. Additional examples are: Milan Cabrnoch (ECR) and Jean Lambert (Greens/EFA) both group coordinators in the parliamentary committee on Employment and Social Affairs (EMPL) as well as heads of the Intergroup 'Ageing and Intergenerational Solidarity'; and Claude Moraes (S&D) group coordinator in the parliamentary committee on Civil Liberties, Justice and Home Affairs (LIBE) and chair of the Intergroup 'Ageing and Intergenerational Solidarity'.
25. Committee on Regional Development.
26. MEPs Oldřich Vlasák (ECR, REGI) 'Urban' Intergroup; Ramona Mănescu (ALDE, REGI) 'Urban' Intergroup; and Lambert van Nistelrooij (EPP, REGI) 'Urban' Intergroup.

References

Abad, D. (2015). *Damien Abad: Député de l'Ain – Portrait*. Retrieved 27 February 2015, from http://www.damien-abad.fr/portrait/.

Ainsworth, S. H., & Akins, F. (1997). The Informational Role of Caucuses in the US Congress. *American Politics Quarterly, 25*(4), 407.

Assemblée Nationale. (2018). *Accueil – Les députés – List des députés par ordre alphabétique – M. Damien Abad*. Retrieved 22 April 2018, from http://www2.assemblee-nationale.fr/deputes/fiche/OMC_PA605036.

Beauvallet, W., Lepaux, V., & Michon, S. (2013). Who Are the MEPs? A Statistical Analysis of the Backgrounds of Members of European Parliament (2004–2014) and of Their Transformations. *Études Européennes*, 1–12.

Beauvallet, W., & Michon, S. (2008). *Women in the European Parliament: Effects of the Voting System, Strategies and Political Resources. The Case of the French Delegation* (GSPE Working Papers), 1–20.

Beauvallet, W., & Michon, S. (2010). Professionalization and Socialization of the Members of the European Parliament. *French Politics, 8*(2), 145–165.

Beauvallet, W., & Michon, S. (2013). MEPs: Towards a Specialization of European Political Work? In J. Rowell & D. Georgakakis (Eds.), *The Field of Eurocracy: Mapping EU Actors and Professionals* (pp. 16–34). Houndmills, Basingstoke, Hampshire and New York, NY: Palgrave Macmillan.

Best, H., & Cotta, M. (2000). *Parliamentary Representatives in Europe 1848–2000: Legislative Recruitment and Careers in Eleven European Countries*. Oxford: Oxford University Press.

Corbett, R., Jacobs, F., & Neville, D. (2016). *The European Parliament* (9th ed.). London: John Harper Publishing.

Corbett, R., Jacobs, F., & Shackleton, M. (2011). *The European Parliament* (8th ed.). London: John Harper Publishing.

Crespo Allen, M. (1996). *Rules on Lobbying and Intergroups in the National Parliaments of the Member States*. Luxembourg: European Parliament.

Deutscher Bundestag. (2014). Datenhandbuch – 3. Alters- und Sozialstruktur – Kapitel 3.4. Dauer der Mitgliedschaft im Bundestag Stand: 14.1.2013 (pp. 1–23). Berlin: Deutscher Bundestag: Parlamentsarchiv und Datenbank MdB-Stamm.

EPP Group in the European Parliament. (2013). *About: Our Members—Danuta Hübner*. Retrieved 10 April 2015, from http://www.eppgroup.eu/mep/Danuta-Maria-H%C3%9CBNER.

European Parliament. (2002). *Activities: 12/A-2002—Bulletin*. Brussels: European Parliament: Directorate for the Planning of Parliamentary Business.

European Parliament. (2003). *Activities: 03/A-2003—Bulletin*. Brussels: European Parliament: Directorate for the Planning of Parliamentary Business.

European Parliament. (2005). *Activities: 08/A-2005—Bulletin*. Brussels: European Parliament: Directorate for the Planning of Parliamentary Business.
European Parliament. (2013a). *About Parliament: Organisation and Work—Intergroups*. Retrieved 24 January 2013, from http://www.europarl.europa.eu/aboutparliament/en/00c9d93c87/Intergroups.html.
European Parliament. (2013b). *MEPs*. Retrieved 16 December 2013, from http://www.europarl.europa.eu/meps/en/map.html.
European Parliament. (2015). *About Parliament: In the Past—Previous Elections—Numbers of Members Per Member States*. Retrieved 9 April 2015, from http://www.europarl.europa.eu/pdf/divers/PDF_Nb_MEP_by_country/elections2009_meps-number_en.pdf.
Fenno, R. F. (1995). *Congressmen in Committees*. Berkeley: Institute for Governmental Studies Press, University of California.
Hammond, S. W. (1998). *Congressional Caucuses in National Policy Making*. Baltimore: Johns Hopkins University Press.
Hix, S. (1999). *The Political System of the European Union*. New York: St. Martin's Press.
Hix, S., Kreppel, A., & Noury, A. G. (2003). The Party System in the European Parliament: Collusive or Competitive? *Journal of Common Market Studies, 41*(2), 309–331.
Hix, S., & Lord, C. (1997). *Political Parties in the European Union*. New York: St. Martin's Press.
Hix, S., Raunio, T., & Roger, S. (1999). *An Institutional Theory of Behaviour in the European Parliament*. Paper Presented at the Joint Sessions of the European Consortium for Political Research.
Intergroup on the Welfare & Conservation of Animals. (2012). *Press Release: New President Takes Helm at Intergroup on the Welfare & Conservation of Animals*. Brussels: Intergroup on the Welfare and Conservation of Animals.
Intergroup on the Welfare & Conservation of Animals. (2013a, April). *About Us: Members—Composition of the Intergroup*. Retrieved 16 December 2013, from http://www.animalwelfareintergroup.eu/about-us/members/composition/.
Intergroup on the Welfare & Conservation of Animals. (2013b, December 12). *Dan Jorgensen, New Danish Minister for Agriculture and Food*. Retrieved 13 December 2013, from http://www.animalwelfareintergroup.eu/2013/12/12/dan-jorgensen-new-danish-minister-agriculture-food/.
Intergroup on the Welfare & Conservation of Animals. (2014). *Intergroup Attendance September 2009—March 2014*. Retrieved 01 August 2014, from http://www.animalwelfareintergroup.eu/wp-content/uploads/2011/08/3-Intergroup-attendance-September-2009-March-2014.pdf.
Judge, D., & Earnshaw, D. (2008). *The European Parliament* (2nd ed.). Basingstoke: Palgrave Macmillan.

Kaeding, M. (2004). Rapporteurship Allocation in the European Parliament: Information or Distribution? *European Union Politics, 5*(3), 353–371.
Kaeding, M., & Obholzer, L. (2012). Pulling the Strings: Party Group Coordinators in the European Parliament. *EIPAScope, 1,* 13–18.
Kauppi, N. (2005). *Democracy, Social Resources and Political Power in the European Union.* Manchester: Manchester University Press.
Kauppi, N. (2011). EU Politics. In A. Favell & V. Guiraudon (Eds.), *Sociology of the European Union* (pp. 150–171). Basingstoke: Palgrave Macmillan.
Mamadouh, V. D., & Raunio, T. (2003). The Committee System: Powers, Appointments and Report Allocation. *Journal of Common Market Studies, 41*(2), 333–351.
McElroy, G. (2006). Committee Representation in the European Parliament. *European Union Politics, 7*(1), 5–29.
Norris, P. (1999). Recruitment into the European Parliament. In R. S. Katz & B. Wessels (Eds.), *The European Parliament, National Parliaments, and European Integration* (pp. 86–102). Oxford: Oxford University Press.
Norris, P., & Franklin, M. (1997). Social Representation. *European Journal of Political Research, 32,* 185–210.
Nugent, N. (2010). *The Government and Politics of the European Union* (7th ed.). Basingstoke: Palgrave Macmillan.
Ringe, N., Victor, J. N., & Carman, C. J. (2013). *Bridging the Information Gap: Legislative Member Organizations as Social Networks in the United States and the European Union.* Ann Arbor: University of Michigan Press.
Sabbati, G. (2014). *European Parliament: Facts and Figures* (No. PE 542.150). Brussels: European Parliamentary Research Service.
Victor, J. N., & Ringe, N. (2009). The Social Utility of Informal Institutions: Caucuses as Networks in the 110th U.S. House of Representatives. *American Politics Research, 37*(5), 742–766.
VoteWatch Europe. (2015a). *Term 7: MEP Caroline Lucas.* Retrieved 25 February 2015, from http://term7.votewatch.eu/en/caroline-lucas.html.
VoteWatch Europe. (2015b). *Term 7: MEP Íñigo Méndez De Vigo.* Retrieved 15 February 2015, from http://term7.votewatch.eu/en/inigo-mendez-de-vigo.html.
Wessels, B. (1997). Germany. In P. Norris (Ed.), *Passages to Power: Legislative Recruitment in Advanced Democracies* (pp. 76–97). Cambridge: Cambridge University Press.
Whitaker, R. (2011). *The European Parliament's Committees: National Party Influence and Legislative Empowerment.* London: Routledge.
Yordanova, N. (2011). Inter-institutional Rules and Division of Power in the European Parliament: Allocation of Consultation and Co-decision Reports. *West European Politics, 34*(1), 97–121.

CHAPTER 5

Finding Allies: The Intergroup as Bridging Social Capital

> [I]t is a good way to get to know people from other groups and people from other committees [...]. So it is like a network creating among members who are interested in one subject and otherwise normally your network is mostly linked to your own committee but in this case no.[1]

Without social relations between individuals 'society would not exist' (Kauppi, 2011, p. 156). Social relationships are fundamental to any social configuration. European Union (EU) Politics and the European Parliament (EP) do not constitute an exemption. The EP conceived of as a social organisation in this book is made up of 736 individuals who bring their own national, political, social and cultural backgrounds to the practice of parliamentary politics at EU level. Thereby, EP representatives are not just members of the institution (i.e. the EP) but belong to a variety of intersecting social groups within the EP. They are members of transnational political groups, of parliamentary committees and delegations, of national political parties, working groups within the EP, and as a matter of fact, of Intergroups. As a result, they engage in various social interactions in their everyday parliamentary work.

As outlined in Chapter 2, social capital comes in many different forms and ways. Initially, it is a symbolic and intangible resource that requires from its holder constant usage and upkeep to sustain its value. A Bourdieusian-inspired reading of the concept defines social capital as close, trusted and durable interpersonal relations that are associated with

L. Landorff, *Inside European Parliament Politics*,
Palgrave Studies in European Political Sociology,
https://doi.org/10.1007/978-3-030-04206-6_5

mutual recognition (Bourdieu, 1986; Kauppi, 2011). A political science-inspired reading offers a distinction between bonding and bridging social capital (Putnam, 2000). The former refers to inward-looking networks that foster homogenous groups and exclusive identities. The latter relates to outward-looking networks that assemble people across various social strata (Putnam, 2000). Understood as open, ad hoc and sporadic interpersonal connections that are similar to relations of (professional) acquaintance, bridging social capital resembles 'weak ties' (Carpenter, Esterling, & Lazer, 1998; Granovetter, 1973; Putnam, 2000). By contrast, bonding social capital, understood as close and trusted contacts, resembles 'strong ties' (Carpenter et al., 1998; Granovetter, 1973).

This chapter argues for a conceptualisation of Intergroups as bridging social capital. In constituting a network beyond 'your own committee' as perceived by the above-cited parliamentarian, Intergroups link Members of the European Parliament (MEPs) to external assets. This means they constitute relationships that link parliamentarians to agents who share the interest in the subject (e.g. animal welfare) but 'who move in different circles' as 'people from other groups and [...] committees'[2] than the individual MEP usually does (Putnam, 2000, p. 23). This insight points to a conceptualisation of the Intergroup as bridging social capital. To underpin this argument, the chapter looks at first at the membership in and composition of Intergroups. Taking into account that social capital comprises trusted and long-lasting personal contacts, it subsequently examines the durability and regularity with which social interactions are practiced by MEPs in Intergroups. Finally yet importantly, the notion of trust, as one important component of social capital is discussed. In this way, the chapter shows that it is predominately networks of outward-looking character, which encompass MEPs across diverse social, political and institutional cleavages. The social relations regularised in Intergroups are predominately of an ad hoc, sporadic nature, which come close to ties of professional acquaintance and interpersonal connections ('weak ties') (Granovetter, 1973). As a result, Intergroups are rather conceived of as bridging social capital of MEPs.

Membership in Intergroups

'Mitmachen kann jeder' argued one interviewee.[3] Statements, such as everyone can participate, presenting the Intergroup as being 'open to all kind[s] of member[s]'[4] and 'open to everybody'[5] convey the impression that Intergroups are of an open, inclusive and outward-looking character. Initially, there are no rules or entry criteria for becoming a member of an Intergroup, except for being an MEP and having an interest in the topic (European Parliament, 2009).[6] MEPs become a member by providing their signature for the Intergroup's official recognition at the beginning of the respective parliamentary term. In comparison with the EP parliamentary committees, where membership is limited and determined by the political groups (Corbett, Jacobs, & Neville, 2016; Yordanova, 2009), Intergroups are voluntary commitments of MEPs. Thus, MEPs decide themselves whether they want to be a member of an Intergroup, and of how many. As a result, among the interviewed MEPs, some were members of up to five Intergroups, which they followed, however, to different degrees.[7] This finding is discussed in more detail below.

Looking at the overall population of MEPs in the 7th EP, 581 out of 754 parliamentarians[8] were registered with an Intergroup (European Parliament, 2013a). Thereby, the Hungarian MEP Csaba Sándor Tabajdi (S&D) stands out with his membership in 10 Intergroups (European Parliament, 2013a). He is followed by a group of nine MEPs who are registered as members in nine Intergroups, among these are the Italian MEP Salvatore Tatarella (EPP), the French MEP Michèle Striffler (EPP) and the Romanian MEP Csaba Sógor (EPP) (see Table 5.1).

The most common practice among MEPs in 2013 was the membership in two Intergroups (European Parliament, 2013a). One hundred and forty-four out of 581 MEPs were registered in two Intergroups (European Parliament, 2013a). This accounts for roughly one fourth of the MEPs being registered as an Intergroup member at that point in time (Fig. 5.1).

The Intergroup 'Animal Welfare' constitutes an exception with regard to membership rules. It is the only Intergroup with its own formal criteria for membership. In 2013, the Intergroup introduced its own rules of procedure, including rules for how to become a member of the Intergroup (Intergroup on the Welfare & Conservation of Animals, 2013).[9] It distinguishes between members and attendees of their meetings. To become a member of the Intergroup, MEPs have 'to actively support and promote animal welfare in the European Parliament', have to 'have applied for this purpose and [need to be] registered on the official list of the Intergroup on the European Parliament website' (Intergroup on the Welfare & Conservation of Animals, 2013, p. 3).

Table 5.1 Membership in EP Intergroups in January 2013

Member of European Parliament	*Number of Intergroups*
1. Tabajdi, C. S.	10
1. Busuttil, S.	9
2. Dorfmann, H.	
3. Franco, G.	
4. Niebler, A.	
5. Papanikolaou, G.	
6. Peterle, A.	
7. Sógor, C.	
8. Striffler, M.	
9. Tatarella, S.	
1. Audy, J.-P.	8
2. Bach, G.	
3. Berman, T.	
4. Dantin, M.	
5. Howitt, R.	
6. Jędrzejewska, S. E.	
7. Morin-Chartier, E.	
8. Pittella, G.	
9. Rübig, P.	
10. Tremosa i Balcells, R.	
11. Tsoukalas, I. A.	
12. Ulmer, T.	
13. Vlasto, D.	
1. Auconie, S.	7
2. Ayala Sender, I.	
3. Badia i Cutchet, M.	
4. Belet, I.	
5. Costa, S.	
6. Fidanza, C.	
7. Gauzès, J.-P.	
8. Göncz, K.	
9. Griesbeck, N.	
10. Koch, D.-L.	
11. Lamassoure, A.	
12. Lambert, J.	
13. McClarkin, E.	
14. Prodi, V.	
15. Rivellini, C.	
16. Rochefort, R.	
17. Scurria, M.	

Source European Parliament (2013a)

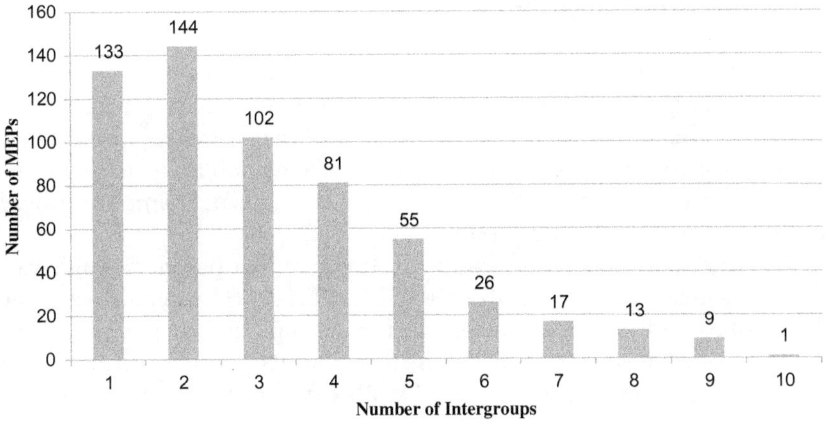

Fig. 5.1 Number of MEPs enrolled in Intergroups (Stand: January 2013) (*Source* European Parliament [2013a])

In contrast to attendees, members have 'the right to vote for the election of the Intergroup' chair (Intergroup on the Welfare & Conservation of Animals, 2013, p. 3). This right is obtained through the participation in at least five meetings during two-and-a-half years (Intergroup on the Welfare & Conservation of Animals, 2013). To become an attendee of the Intergroup, MEPs need to attend one meeting during the entire parliamentary term. The attendee will be then included in the mailing list and consequently, receives all information about the activities of the Intergroup (Intergroup on the Welfare & Conservation of Animals, 2013). These rules were introduced in order to organise the elections of Intergroup chairs more systematically and to ensure that only Intergroup members vote for an Intergroup chair.[10] This rule became necessary after an MEP had been elected as Intergroup chair with the help of MEPs who were not members of the Intergroup and who only attend the session on the election of the chair in order to vote for the respective MEP.[11]

This observation provides an empirical hint to the perception of an Intergroup chair constituting a valued resource in the EP, i.e., constituting institutionalised political capital for MEPs. This aspect is discussed again in more detail in Chapter 7. Given, however, that the Intergroup 'Animal Welfare' meets on a monthly basis, both criteria for becoming a member or an attendee are interpreted as very low and easy entry criteria. This speaks again for the inclusive character of an Intergroup.

What speaks further for the inclusive, open nature of Intergroups is that some interviewees regret that they cannot exclude anyone from their meetings (e.g. in this particular case, parliamentarians who were not sympathetic to the cause of the Intergroup).[12] As a consequence, MEPs decided to be more discreet in the conduct of their Intergroup meetings. This meant to no longer advertise their meetings publically, to avoid the attendance of certain MEPs.[13] This practice, in turn, points to a more exclusive character of Intergroups.

Information about Intergroup meetings is distributed through various channels. Those MEPs who are officially registered with the Intergroup and are included on the Intergroup's internal mailing lists, receive information about the Intergroup and its activities. The mailing lists are usually maintained by the MEP's office of the Intergroup chair or the external secretariat. In addition, some Intergroups also announce their meetings on their website (e.g. the Intergroups on 'Animal Welfare' and 'Urban'). As outlined in Chapter 3, around one-half of the officially recognised Intergroups have their own website (i.e. 13 out of the 27), while two additional Intergroups have a Facebook site to communicate about the Intergroup. Moreover, Intergroup meetings are also announced within the EP in showcases (e.g. the Intergroups on 'Animal Welfare', 'Climate Change, Biodiversity and Sustainable Development' and 'Water'). For this information, however, one has to gain access to the EP premises in the first place. This is, of course, secured for MEPs. Non-parliamentarians or external visitors need to obtain accreditation to enter the buildings of the Parliament. To obtain accreditation to the EP, direct contact (i.e. social capital) to the MEP's office chairing the Intergroup or to a parliamentarian, who is a member of an Intergroup, is needed. These MEPs may organise accreditation to the EP. Thus, Intergroups as social capital become of exclusive character when it comes to the conduct and attendance of their meetings. In theory, meetings can be attended by anyone, given one knows when and where these take place. For half of the Intergroups, the information about meetings is publicly accessible.

Composition of Intergroups

How homogenous or heterogeneous are Intergroups in terms of their members? Are the MEPs gathering in Intergroups birds of a feather?

The majority of interviewees[14] described their fellow colleagues in the Intergroup as 'like-minded people',[15] as people having the same interest. Hence, the shared interest in the topic is one common denominator among the MEPs engaging in Intergroups. It emerged, however, from the interviews that despite the shared interest in the topic, MEPs do not necessarily share the beliefs, ideas or approaches to a certain issue, problems or solutions to problems within the overall theme of the Intergroup. For instance, parliamentarians in the 'Viticulture' Intergroup had different opinions on the liberalisation of planting rights. Some MEPs were in favour of the new regulation proposed by the European Commission, while others adhered to the existing system.[16] While most of the members in the 'Animal Welfare' Intergroup engage for animal protection, it is also farmers and animal welfarists who are divided on the issue of battery cages for laying hens.[17] Thus, Intergroups differ here from advocacy coalitions as a composition of people who share 'a set of normative and causal beliefs' and who engage in collective actions to 'transform their beliefs into public policy programs' (Sabatier, 1988, p. 133). Since Ringe, Victor, and Carman (2013) reach the same conclusion on shared policy priorities but different policy preferences among MEPs in Intergroups, this qualifies as a more general trend within Intergroups.

With regard to their socio-demographic characteristics, Chapter 4 has shown that the most active MEPs in the four selected Intergroups are heterogeneous in terms of their educational backgrounds, nationality and gender. By contrast, they are homogenous with regard to their professional backgrounds. The 'Urban' Intergroup gathers experienced local and regional politicians and urban-related professionals. At the same time, the 'Viticulture' Intergroup gathers MEPs with a predominately agricultural and vintner's background, while the 'Trade Union' Intergroup gathers MEPs who all have a strong trade union affinity or affiliation. This may point to an interpretation of Intergroups as epistemic communities, understood as networks of professionals (see Haas, 1992). This aspect is further discussed in the upcoming Chapter 6 on the Intergroup as informational capital of MEPs. Only the professional backgrounds of the MEPs in the Intergroup on 'Animal Welfare' are diverse, including former lecturers and researchers, lawyers and judges, farmers and environmental officers. One reason given by interviewees for the heterogeneity of professional backgrounds is that animal welfare denotes a rather universal topic for which various social groups with diverse political and professional backgrounds may engage.[18]

Moreover, MEPs in Intergroups are heterogeneous in terms of their political trajectories and affiliations as well as in terms of the positions they occupy within the transnational field. The four chosen Intergroups assemble a mix of experienced, long-serving MEPs and parliamentary novices. Furthermore, the majority of interviewees highlighted the cross-party/cross-committee[19] character of their respective Intergroup, gathering MEPs from different political groups, parliamentary committees and member states. Thereby, Intergroups transcend established formalised institutional structures. With regard to the four chosen Intergroups, the most active MEPs in the 'Urban' Intergroup come from five different parliamentary committees and political groups. In the Intergroup 'Animal Welfare', MEPs come from three different committees, six different political groups and six member states. In the Intergroup 'Viticulture', it is MEPs from eight different parliamentary committees and four different political groups interacting with each other (see Table 5.2).

The 'Trade Union' Intergroup deviates in its composition slightly from the other three selected Intergroups. Its most active members share membership in the Group of the Progressive Alliance of Socialists and Democrats (S&D). Moreover, they are from the same parliamentary committee. This is the Committee on Employment and Social Affairs (EMPL). The exceptions are the Luxembourgish MEP Georges Bach as a member of the Committee on Transport and Tourism (TRAN) and the Austrian MEP Evelyn Regner serving in the Committee on Legal Affairs (JURI). Both MEPs, however, serve as substitutes in the EMPL committee during the 7th EP (European Parliament, 2014b, 2014c).

Furthermore, members of the 'Trade Union' Intergroup referred to the cross-committee character of the Intergroup in terms of the parliamentary reports and opinions that are discussed during Intergroup meetings, as well as with regard to the invited rapporteurs and shadow-rapporteurs who come from different parliamentary committees (e.g. EMPL, ITRE[20] and TRAN).[21] In line with this observation, the attendance lists[22] show that members of the Greens/EFA Group, of the Liberal Group (ALDE) and the European United Left–Nordic Green Left (GUE/NGL) do also attend meetings of the 'Trade Union' Intergroup but they do to a lesser extent than S&D members. As an example, the Greens/EFA MEP who joined most frequently Intergroup meetings attended seven out of 31 meetings during the first two-and-a-half years of the 7th EP, and sent an assistant to 13 meetings in total.[23] Similarly, parliamentarians from the GUE/NGL joined at most four meetings

Table 5.2 Cross-party and Cross-committee Character of Four Intergroups (2009–2014)

	Animal Welfare	*Viticulture*	*Trade Union*	*Urban*
Political groups	EPP-ED, ALDE, S&D, GREENS/EFA, ECR, EFD	EPP-ED, ALDE, Greens/EFA, EFD	EPP-ED, S&D	EPP-ED, ALDE, S&D, Greens/EFA, ECR
Parliamentary committees	AGRI[a], ENVI[b], EMPL[c]	ECON[d], FEMM[e], ENVI, AGRI, LIBE[f], DEVE[g], TRAN[h], EMPL	EMPL, TRAN, JURI[i]	REGI[j], CULT[k], LIBE, ECON, ENVI
Member states	6	4	7	9

[a]Agriculture and Rural Development
[b]Environment, Public Health and Food Safety
[c]Employment and Social Affairs
[d]Economic and Monetary Affairs
[e]Women's Rights and Gender Equality
[f]Civil Liberties, Justice and Home Affairs
[g]Development
[h]Transport and Tourism
[i]Legal Affairs
[j]Regional Development
[k]Culture and Education

during the period from September 2009 to April 2012. In comparison with the three other Intergroups, the 'Trade Union' Intergroup appears to be less heterogeneous in its composition, gathering primarily S&D and EMPL members who are, however, from different member states.

In sum, the analysis shows that Intergroups bridge social, national, institutional and political cleavages.

The dominant habitus of the field, i.e., the specific, internalised culture of the EP that regulates interactions of MEPs, provides that MEPs are grouped along their 'political affinities' (Corbett, Jacobs, & Shackleton, 2011, p. 78) in transnational political groups and conduct their legislative work within the parliamentary committees. Committee composition is regulated by the EP's Rules of Procedure (see Rule 186, European Parliament, 2009) and reflects roughly 'the ideological balance of the wider Parliament', while being simultaneously characterised by national and political heterogeneity (Burns, 2013, p. 166; Neuhold, 2001). Parliamentary committees are perceived as closed subfields in this study (see Chapter 2 again). They are limited in numbers and members. Moreover, the assignment to the parliamentary committees is controlled by party groups or respectively by national party delegations providing the transnational political groups with proposals for committee nominations (Bowler & Farrell, 1995; Corbett, et al., 2011). The statements above demonstrate that through Intergroups, MEPs link to parliamentarians from different parliamentary committees and political groups. Hence, they link to colleagues who 'normally', given the dominant habitus of the field, move in different subfields or respectively in circles different from their own within the transnational field. In this way, Intergroups provide MEPs with access to committees that they are not a member of.[24] This access to closed subfields constitutes a valuable resource in terms of influencing the information flow as well as the activities of parliamentarians, in particular of rapporteurs, in these respective committees. The upcoming Chapters 6 and 7 will demonstrate how Intergroups, as bridging social capital, are used to gain informational capital as well as political capital.

Regular Interpersonal Connections

MEPs' daily work life is not only characterised by multiple memberships in various political and social groups but also by a 'scarcity of time' and enormous amounts of travelling and mobility (Bale & Taggart, 2006; Wodak,

2009, p. 115). Their work life and time is divided between: their constituencies, the plenary sessions in Strasbourg, France that take place 12 times a year, as well as the additional plenary sittings, committee and political group meetings that take place in Brussels, Belgium (European Parliament, 2015). In addition, there is time allocated to the work in the interparliamentary delegations. With regard to Intergroup meetings, the official EP rules on Intergroups outlined in Chapter 3 prescribe MEPs to meet on Thursday during the monthly plenary week in Strasbourg, France. Hence, the habitus of the transnational field, providing the guidelines for legitimate behaviour, regulates the social interactions of MEPs in Intergroups by prescribing a particular spot for these practices in the parliamentary calendar.

Fieldwork conducted for this book, however, showed that MEPs work around these rules. Intergroup meetings are held in Brussels.[25] They are partly held under different headings, declared as meetings of individual MEPs.[26] Intergroups, such as the 'Disability', 'Western Sahara' and 'Tibet' Intergroup, convene meetings on demand and on ad hoc basis in response to political events (such as human rights violations), debates and legislation in the EP on the respective topic.[27]

Comparing the frequency of Intergroup meetings with the social interactions MEPs maintain in other (social) groups (e.g. political groups or parliamentary committees), interactions regularised in and through Intergroups feature less frequently. The transnational political groups conduct their meetings during the monthly 'Group week' in Brussels over two to three days (Corbett et al., 2011). Parliamentary committee meetings take place during the two committee weeks in Brussels. Some might meet twice a month with meetings lasting two, three or four half days, while others meet once a month for up to four half days (Corbett et al., 2016). On the contrary, more than half of the 27 officially registered Intergroups meet at least monthly or every other month, while those remaining meet four or less times a year (see Appendix A). In addition, MEPs meet in their national delegations twice a month, one time during the 'Group week' in Brussels and again during the plenary session in Strasbourg (Corbett et al., 2016). Consequently, Intergroups constitute less investment in time on the side of the MEP.

Furthermore, Intergroup meetings differ in the way in which they are conducted. In doing so, they also offer different opportunities for MEPs to regularise social interactions with other MEPs and to build up social capital. The meetings of the Intergroups 'Animal Welfare', 'Viticulture' and 'Urban' take place during the EP plenary sessions in

Strasbourg. While the Intergroups 'Animal Welfare' and 'Urban' meet (nearly) every month, the Intergroup 'Viticulture' meets every other month.[28] The Intergroup 'Trade Union' convenes monthly meetings of its Bureau, resembling the executive of the Intergroup,[29] in Brussels. In addition, the Intergroup holds four to five plenary meetings a year.[30] These are conducted in Strasbourg. The Bureau meetings are reserved for 'a restricted group'.[31] They gather one or two representatives of the main political groups, representatives of the European Trade Union Confederation (ETUC), the staff of the political groups providing the secretariat for the Intergroup, and assistants of MEPs.[32] Rapporteurs and shadow-rapporteurs are invited to these meetings to present and discuss respective reports in the presence of trade union representatives.[33] The plenary meetings are public meetings.[34] They serve the purpose of presenting the positions of the trade unions to a wider audience and to debate on more general topics.[35]

The meetings of the Intergroup 'Animal Welfare' are usually split into two presentations, one being almost always reserved for a representative of the Eurogroup for Animals.[36] Meetings last around an hour on Thursday mornings between 10.00 and 11.00 am prior to the voting time during the Strasbourg session. In contrast, meetings of the Intergroup 'Viticulture' take place on Wednesday in the early evening between 5.00 and 6.00 pm (see Appendix C for an agenda of the Intergroup 'Viticulture') and are followed by a reception (e.g. food and wine tasting). Bureau meetings of the 'Trade Union' Intergroup have been held on Tuesday mornings between 09.00 and 10.00 am in Brussels, occasionally also on Tuesday afternoon or on Wednesday mornings between 08.30 and 09.30 am. Taking into account the Parliament's timetable, the majority of these Bureau meetings took place in the early mornings of the 'Group week', and thus prior the meetings of the transnational political groups. The majority of plenary meetings has been held on Thursday mornings in line with the official rules on Intergroups prescribing meetings to be held during the part-time sessions in Strasbourg.[37]

Field research revealed that while MEPs in the Intergroup 'Animal Welfare' hastily left their Intergroup meetings on Thursday mornings to attend the subsequent voting session in the EP, MEPs in the Intergroup 'Viticulture' and their guests joined the following reception.[38] The reception offered external guests the opportunity to talk to MEPs, to exchange business cards and presumably present their cause to MEPs. This practice has been also observed after meetings of the Intergroups 'Water', and 'Climate Change, Biodiversity and Sustainable Development'.[39] For an overview of the meetings of the four selected Intergroups and their topics, see Appendix C. Moreover, it has been observed as a common practice that MEPs do not stay for the entire length of the meetings. By contrast, Intergroup meetings were characterised by a coming and going of MEPs.[40] Some MEPs just stayed for a couple of minutes, half an hour or for one presentation. This practice has also been confirmed by interviewees.[41] These observations already point to an interpretation of Intergroups being not primarily used by MEPs to build up long-lasting and trusted interpersonal relations, and thus social capital understood as close group ties.[42]

With regard to the general attendance of Intergroup meetings (limited here to the 7th EP), interviewees across Intergroups unanimously stated that attendance varies from meeting to meeting and with the topics. The majority of those MEPs inscribed in Intergroups only goes to the meetings that they have a particular interest in.[43] Thereby, one important finding of this book is that MEPs' attendance of Intergroup meetings is significantly lower than the official membership numbers, provided by the EP, suggest (European Parliament, 2013a).

For the four Intergroups under scrutiny, the official membership numbers were as follows: 95 MEPs have subscribed to the Intergroup 'Viticulture', 61 to the Intergroup 'Urban', 44 MEPs have subscribed to the Intergroup 'Animal Welfare' and 20 MEPs to the Intergroup 'Trade Union' in the 7th EP (European Parliament, 2013a). Based on these figures, it could be assumed that MEPs in the Intergroup 'Viticulture' may extend their social and personal relations by up to 94 parliamentarians. This constitutes a larger social group than the largest parliamentary committee. Depending on the size of the committee, parliamentarians 'normally' interact with 23 (e.g. Fisheries Committee) or 75 colleagues (e.g. Foreign Affairs Committee) of different nationalities and party groups (Corbett et al., 2011). By contrast, between five to 10 parliamentarians joined on average the meetings of the 'Viticulture' Intergroup.[44] The attendance of MEPs in the Intergroup 'Animal Welfare' ranged from eight to 23 parliamentarians (Intergroup on the Welfare & Conservation of Animals, 2014). Similar patterns have been observed in the 'Trade Union' and 'Urban' Intergroup. In the 'Trade Union' Intergroup attendance of MEPs varied from five to sixteen[45] with only the two co-chairs Alejandro Cercas (S&D) and Elisabeth Morin-Chartier

(EPP-ED) being present for all 31 meetings documented for the time between September 2009 and April 2012. For the 'Urban' Intergroup around 10 MEPs joined meetings on a regular basis.[46]

Thus, fieldwork revealed that MEPs are listed as members of an Intergroup without having ever attended a meeting of the Intergroup or having shown any other commitment in this respect. As a result, this study stresses that being listed as a member of an Intergroup cannot be equated with the actual practice or participation of an MEP in an Intergroup. Consequently, the official membership lists provided by the EP shall be rather understood as lists of supporters of the Intergroup.

In contrast, attending assistants of MEPs and external guests constituted the majority of Intergroup attendees who also stayed for the entire length of the meetings. Having this said, it is a common practice of MEPs to send their assistants as substitutes to Intergroup meetings.[47] In almost one-third of the meetings conducted by the 'Animal Welfare' Intergroup between September 2009 and March 2014, assistants either outweighed MEPs[48] or were represented equally.[49] Similar patterns were revealed in the 'Trade Union' Intergroup.[50] With regard to the Intergroup 'Viticulture', several interviewees confirmed this practice.[51] In the overall context of the EP and the MEP's individual work, it is not unusual for accredited assistants to attend meetings when their respective MEP is prevented (Corbett et al., 2016). It is, however, interesting to note that in some offices assistants were deliberately assigned with the task to follow-up on the respective Intergroup.[52] Their job portfolio as an assistant included tasks such as attending Intergroup meetings, briefing the MEP about Intergroup activities, and to communicate about the MEP's involvement in the Intergroup. Hence, some MEPs made the Intergroup a practice and responsibility of their assistants. For an interesting insight into the role and tasks of assistants, see the work by Busby (2013) or Michon (2008).

Durable Interpersonal Connections

As previously stated in Chapter 4, the EP as a social organisation is characterised by a high turnover of its personnel with every parliamentary term. The statistical analysis of the sociopolitical features of Intergroup chairs and members has shown that the majority of chairs and co-chairs of the 27 Intergroups as well as the most active members of the four selected Intergroups under scrutiny served either in their first or second term in the EP. Within the four selected Intergroups, MEPs in their first mandate outweighed those in their second mandate, with the exception of the MEPs in the Intergroup 'Animal Welfare'. Given the lack of membership lists for the past parliamentary terms (e.g. from the 6th legislative term on back) no statements can be made with regard to the (in)stability of overall Intergroup memberships. In the light of the finding that official membership lists do not reflect actual participation in Intergroups, it is also questionable to what extent these lists could provide a realistic picture on the (in)stability of membership. The picture looks different in the case of the Intergroup chairs, where documentation is available.

Tracing Intergroup chairs from the 5th to the 7th EP (from 1999 to 2014), reveals that chairmanships fluctuate from one parliamentary term to another (European Parliament, 2002, 2003, 2005, 2013a, 2014a). Only three of the current MEPs active as chairs in the 7th parliamentary term have served for three successive parliamentary terms in the same position and thus display a stable leadership. These are the Intergroups 'Viticulture' chaired by the Luxemburgish MEP Astrid Lulling since 1999 (European Parliament, 2002, 2003, 2005),[53] 'Tibet' presided by the German MEP Thomas Mann since 1999 (European Parliament, 2013c) and the 'Climate Change, Biodiversity and Sustainable Development' Intergroup led by the Scottish MEP Struan Stevenson since 1999 (European Parliament, 2013b).[54] In the 7th EP, five Intergroup chairs have left the EP. Among them were the Spanish MEP Iñigo Méndez de Vigo, chair of the Intergroup 'Extreme Poverty and Human Rights'; the Finnish MEP Carl Haglund, co-chair of the Intergroup 'Traditional National Minorities'; the Italian MEP Mario Mauro, co-chair of the Intergroup 'Social Economy' as well as the Danish MEP Dan Jørgensen and the French MEP Damien Abad, see also Chapter 4 again.[55]

Moreover, the change in Intergroup leaderships is also a result of its internal organisation described previously in Chapter 3. In the Intergroups 'Trade Union', 'Animal Welfare' and 'Traditional Minorities, National Communities and Languages' the chairmanships rotate every two-and-a-half years (i.e. halfway through the parliamentary term). In doing so, they resemble practices and routines regularised at the official structure of the EP, i.e., the election of 'formal office holders' such as the EP leadership, parliamentary committee chairs and vice-chairs, every two-and-half years (Corbett et al., 2016, p. 151). In terms of durability, it shows, however, that only a tiny minority of MEPs practices his or her

Intergroup commitment as chair constantly over time. In contrast, there is a high fluctuation among Intergroup chairs from one legislative term to another.

In sum, the majority of MEPs who are registered as members of an Intergroup practice their engagement on an ad hoc, flexible and sporadic basis or delegate it to their assistants. Only a very small percentage of MEPs practices his or her Intergroup activities in person and on a regular basis. These observations support again the notion of the Intergroup as bridging social capital, coming close to 'weak ties', i.e. a 'network of professional acquaintance' consisting of sporadic and ad hoc contacts rather than durable interpersonal ties (Carpenter et al., 1998; Granovetter, 1973; Putnam, 2000, p. 21).

The Notion of Trust

Defining social capital as 'relations of trust and durable interpersonal connections and recognition' (Kauppi, 2011, p. 156), the role of trust needs to be discussed in the context of Intergroups. The notion of trust was only explicitly used by a few interviewees.[56] One described 'the added value' of an Intergroup as being 'people from different groups meet, become more friendly, [...] develop trust between themselves [...]'.[57] Another MEP referred to a 'deep sense of mutual respect and trust'[58] among the MEPs in the Intergroup.

The previously mentioned observations, i.e., the low investment of time in the Intergroup by the majority of MEPs, the low attendance rates, and the ad hoc joining of meetings in connection with the nature of social capital as an intangible and unstable resource that requires 'constant upkeep and usage' to sustain its value (Kauppi, 2011, p. 156) point to the subordinate role that trust plays with regard to MEPs' engagement in Intergroups. What is notable in this context is that in particular members of the 'Trade Union' Intergroup referred to trust. I.e., the Intergroup that is the most homogenous in terms of membership in political groups (i.e. S&D Group) and parliamentary committees (i.e. EMPL committee) among the four selected Intergroups. This means that these MEPs cultivate also social contacts beyond the Intergroup, or respectively initially through their political group and committee work. Moreover, interviewees cultivated these interpersonal relations across these three social groups over a longer period of time. This corresponds with the statements that the development of a 'deep sense of mutual respect and trust [...] [is] not easy to build that comes from many, many hours of dialogue and from past experience'.[59] Thus, in the case of the MEPs in the 'Trade Union' Intergroup, there are indicators for the development of social relations, understood as durable interpersonal relations. In addition, fieldwork revealed further that the different offices of those MEPs leading the Intergroup work closely together, as do the respective assistants. This shows regular social interactions, and thus a constant investment in these social relationships.

The reasons for why interviewees referred to different degrees to trust within Intergroups are manifold. For one thing among the interviewees were MEPs who served their first mandate in the EP, and thus in an Intergroup. Arguing that the establishment of trust and mutual recognition takes 'many, many hours of dialogue',[60] these MEPs simply have not yet had the time to build up this trust and recognition. Moreover, as outlined before, the majority of MEPs joins Intergroup meetings ad hoc and ad libitum. Among the interviewed parliamentarians were also MEPs who only very sporadically joined meetings of the respective Intergroup. Consequently, these MEPs have not made the investment in time to develop relations of mutual trust and recognition. What should be maintained at this point is the following: through Intergroups MEPs establish and maintain social relations with colleagues whose interest and opinion they share (e.g. political allies), but also with MEPs whose opinion they do not share (e.g. political opponents). This supports the perspective of Intergroups as bridging politically heterogeneous groups, demonstrating the inclusive character. The homogenous aspect—the like-mindedness—relates primarily to the common interest in the topic and shared professional backgrounds. Durable interpersonal relations of trust and mutual recognition constitute rather an exception. They might occur among long-serving MEPs sharing membership in the same Intergroup, transnational political group and parliamentary committee as indicated for the members of the 'Trade Union' Intergroup. Hence, these parliamentarians are part of the same intersecting social groups over a longer period of time. This allows them to build trusted and long-lasting interpersonal relations, to develop and cultivate social capital as defined by the Bourdieusian reading of the concept. In contrast, they are looser, sporadic contacts between parliamentarians who move in different subfields of the transnational field.

Relations with Civil Society

To explore social practices in Intergroups only from the perspective of parliamentarians would be short-sided. Representatives of civil society organisations (CSOs) are frequent and regular attendees of Intergroup meetings (see Appendix C). They are, however, not members of the Intergroup as membership in the officially recognised Intergroups is restricted to MEPs (Chapter 3).

Representatives of CSOs include here 'trade unions, employers' and producers' organisations, non-governmental organisations representing general interests […]; professional associations and grassroot organisations' (Kohler-Koch & Quittkat, 2009, p. 14). In the 'Trade Union' Intergroup the speakers are, with the exception of the plenary meetings in Strasbourg, exclusively representatives of the European Trade Union Confederation (ETUC) and its member organisations, such as the European Trade Union Institute (ETUI) or the European Transport Workers' Federation (EFT). In contrast, in the Intergroup 'Viticulture' it is primarily representatives of professional organisations, such as the Assembly of European Wine Regions (AREV), and business interest associations, such as the Confédération Nationale des producteurs de vins et eaux-de-vie de vin à Appellations d'Origine Contrôlées (CNAOC). With the restriction that not all meeting protocols of the Intergroup could be obtained, it is notable that there is a slight dominance of French professional and business interest associations engaging in the Intergroup 'Viticulture' (see Appendix C). In the Intergroup 'Animal Welfare', a variety of international, national, regional and local animal welfare organisations are present. Among those, the Eurogroup for Animals, which also provides the secretariat for the Intergroup, is the most active participant. It contributes a presentation to nearly every meeting. Other frequent guests and speakers are representatives of the Humane Society International (HSI) and the International Fund for Animal Welfare (IFAW). Moreover, representatives of research institutes, such as the Centre for Alternatives to Animal Testing (CAAT) at the Johns Hopkins University in Baltimore, USA, as well as practitioners, such as veterinarians and farmers, are regular attendees of Intergroup meetings (see Appendix C). In the 'Urban' Intergroup, it is mostly urban-related professionals, such as 'the architects, the urbanists, city planners, the tenants, the owners of the land, the transport people',[61] representatives of the European

Metropolitan Network Institute (EMI), of national and regional housing federations (see Appendix C).

In the light of these statements, the development and maintenance of social capital through Intergroups should not only be understood as exclusively among MEPs, but also with regard to representatives of civil society, as well as from the perspective of CSOs extending their interpersonal relations via Intergroups into the EP as a transnational field. For a more detailed account of civil society engagement in Intergroups, see Landorff (Accepted/In press). In this context, frequent descriptions of the Intergroup as a place 'to link',[62] as a 'bridge'[63] to the outside world, between decision-makers and partners, as a 'two-way conduit'[64] and as an 'interface [...] between the Parliament and the citizens [...] through the NGOs'[65] support the interpretation of the Intergroup as bridging social capital. In terms of the scope, this is in terms of the attendance of Intergroup meetings by civil society representatives, by representatives of EU institutions (see Chapter 6), and MEPs across political groups and parliamentary committees, the Intergroup has an outward-looking character, transcending political, social, national and institutional cleavages.

Given the match of previous professional occupation and Intergroup membership (Chapter 4) for some MEPs, one would assume that these MEPs may use their previously acquired interpersonal contacts in the context of the Intergroup. From the interviews, however, only a few isolated statements provided support for this assumption.[66] In contrast, interviewees claimed to seek additional contacts to fellow parliamentarians with similar interests, to CSOs and experts, as they were lacking these contacts in the first place.[67]

All forms of capital have to be used in order to be of value to their holder. Initially, 'the value of social capital depends on the size of the network of connections' the actors can effectively mobilise (Bourdieu, 1986, p. 51). In the political context, interpersonal ties regularised in informal groupings are primarily important in terms of channelling and exchanging information on legislation and voting (Caldeira & Patterson, 1987; Fiellin, 1962). In other words, bridging social capital is good for creating 'linkage to external assets and for information diffusion' (Putnam, 2000, p. 22). Next to these prominent functions, interpersonal ties may also serve as channels for the formation of coalitions and compromises, as tools for socialisation or may serve legislators in terms of their career development within or beyond the institution (see Fiellin, 1962; Scarrow, 1997).

Fieldwork showed that information diffusion (including the exchange of voting cues and political stances, i.e., organisational knowledge, but also expert knowledge) is the dominant purpose attributed to the Intergroup by the majority of interviewees.[68] Consequently, the upcoming Chapter 6 is dedicated to the Intergroup as informational capital. This is followed by the purpose of forming coalitions or majorities.[69] Chapter 7 on the conversion and mobilisation of the different forms of resources into political capital will notice this finding. In this context, the conversion of bridging social capital into political capital for the purpose of MEPs' career development will be discussed as well. Fieldwork did not provide evidence to support the assumption of Intergroups as a place for socialisation.[70] This finding goes hand in hand with the conceptualisation of Intergroups as primarily bridging social capital instead of bonding social capital. This chapter has shown that only a small group of MEPs attends meetings on a regular basis, while the majority joins on an ad hoc basis. Furthermore, the observation of Intergroup meetings revealed a large presence of CSO representatives and MEPs' assistants during these meetings. It also showed that meetings were dominated by presentations of CSO representatives, rapporteurs or MEPs, leaving not much space and time for interactions among parliamentarians during the meetings. Moreover, parliamentarians immediately left the room after the closure of the meeting or even before. As the only Intergroup among the four selected, the Intergroup 'Viticulture' may provide opportunities for socialisation as it organises receptions after its meetings where MEPs and attending guests have a glass of wine.[71] Based on the observations made during these receptions, it appears, however, that it is more MEPs and CSO representatives getting to know each other than parliamentarians among each other.

Conclusion

This chapter explored Intergroups as social capital of MEPs. Based on different coinages of the concept present in sociology and political science, it analysed the nature of interpersonal relations being regularised by MEPs in Intergroups. It focused thereby on the membership criteria, and thus on the exclusiveness or inclusiveness of Intergroups. It looked at the composition of Intergroups, i.e., on the homogeneity or heterogeneity of Intergroup members in terms of their socio-demographic and political characteristics. As a result, the chapter showed that the examined Intergroups are predominately of an outward-looking, inclusive and heterogeneous character. With no strict entry criteria, they assemble MEPs from different political groups and parliamentary committees, with different nationalities, length of services in the EP, gender and educational backgrounds. In this context, the chapter highlights the cross-party, cross-committee character of Intergroups, linking MEPs across various social groups to colleagues who 'normally' move in different subfields of the EP (i.e. parliamentary committees and political groups). Moreover, the chapter accounted for those relations practiced by MEPs with civil society.

Additionally, it analysed the regularity and durability with which those social interactions in Intergroups take place and discussed the notion of trust as a basic component of social capital in the context of Intergroups. In this way, the chapter showed that the majority of MEPs practices his or her Intergroup activities in a sporadic, ad hoc fashion with no long-term commitment over several legislative terms among the majority of Intergroup chairs. Consequently, an important finding of this study is that only a fraction of those MEPs inscribed in Intergroups practices their membership on a regular and durable basis. The analysis showed further that trust plays only a marginal role in Intergroups and is only noticed by a small number of MEPs. Only those parliamentarians who share membership in various social groups, e.g. political groups, parliamentary committees and Intergroups, over several mandates associated trust with the Intergroup (e.g. 'Trade Union' Intergroup). As a result, this chapter argues for an interpretation of Intergroups as bridging social capital as opposed to bonding social capital.

Notes

1. See Interview MEP 2.
2. See Interview MEP 2.
3. See Interview MEP 17; translation by the author, 'everyone can participate'.
4. See Interview MEP 4.
5. See Interview MEP 20.
6. See also Interviews MEPs 5, 19.
7. See Interviews MEPs 8, 18.
8. Between 2011 and 2013 the EP had 754 MEPs, see Corbett et al. (2016, p. 27).
9. See Interview CSO 1.
10. See Interview CSO 1.

11. See Interview CSO 1.
12. See Interview MEP 7.
13. See Interview MEP 7.
14. See Interviews MEPs 1, 2, 4, 8, 9, 10, 13, 14, 15, 19, 20, 21; CSO 1, 2.
15. See Interview MEP 14.
16. See Interview MEP 19. For further insight into the liberalisation of planting rights, see European Commission. (8 January 2016). *Agriculture and Rural Development: Wine*. Retrieved 18 March 2016, from http://ec.europa.eu/agriculture/wine/.
17. See Interview MEP 12.
18. See Interview MEP 2.
19. See Interviews MEPs 1, 2, 3, 4, 5, 6, 8, 9, 10, 11, 12, 13, 14, 15, 17, 18, 19, 20, 21.
20. Industry, Research and Energy.
21. See Interviews MEP 13; CSO 2.
22. Covering the period between September 2009 and April 2012.
23. Statement based on attendance sheets of the 'Trade Union' Intergroup covering the period between September 2009 and April 2012.
24. See Interviews MEPs 1, 2, 10, 14.
25. See Interviews MEPs 8, 20, and attended meetings of the Intergroups 'Trade Union' 16 October 2012 in Brussels, 'Water' 27 March 2013 in Brussels and 'Climate Change, Biodiversity and Sustainable Development' 7 May 2013 in Brussels.
26. See Interview MEP 8.
27. See Interviews MEPs 9, 10, 11.
28. See Interview MEP 7.
29. See Interview MEP 13.
30. See Interviews MEP 13; CSO 2, 5.
31. See Interview CSO 5.
32. See Interview MEP 13; Minutes of the 'Trade Union' Intergroup (2009–2012), see Appendix C.
33. See Interviews MEP 13; CSO 2, 5.
34. See Interviews MEP 13; CSO 2, 5.
35. See Interviews MEP 13; CSO 2, 5.
36. See Interviews CSO 1; MEP 2.
37. With the exception of plenary meetings conducted in November 2009 and February 2010. These were conducted on a Wednesday afternoon, see Appendix C.
38. See meetings of the Intergroups 'Animal Welfare' and 'Viticulture' on 12 and 13 September 2012 in Strasbourg.
39. See meetings of the Intergroups 'Climate Change, Biodiversity and Sustainable Development'/Sub-Group 'Islands' on 7 May 2013 and 'Water' on 27 March 2013 in Brussels.

40. See meetings of the Intergroups 'Animal Welfare', 'Viticulture', 'Traditional Minorities, National Communities and Languages', 'Water' and 'Climate Change, Biodiversity and Sustainable Development'/Sub-Group 'Islands'. For a complete overview of attended Intergroup meetings, see Appendix C.
41. See Interviews MEP 15; CSO 1.
42. See also Interview MEP 14.
43. See Interviews MEPs 2, 3, 5, 7, 10, 12, 13, 15, 16, 18, 19, 20.
44. See Interview MEP 18.
45. Statement based on attendance sheets of the 'Trade Union' Intergroup covering the period between September 2009 and April 2012.
46. Informal talk with assistant—Interview MEP 1.
47. See Interviews MEPs 4, 5, 10, 18, 19, 20; CSO 4.
48. In 11 out of 47 meetings.
49. In 7 out of 47 meetings.
50. In 12 out of 32 meetings between September 2009 and April 2012, assistants outnumbered attending parliamentarians.
51. See Interviews MEPs 18, 19. Attendance sheets could not be obtained for the Intergroup 'Viticulture' despite several requests to the bureau of the Intergroup. For the Intergroup 'Urban' no insights on this aspect could be gained.
52. This practice has been observed in the offices of MEPs 19, 5 and 14.
53. See Interview CSO 6.
54. See Interview MEP 3.
55. See also Interview MEP 21.
56. See Interviews MEPs 4, 13, 20.
57. See Interview MEP 20.
58. See Interview MEP 13.
59. See Interview MEP 13.
60. See Interview MEP 13.
61. See Interview MEP 1.
62. See Interviews MEPs 4, 8.
63. See Interviews MEPs 1, 18, 19.
64. See Interview MEP 13.
65. See Interview MEP 3.
66. See Interview MEP 19.
67. See Interviews MEPs 13, 14, 15, 17, 18.
68. See Interviews MEPs 1, 2, 3, 4, 5, 7, 8, 10, 12, 13, 14, 15, 16, 17, 18, 21.
69. See Interviews MEPs 2, 7, 11, 17, 21.
70. See Interviews MEPs 14, 15.
71. See, e.g., Interview CSO 6.

References

Bale, T., & Taggart, P. (2006). *First-Timers Yes, Virgins No: The Roles and Backgrounds of New Members of the European Parliament* (SEI Working Paper No. 89), 1–30.

Bourdieu, P. (1986). The Forms of Capital. In J. G. Richardson (Ed.), *Handbook of Theory and Research for the Sociology of Education* (pp. 1–16). London: Greenwood Press.

Bowler, S., & Farrell, D. M. (1995). The Organizing of the European Parliament: Committees, Specialization and Co-ordination. *British Journal of Political Science, 25*(02), 219–243.

Burns, C. J. (2013). The European Parliament. In M. Cini & N. Perez-Solorzano Borragan (Eds.), *European Union Politics* (4th ed., pp. 159–171). Oxford: Oxford University Press.

Busby, A. (2013). *The Everyday Practice and Performance of European Politics: An Ethnography of the European Parliament* (PhD thesis). University of Sussex, Sussex.

Caldeira, G. A., & Patterson, S. C. (1987). Political Friendship in the Legislature. *The Journal of Politics, 49*(04), 953–975.

Carpenter, D. P., Esterling, K. M., & Lazer, D. M. J. (1998). The Strength of Weak Ties in Lobbying Networks: Evidence from Health-Care Politics in the United States. *Journal of Theoretical Politics, 10*(4), 417–444.

Corbett, R., Jacobs, F., & Neville, D. (2016). *The European Parliament* (9th ed.). London: John Harper Publishing.

Corbett, R., Jacobs, F., & Shackleton, M. (2011). *The European Parliament* (8th ed.). London: John Harper Publishing.

European Commission. (8 January 2016). *Agriculture and Rural Development: Wine*. Retrieved 18 March 2016, from http://ec.europa.eu/agriculture/wine/.

European Parliament. (2002). *Activities: 12/A-2002—Bulletin*. Brussels: European Parliament: Directorate for the Planning of Parliamentary Business.

European Parliament. (2003). *Activities: 03/A-2003—Bulletin*. Brussels: European Parliament: Directorate for the Planning of Parliamentary Business.

European Parliament. (2005). *Activities: 08/A-2005—Bulletin*. Brussels: European Parliament: Directorate for the Planning of Parliamentary Business.

European Parliament. (2009). *Rules of Procedure: 7th Parliamentary Term December 2009*.

European Parliament. (2013a). *About Parliament: Organisation and Work—Intergroups*. Retrieved 24 January 2013, from http://www.europarl.europa.eu/aboutparliament/en/00c9d93c87/Intergroups.html.

European Parliament. (2013b). *MEPs: Struan Stevenson*. Retrieved 13 December 2013, from http://www.europarl.europa.eu/meps/en/4546/STRUAN_STEVENSON_home.html.

European Parliament. (2013c). *MEPs: Thomas Mann*. Retrieved 20 December 2013, from http://www.europarl.europa.eu/meps/en/1922/THOMAS_MANN_home.html.

European Parliament. (2014a). *About Parliament: Organisation and Work—Intergroups*. Retrieved 19 May 2014, from http://www.europarl.europa.eu/aboutparliament/en/00c9d93c87/Intergroups.html.

European Parliament. (2014b). *MEPs: Evelyn Regner*. Retrieved 24 November 2014, from http://www.europarl.europa.eu/meps/de/96998/EVELYN_REGNER_cv.html.

European Parliament. (2014c). *MEPs: Georges Bach*. Retrieved 24 November 2014, from http://www.europarl.europa.eu/meps/en/97293/GEORGES_BACH_history.html.

European Parliament. (2015). *MEPs: Browse Map*. Retrieved 12 November 2015, from http://www.europarl.europa.eu/meps/en/map.html.

Fiellin, A. (1962). The Functions of Informal Groups in Legislative Institutions. *The Journal of Politics, 24*(1), 72–91.

Granovetter, M. S. (1973). The Strengths of Weak Ties. *American Journal of Sociology, 78*(6), 1360–1380.

Haas, P. M. (1992). Introduction: Epistemic Communities and International Policy Coordination. *International Organization, 46*(1), 1–35.

Intergroup on the Welfare & Conservation of Animals. (2013). *Rules of Procedure*. Retrieved 31 May 2014, from http://www.animalwelfare-intergroup.eu/wp-content/uploads/2013/01/Rules-of-procedure-final-11-01-2013.pdf.

Intergroup on the Welfare & Conservation of Animals. (2014). *Intergroup Attendance September 2009–March 2014*. Retrieved 01 August 2014, from http://www.animalwelfareintergroup.eu/wp-content/uploads/2011/08/3-Intergroup-attendance-September-2009-March-2014.pdf.

Kauppi, N. (2011). EU Politics. In A. Favell & V. Guiraudon (Eds.), *Sociology of the European Union* (pp. 150–171). Basingstoke: Palgrave Macmillan.

Kohler-Koch, B., & Quittkat, C. (2009). What is civil society and who represents civil society in the EU?—Results of an online survey among civil society experts. *Policy and Society, 28*(1), 11–22.

Landorff, L. (Accepted/In press). Intergroups as alternative venues in the European Parliament: Lessons for civil society. In U. Liebert & A. Jenichen (Eds.), *Europeanisation and Renationalisation: Learning from Crises for Innovation and Development*. Leverkusen: Barbara Budrich Publishers.

Michon, S. (2008). Assistant parlementaire au Parlement européen: un tremplin pour une carrière européenne. *Sociologie du Travail, 50*(2), 169–183.

Neuhold, C. (2001). The 'Legislative Backbone' Keeping the Institution Upright? The Role of European Parliament Committees in the EU Policy-Making Process. *European Integration Online Papers (EioP), 5*(10), 1–29.

Putnam, R. D. (2000). *Bowling Alone: The Collapse and Revival of American Community*. New York: Simon & Schuster.

Ringe, N., Victor, J. N., & Carman, C. J. (2013). *Bridging the Information Gap: Legislative Member Organizations as Social Networks in the United States and the European Union*. Ann Arbor: University of Michigan Press.

Sabatier, P. A. (1988). An Advocacy Coalition Framework of Policy Change and the Role of Policy-Oriented Learning Therein. *Policy Sciences, 21*(2/3), 129–168.

Scarrow, S. E. (1997). Political Career Paths and the European Parliament. *Legislative Studies Quarterly, 22*(2), 253–263.

Wodak, R. (2009). *The Discourse of Politics in Action: Politics as Usual*. New York: Palgrave Macmillan.

Yordanova, N. (2009). The Rationale Behind Committee Assignment in the European Parliament: Distributive, Informational and Partisan Perspectives. *European Union Politics, 10*(2), 253–280.

CHAPTER 6

Seeking Information: The Intergroup as Informational Capital

> [I]t is a forum for education [...] I learn about shark finning and that sort of thing there.[...] I go along there because I think that it increases my knowledge [...].[1]

> I mean knowledge [...] through the Intergroup meetings I have the information on what is going on in other committees.[2]

> [...] we can predict very accurately how many members we will be able to mobilize to support a particular position [...].[3]

Conventional wisdom tells us 'knowledge is power'. From informational theories of legislatures, we know that 'expertise is universally needed in most legislatures but not uniformly distributed' (Krehbiel, 1992, p. 68).[4] Some legislators 'have better knowledge than others about the relationship between policies and outcomes' (e.g. possess better policy information), while others again have better knowledge about 'what policies other legislators want' (e.g. political information) (Krehbiel, 1992, p. 68). Hence, legislative work is characterised by uncertainty and information asymmetry where some players in the field possess better, more complete policy and political information than others, and hence have more power. The European Parliament (EP) is not different from other legislatures in this regard. Shaped by the informational rationale of legislative organisation,[5] 'information is a highly valued good in [EP] legislative politics' (Ringe, Victor, & Carman, 2013, p. 25).

L. Landorff, *Inside European Parliament Politics*, Palgrave Studies in European Political Sociology, https://doi.org/10.1007/978-3-030-04206-6_6

The profession of Members of the European Parliament (MEPs) and their everyday work life have changed over time in line with the EP's increase in competences and members. The work of an MEP is no longer a part-time occupation but a full-time job that requires MEPs not only to divide their time between multiple geographical workplaces but also to specialise in particular policy areas (Corbett, Jacobs, & Neville, 2016; Kauppi, 2011). Still, MEPs choose to practise their mandate in different ways. Some members 'remain generalists, whereas others become specialists', and some advance 'functional rather than policy specialities' (Corbett, Jacobs, & Shackleton, 2011, p. 65). However, all of them are faced with the challenging task of voting on highly technical legislative acts and making well-informed decisions on a very broad range of policy issues (Ringe, 2010). Following again conventional wisdom (e.g. that one cannot be an expert in everything); MEPs need to have their own, additional sources of information when they make decisions on policy issues that are beyond their own areas of expertise. MEPs can draw on various knowledge sources, for example, on parliamentary committees, which as the 'legislative backbone' of the Parliament, serve as the 'main repositories of policy expertise' (Ringe, 2010, p. 20; Westlake, 1995, p. 191).

Building on the conceptualisation of Intergroups as bridging social capital, this chapter argues for a conceptualisation of Intergroups as informational capital. In this way, the chapter shows how bridging social capital is converted into informational capital. Inspired by the informational rationale of legislative organisation and Wodak's (2009) ethnographic research on the everyday life of MEPs, this chapter presents an innovative conceptual modification of the Bourdieusian concept of informational capital. In view of the above quoted parliamentarians heading this chapter, referring to knowledge about shark finning, to information about what is happening in other parliamentary committees as well as to numbers of MEPs supporting a particular position in the Parliament, previous conceptualisations of informational capital appear to be too neat (Bernhard, 2012, 2015; Bourdieu, Wacquant, & Farage, 1994). Recalling the nature of the EP as a legislature with no overall majority of one political group, with no fixed opposition and where an effective MEP has to be 'good at explaining, persuading, and negotiating' (Corbett et al., 2011, p. 9), informational capital referring primarily to statistical data does not meet the requirements which MEPs face in their everyday parliamentary work. By contrast, knowledge about the position and thinking of others and about how to convince parliamentary colleagues is as necessary as substantial knowledge (including statistical data, numbers and figures) for achieving consensus and creating majorities across heterogeneous political groups. As a result, this chapter discusses each of Wodak's (2009) three dimensions of knowledge, namely expert, organisational and political knowledge, in the context of Intergroups. All of these three forms of knowledge are intertwined, and MEPs acquire and draw on them to varying degrees. In this manner, this study provides a more comprehensive and holistic conceptualisation of not only information but knowledge going beyond the terms of policy information and political information used in theories of legislative organisation (see Krehbiel, 1992). Knowing that the parliamentary committees serve as the main arenas for MEP's specialisation, the chapter also provides an insight into the advantages of Intergroups as informational capital vis-à-vis established knowledge bases in the EP. In this context, the discussion shows that the accumulation of informational capital takes place against the backdrop of MEPs perceiving those topics addressed in Intergroups as themes that are sidelined in parliamentary committees, and on the EP's agenda. MEPs perceive a dominance of certain interests, which are represented in and by the EP, to the detriment of others. This is reflected in statements, that MEPs would only talk about the 'banking system' in the Parliament and very rarely 'about the social right[s]', the rights of workers and workers' organisations in general[6] or in MEPs noticing a dominance of agricultural topics vis-à-vis topics concerning urban areas in the Parliament.[7] As a result, MEPs seek to acquire informational capital on these dominated themes.

Acquisition of Expert Knowledge

Expert knowledge is reflected in MEPs being specialised in 'specific policy domains' (e.g. in agricultural, regional or social policy) (Wodak, 2009, p. 46) and thus, includes what is understood by policy information, policy-oriented and substantive information in informational theories of legislatures.

The majority of interviewees linked their participation in Intergroups to the wish or need to learn and inform themselves about the specific policy issue,[8] and to increase their knowledge with 'new facts, new data and new studies' as expressed by interviewees.[9] The wish to learn and inform themselves goes hand in hand with the perception of the Intergroup as a 'place for discussion'[10] and exchange[11] and as a 'forum of education'[12] where a process of learning takes place. Thereby, the discussions within Intergroups are on 'very specific detailed issues',[13] where specific means being 'concentrated on concrete subject[s]'[14] and concerned with predominately very technical topics,[15] such as the level of sulphur dioxide in organic wine, the geographical indications of aromatised wine, or alternatives to animal testing, just to provide some examples from the Intergroups 'Viticulture' and 'Animal Welfare'; see Appendix C for a full record of topics of Intergroup meetings.

The analysis of Intergroup minutes reveals that the subject of debate and exchange varies across and within Intergroups. In the 'Trade Union' Intergroup, current legislative dossiers were the exclusive subjects of discussion. Out of 21 discussed reports,[16] twelve of them were subject to the ordinary legislative procedure (COD), while nine of them were own-initiative reports[17] (see Appendix D). The meetings of the 'Urban' Intergroup focused primarily on the evaluation of current, and the alignment of the future, EU Cohesion Policy. In the Intergroup 'Animal Welfare', discussions on EP reports, specific case studies, research reports as well as the enforcement and implementation of current European Union (EU) legislation appeared to be broadly balanced (see Appendix C). Out of 11 discussed reports, five were subject to the ordinary legislative procedure (COD), while six were own-initiative reports (see Appendix D; Intergroup on the Welfare & Conservation of Animals, 2014). The debates in the Intergroup 'Viticulture' were dominated by the reform of the common market organisation (CMO) for wine. Several meetings were dedicated to the topic, including a number of presentations on the single CMO report by the French MEP and Intergroup vice-president Michel Dantin (see, e.g. Intergroup meeting on 12 September 2012 in Strasbourg, France in Appendix C). Consequently, MEPs acquire and exchange very specific, technical and scientific knowledge in and through Intergroups, containing also numbers, facts and indicators. This type of knowledge resembles previous conceptualisations of informational capital (Bernhard, 2012, 2015; Bourdieu et al., 1994).

While acquiring new expert knowledge, some of the MEPs contribute also their own (professional) knowledge on the issue to the debates.[18] The analysis of social and professional backgrounds of Intergroup members revealed a link between their previous occupation and their current Intergroup activities (see Chapter 4). For instance, many members of the 'Urban' Intergroup had posts as mayors or city counsellors prior their first mandate in the EP. The most active members of the 'Viticulture' Intergroup have social or professional backgrounds in the vine-growing sector. Likewise, the majority of 'Trade Union' Intergroup members have a trade union record (see Chapter 4). Those MEPs contribute to the discussion their practical expert knowledge linked to the management and administration of cities, the production of wine or the rights and interests of workers, and they utilise this professional knowledge to push for their respective interests.[19] Again, it is stressed that MEPs appear to seek membership in those Intergroups where they can draw on their own previous work experience.

Nevertheless, in the overall picture, expert knowledge is predominately provided by external invitees,[20] i.e. by speakers of civil society organisations (CSOs), scientific experts and practitioners. Thus, to speak of Intergroups as epistemic communities,[21] that is as networks of knowledge-based experts who share a 'set of normative and principled beliefs, which provide a value-based rationale for the social action of community members' (Haas, 1992, p. 3), would be misleading. While there are individual parliamentarians across the Intergroups who can be perceived as professional experts given their previous occupation, the practice is that 'experts are normally invited experts',[22] and invited guests change with the topics of Intergroup meetings. Moreover, interviews with MEPs revealed that Intergroup members share in the first place the interest in the topic but not necessarily the solutions or 'practices associated with a set of problems' or attached to the issues discussed in the Intergroup (Haas, 1992, p. 3). In contrast, this book argues that it is both expert and non-expert parliamentarians who meet in Intergroups.

Acquisition of Organisational Knowledge

Organisational knowledge designates 'shared knowledge about preceding events and debates, rules and routines, and about the positions and opinions of specific MEPs' or political groups (Wodak, 2009, p. 46). In terms of the EP, knowing about the positions of different actors within the transnational political field is of utmost importance. Thereby, it concerns not only the positions of MEPs and political groups, but also the positions of civil society organisations and their representatives, as well as of representatives of other EU institutions given the transnational and overlapping character of the EP as a political field with its permeable boundaries. In doing so, it includes the term political information used by theorists of informational theory of legislatures that designates 'strategic information about policy positions of other decision-makers' (Ringe et al., 2013, p. 4).

Views and Positions of Civil Society

The analysis of attendance sheets and minutes as well as the observation of Intergroup meetings revealed that representatives of civil society are regular attendees and speakers at Intergroup meetings (see also Chapter 5).

The analysis of the meeting protocols of the 'Trade Union' Intergroup from September 2009 to March 2013 revealed that in most cases the representatives of the European Trade Union Confederation (ETUC) opposed the legislative proposals coming from the European Commission. Noticeable examples are the three draft directives on conditions of entry and residence of third-country nationals in the framework of an intra-corporate transfer (ICT), on seasonal workers, and on single application procedures for a single permit discussed in June and December 2010 as well as in June 2011 (see Appendix C). With regard to the single permit, ETUC representatives demanded to delete the three exclusions 'included in the proposed directive concerning third-country seasonal workers, posted workers and people working in the EU under GATT agreements', and 'to ensure the same rights to all workers legally residing in the EU, without any restriction' (Trade Union Intergroup, 2010c, pp. 1–2). In addition, ETUC representatives were pushing continuously for a revision of the Posting of Workers Directive, see the meetings in April 2012, March 2011 and June 2010 (Trade Union Intergroup, 2010b, 2010c, 2010d, 2011, 2012). Thereby, the chair of the European Federation of Building and Woodworkers' (EFBWW) building committee, John Kerstens, called on the EP 'to counterweigh the Commission's minimalistic approach and the Council' (Trade Union Intergroup, 2010d, p. 3). Hence, within the transnational field, the opposite poles are occupied by the MEPs and trade unions in the Intergroup, and the European Commission and Council.

Animal welfare CSOs, such as the Eurogroup for Animals, used the Intergroup to push the European Commission, e.g. on the enforcement of the battery cage ban for laying hens or for a new EU Animal Welfare Strategy (Intergroup on the Welfare & Conservation of Animals, 2011c, 2012a, 2012b). The Humane Society International (HSI) pushed for the preservation of the EU ban on the trade with seal products in the context of the World Trade Organisation (WTO) consultations with Canada (Intergroup on the Welfare & Conservation of Animals, 2011b).

Views and Positions of the European Commission

In particular, members of the Intergroups 'Urban' and 'Animal Welfare' emphasised that through the Intergroup they are provided with direct access to the European Commission.[23] The analysis of meeting minutes revealed that primarily policy officers or heads of units of Directorate-Generals (DGs) for Regional and Urban Policy (REGIO), Mobility and Transport (MOVE) as well as for Energy (ENER) are regular speakers at meetings of the 'Urban' Intergroup (Urban Intergroup at the European Parliament, 2014a). In the 'Animal Welfare' Intergroup, it is primarily representatives of the DGs Health and Consumers (SANCO), Environment (ENV), Maritime Affairs and Fisheries (MARE), Agriculture and Rural Development (AGRI) as well as of Research and Innovation (RTD) exchanging with MEPs and animal welfare organisations (Intergroup on the Welfare & Conservation of Animals, 2014). In addition, extraordinary meetings with the European Commissioner for Health John Dalli, and his successor Tonio Borg, were organised by members of the Intergroup. These provided parliamentarians with the opportunity to inquire directly about, e.g. the state of play concerning the possible framework law on animal welfare (Intergroup on the Welfare & Conservation of Animals, 2013c).

Getting to know the views and positions of civil society and of representatives of the European Commission goes hand in hand with the information on forthcoming actions concerning legislation. Through the exchange with the Eurogroup for Animals, MEPs in the Intergroup 'Animal Welfare' get to know about actions and plans of the European Commission, while the Eurogroup for Animals in exchange gets to know what is going on in the EP regarding the issue.[24] Accordingly, the issue is timed on the agenda of the Intergroup.[25]

A similar pattern has been noticed in the 'Urban' Intergroup where meetings are, inter alia, organised in response to new legislative proposals from the European Commission concerning urban areas in order to allow the Commission to explain its views on the proposal.[26] In the 'Trade Union' Intergroup, MEPs and the ETUC jointly align the agenda of the Intergroup to the working programme of the Commission in order to 'be prepared' and have enough time for the 'process of feeding information to members', i.e. to brief them on the subject and upcoming proposals from the European Commission).[27] These statements provide new insights into the practices occurring prior to the committee stage, in preparation to committee meetings and along them.

The fact that representatives of the European Commission are less present in the meetings of the Intergroups 'Viticulture' and 'Trade Union' (see Appendix C) does not mean that those MEPs do not gain knowledge on the respective views and positions. Instead, it is a regular practice that MEPs (sometimes in their functions as rapporteur) inform their colleagues about the position of the European Commission and the Council on the subject matter. For instance, MEP Hughes reported back to his colleagues in the 'Trade Union' Intergroup about a meeting with the president of the European Commission José Manuel Barroso (Trade Union Intergroup, 2010a). Similarly, French MEP Mathieu Houillon, in her function as LIBE committee rapporteur, informed MEPs in the 'Trade Union' Intergroup about the European Commission presenting 'an ad hoc proposal on seasonal workers' on July 8th, as well as a specific directive on posted workers in the near future (Trade Union Intergroup, 2010c, p. 2). MEP Lulling, chair of the 'Viticulture' Intergroup, informed members about the progress made by the High Level Group on Wine established by the European Commission (see Appendix C meeting on 19 April 2012).

Views of MEPs and Rapporteurs

As mentioned previously, EP reports and legislative proposals from the European Commission are primarily subject to debate in the 'Trade Union' and 'Animal Welfare' Intergroup.[28] Hence, through the Intergroups, MEPs inform themselves about the state of play of EP reports. They learn from their fellow MEPs (e.g. rapporteurs and shadow-rapporteurs) about their approach to the report and the state of affairs. They are informed about contentious points, deadlines for tabling amendments, votes in the parliamentary committees and the plenary,[29] as well as about majorities or oppositions towards the report within the EP. Thereby, learning and exchange of information occur mutually since rapporteurs and shadow-rapporteurs also receive an insight into potential opposition or support for their report through the feedback from their colleagues in the Intergroup.

An example is the report by the Portuguese MEP Edite Estrela[30] that has been discussed in the 'Trade Union' Intergroup (Trade Union Intergroup, 2009, 2010b). While the Portuguese rapporteur stressed that the introduction of paternity leave of two fully paid weeks minimum is key to her voting in favour of this report, the French EPP member and co-chair of the Intergroup Morin-Chartier stated that 'the EPP was against the inclusion of a paternal leave in this specific directive and against the extension of the maternity leave to 20 weeks' (Trade Union Intergroup, 2010b, p. 2). Furthermore, she informed the rapporteur that 'the report as drafted could not be supported by the majority of the Parliament and further negotiations were necessary' (Trade Union Intergroup, 2010b, p. 2).

Next to the views and positions of rapporteurs and shadow-rapporteurs, parliamentarians get to know how MEPs in other committees, working on the same issue, think about the subject. For instance, a member of the 'Animal Welfare' Intergroup gets to know colleagues in the AGRI committee working on animal welfare-related issues through the Intergroup.[31] Through the cross-committee and bridging character of the Intergroup, MEPs gain information 'on what is going on in other committees', both in terms of thinking and in terms of actual legislation on, for example, cities and urban areas that is worked out in different parliamentary committees, and the consequences these different legislative acts have.[32] In this way, bridging social capital is converted into informational capital. Another example for the acquisition of organisational knowledge, and the conversion of social bridging capital into informational capital, concerns the exchange and coordination of voting cues. In this context, the Intergroup is referred to as a 'very powerful tool' through which those who engage in the Intergroup 'can predict very accurately how many members we will be able to mobilise to support a particular position'.[33] Moreover, the Intergroup helps to coordinate 'to some extent our votes in committees or in the plenary'.[34] In this manner, the exchange across political groups in the Intergroup provides feedback—'a very accurate breakdown of the numbers they [MEPs] can deliver from their group for a particular issue'.[35] Given, however, that this observation emerged primarily in the context of the 'Trade Union' Intergroup, the statements concerning the exchange of information on voting cues have to be treated with caution. As demonstrated in Chapters 4 and 5, the 'Trade Union' Intergroup is particular in terms of its composition, gathering primarily MEPs from the S&D Group and the EMPL committee. As a result, the interpersonal relationships appear to be closer and more exclusive as compared to those social relations described and regularised in the other three Intergroups. In this context, bridging social capital is converted into organisational knowledge and becomes an asset in the process of forecasting votes, and subsequently in the mobilisation of votes for a particular position. Hence, for the rapporteur, this organisational knowledge in the form of voting cues denotes a valuable asset. It provides knowledge for the rapporteur concerning which MEPs and political groups still need to be convinced of his or her position,[36] and how the majorities concerning the respective report are distributed in the EP.

In sum, through the Intergroup MEPs interact with parliamentarians they would not normally interact with due to different and limited committee memberships. MEPs usually serve on one committee as a permanent member. The allocation to committees is regulated and restricted by the political groups. Through the Intergroup, MEPs are able to identify like-minded and not like-minded parliamentarians out of the overall EP population of 736 MEPs (7th term). They gain organisational knowledge on potential allies with whom alliances can be built and on opponents concerning the issue who still need to be convinced.

Acquisition of Political Knowledge: The 'Know-How' of How to Convince Others

Identifying supporters and opponents of one's position is one side of the coin. Convincing your colleagues of your view is the other one. While national parliamentarians are supposed to be good at debating and need to score over their opponents, an MEP needs to be good at explaining and negotiating to establish consensus and to create needed majorities (Corbett et al., 2016). Hence, knowing how to induce cooperation is a very valuable asset and skill in the EP as a transnational field.

Political knowledge as the 'know-how' of how to convince, advise and persuade others presumes knowledge of strategies and tactics, of positions and ideologies (Wodak, 2009). It includes knowledge of the strong and weak points of colleagues; hence, 'one has to know the rules of the game' (Wodak, 2009, p. 46). Therefore, winning the game—the struggle over influence and dominance—'has only a little to do with luck and a lot to do with strategies' and the ability 'to read the game and the other player', and having 'a feel for the game' (Wilken, 2008, p. 91). In doing so, political knowledge, understood as the 'know-how' of how to persuade others and forge alliances, is also linked to the habitus of the individual (i.e. the MEP).

This means, it is linked to the 'structuring mechanism that operates from within agents' (Bourdieu & Wacquant, 1992, p. 18).

Fieldwork revealed that it is primarily the Intergroup chairs who possess the skill to convince and persuade. For instance, in the case of the chair of the Intergroup 'Viticulture' MEP Astrid Lulling, interviewees have highlighted her persuasiveness.[37] Initially, the very fact that MEPs actively establish and maintain Intergroups is interpreted as one sign that these MEPs have a 'feeling for the game' (i.e. pursuing the Intergroup as a practice, as a strategy to pursue their own policy priorities). This interpretation is also supported by interviewees with regard to the 'Trade Union' Intergroup. They described the Intergroup as a tool-kit—'as a means we need to use to achieve the ends and the end justifies the means'.[38] As described previously, Intergroups allow MEPs to identify like-minded MEPs across political groups and committees. They further allow them to expand their social capital as well as informational capital (i.e. primarily expert and organisational knowledge) while they only make low investments (in terms of time and resources) themselves. Maintaining an Intergroup is interpreted here as agents being able 'to act and to develop relevant political strategies' (i.e. the set-up of an Intergroup for the specific topic), which presupposes 'having the practical sense of political games in the European space' (Beauvallet & Michon, 2010, p. 158).

Returning to those MEPs who displayed or have been attributed with the power of persuasion, this political knowledge has been linked by interviewees to the seniority of the MEPs as well as to previous national parliamentary experience.[39] This political knowledge is reflected in knowing how to make laws, knowing how to organise majorities, and in having their own formula in the Intergroup of how to stifle legislative proposals coming from the European Commission before they become real.[40]

These elaborations point to the possession of political knowledge, the knowledge of how 'to prepare and influence decision-making' or respectively policymaking, and how to advise and start convincing their parliamentary colleagues of their opinion (Wodak, 2009, p. 46). It supports the interpretation that Intergroup chairs have the knowledge of strategies and tactics and 'a feel for the game' (Wilken, 2008, p. 91). In addition to the finding that political knowledge is primarily attached to Intergroup chairs, three further comments have to be made in terms of persuasion and convincing taking place in Intergroups.

First, interviews indicate that convincing of MEPs by MEPs in the Intergroup takes place less. Interviewees associated with the Intergroup 'Animal Welfare' stated that Intergroup meetings are not conclusive, arguing that the 'work of the Intergroup is not targeted at reaching any consensus or any compromise, it is not necessary' because 'all people are like-minded'.[41] Instead 'you leave [the meeting] and you do your own thing based on the input you get from the experts and from other [...] members of the house'.[42] Similarly, interviewees associated with the Intergroup 'Trade Union' stated: '[W]e discuss things and then it's up to the members themselves, I would think to make their choice'.[43] This, of course, does not rule out that MEPs make their choice after having been convinced by what they have heard in the Intergroup. These statements do not, however, point to collective position building in the Intergroup. Instead, they point to individual opinion-formation, which does not necessarily have to lead to consensus building.

Second, interviews indicate that persuasive efforts take place more between MEPs and civil society representatives, as for instance in the 'Trade Union' Intergroup, where MEPs and trade union representatives attempt to establish a consensus among each other.[44] This, however, does also not always happen. By contrast, meetings were conducted where both sides presented their opinions and where no agreements were reached.[45]

Third, interviews indicate that the persuasion of MEPs by MEPs takes place beyond the Intergroup. It takes place by MEPs selling the position acquired or established in the Intergroup inside their own political groups to subsequently organise majorities for the respective issue.[46] Hence, according to this study, the persuasive efforts are carried out outside the Intergroup.

While these three comments are based on individual statements by MEPs, these impressions are further substantiated through the attendance of Intergroup meetings.[47] These meetings have been characterised by mere presentations of either very technical facts or processes, perspectives and opinions, followed by short question and answer sessions with or without the participation of MEPs, rather than by an engagement in an argument by MEPs and other attendees. Again, as stated previously, this does not rule out that MEPs act and make decisions after having been convinced by what they have heard in the Intergroup.

Relating these findings to the study of Ringe et al. (2013, pp. 13, 203) which positions Intergroups 'as arenas for contestation, bargaining, political coordination and the exchange of political information across party groups' as well as a 'place for search of consensus and compromise', only the aspects of political coordination and the exchange of both expert knowledge as well as organisational knowledge containing political information, are confirmed by the results of this study. Reasons for the different interpretations and results may be attributed to the sampling of different Intergroups and thus, different interview partners, and the fact that Intergroups vary significantly in their activities, objectives and scope. Moreover, Ringe et al. (2013) base their findings on interview data only. This book draws also on data generated through the personal attendance of Intergroup meetings, which provides different insights and complements interview statements. In this way, the book provides a more holistic picture of MEPs' engagement in Intergroups.

In sum, it is concluded that MEPs gain and exchange informational capital, including expert knowledge (which they partly contribute themselves) and organisational knowledge. It is further argued that they already possess some political knowledge on how to mobilise support and identify allies within the EP—the mere fact of establishing an Intergroup substantiates this claim. So how do Intergroups as sources of informational capital relate to the established and conventional knowledge bases in the EP?

In the EP, the accumulation of informational capital is regulated through the dominant habitus of the field. As outlined in Chapter 2, the habitus of the field constitutes 'its specific internalized culture' that assigns roles to MEPs, provides guidelines for legitimate behaviour and hence, constrains and empowers parliamentarians in their actions (Kauppi, 2005, p. 46). In line with the dominant habitus of the EP, resource accumulation is regulated by the political groups which control committee assignments and thus, control the assignment to places of specialisation.

Within the transnational field, MEPs can draw on various knowledge sources, for example, on the parliamentary committees, on committee staff, experts or sectoral representatives in public hearings or workshops, lobby groups, as well as their personal assistants (see Neuhold, 2001; Whitaker, 2011). Given the diversity and number of sources of knowledge available to MEPs, one wonders why MEPs perceive an additional need to establish and participate in informal cross-party/cross-committee groups where they interact with representatives from civil society as well as with representatives of other EU institutions?

Intergroups Versus Established Knowledge Sources

The accumulation of expert knowledge on policy issues is primarily regulated through interactions taking place within parliamentary committees, where MEPs 'acquire and make use of existing expertise in specific policy areas' (Ringe, 2010, p. 21). In addition, MEPs can also draw on the EP committee secretariat. Compared to the US Congress's full-time staff, the size of committee staff in the EP is rather small with five to 15 administrators depending on the committee (Corbett et al., 2016). Committee staff assists MEPs in their function as rapporteurs or opinion-givers by providing scientific and technical information as well as political advice (Neuhold, 2001; Winzen, 2011). Hence, they serve as a source for both expert and organisational knowledge. Furthermore, public hearings and workshops organised within the scope of MEPs' committee work provide parliamentarians with the opportunity to receive 'independent expertise and advice' from experts or sectoral representatives, and 'to enter into dialogue with interested parties' (Corbett et al., 2016, p. 186).

However, the topics addressed by MEPs in Intergroups are very much topics of their own personal interest.[48] At the same time, these topics, despite being generally considered as important, seem rather to present 'des opinions souvent minoritaires au sein du Parlement européen' as Dutoit (2009, p. 23) indicates. Interviewees referring to them as 'low profile issue'.[49] These are topics which are not of high priority in the Parliament, and to which not enough committee time is dedicated according to the MEPs.[50] Moreover, the EP committee secretariat consists rather of generalists than of specialists (Corbett et al., 2016). This conflicts with the motivation of MEPs to discuss in Intergroups very specific, detailed and to some degree very technical subjects.

Furthermore, the subjects addressed in Intergroups fall under the jurisdiction of several parliamentary committees.[51] Subjects discussed in the 'Urban' Intergroup are covered by the REGI, TRAN and ENVI committee. Issues discussed in the 'Animal Welfare' Intergroup are subject to the AGRI (see the protection of animals used for scientific purposes Intergroup on the Welfare & Conservation of Animals, 2013a), ENVI (see invasive alien species Intergroup on the Welfare & Conservation of Animals, 2013b) and TRAN committee (see the protection of animals during transport Intergroup on the Welfare &

Conservation of Animals, 2011a). MEPs who are interested in a topic would need to draw on the expert knowledge of several committees. However, this is hardly possible given the guidelines for legitimate behaviour in the field (i.e. that MEPs are usually only a member of one or two committees). The Intergroup provides them with one place to acquire the expert knowledge they desire, which saves time and resources. Moreover, they receive an overview of all legislative and non-legislative activities going on across several committees, which puts them in a better position vis-à-vis other agents in the field (e.g. colleagues who just possess knowledge about individual, separate committees).

Bypassing these structural constraints of knowledge accumulation through the Intergroup is one part of the story. The other part links back to voicing 'des opinions souvent minoritaires' (Dutoit, 2009, p. 23). With their Intergroup activities, MEPs seek to make marginalised perspectives more present, more dominant in the EP or to introduce even a new perspective.[52] Experiencing that it is very difficult to have something non-legislative discussed in the committees—to 'hav[e] an open debate about something that is not related to the Parliament's agenda',[53] parliamentarians use the Intergroup to communicate and present those opinions they feel are marginalised within the field. In the 'Animal Welfare' Intergroup, MEPs communicate a different perspective, that is, a perspective different to the dominant view advocated in the AGRI committee on animals. While Intergroup participants look at animals from the human perspective, being interested in 'what is good for animals', the 'AGRI committee is more interested into look[ing] at animals from the perspective of farmer[s and the] food industry [...]'.[54] In the 'Urban' Intergroup, MEPs struggle to establish a new and European perspective (e.g. the urban dimension in structural funds) and push for the creation of a European urban policy 'after years of discussion about the urban dimension of different European policies' (Urban Intergroup at the European Parliament, 2014b).[55] In the 'Trade Union' Intergroup, the perception that drives the MEP to engage for the Intergroup is that in the EP one is 'only chatting about the banking system and economic [sic!]' and very rarely 'about the social right[s]', the rights of workers and workers' organisations in general.[56]

To introduce a new perspective or make a marginalised opinion stronger, new and different knowledge is needed. Through the exchange with CSOs and research institutes, MEPs receive 'new facts, new data'[57] to substantiate their perspective and claims. Likewise, members of the 'Urban' Intergroup learn about the situation on the ground and receive expert knowledge through the presentations by urban-related professionals and practitioners on the usage of EU structural funds at regional and local level.[58] They gain an overview of the situation across EU member states, which put those MEPs in a better position about knowing the consequences of EU legislation and defining new approaches to EU urban policies.[59] Hence, one benefit of Intergroups as a means of acquiring informational capital is based on the acquisition of new, original expert knowledge, which is not available in this neat and compact form for MEPs in the parliamentary committees.

The other benefit refers to a different organisational knowledge accumulated in and through Intergroups, that is, a better knowledge about the positions and views of fellow MEPs as the result of the established trust and mutual respect among Intergroup members that does not exist in the parliamentary committees. While MEPs perceive not to be 'completely among friends' in the parliamentary committees with MEPs from all 'the political perspectives' being present and with 'some very strange ones from the far right, from the ECR Group [...]',[60] the working atmosphere in the Intergroup is characterised by a 'more open intimate trusting exchange'.[61] Interviewees trace this mutual trust and respect among Intergroup members back to long-term involvement in the Intergroup and EP as well as to past experiences and 'many, many hours of dialogue' which showed that 'these people are being honest'.[62] This trust makes MEPs say things in the Intergroup that they would not say in full committee, and thus represents additional organisational knowledge that MEPs gain in Intergroups.[63] This insight is, however, limited to members of the 'Trade Union' Intergroup, see Chapter 5 again.

Through the interaction with colleagues from different political groups and committees, representatives of civil society and EU institutions, MEPs accumulate and exchange expert and organisational knowledge on a topic of their personal interest. In contrast to the parliamentary committees where MEPs 'have to deal with what comes',[64] they choose what they want to discuss in the Intergroup. Furthermore, Intergroups are 'open to everybody'[65] in terms of membership. Being an MEP, having an interest in the topic and a formal signature on a membership list at the beginning of each parliamentary term suffices to become a member. That means easy access and unlimited membership, while committee membership is regulated and restricted by the political groups. Since Intergroup meetings take place (depending on the Intergroup) on a monthly basis, every two months or even just three or four times a year, they involve rather little investment of time on the side of the MEPs. In this context, Intergroups constitute for MEPs an additional source of information—additional, complementary to the established knowledge bases in the EP (e.g. parliamentary committees), that is of easy access and involves low investment of resources on the side of the MEP.

Conclusion

This chapter explored Intergroups as informational capital of MEPs. Inspired by insights from ethnographic studies on MEPs' daily knowledge management and informational theories of legislative organisation, this chapter offers an original adaptation of the Bourdieusian concept of informational capital including three types of knowledge: expert, organisational and political knowledge.

The analysis revealed primarily the acquisition and exchange of expert and organisational knowledge in Intergroups. This means that MEPs discuss very specific and partly very technical topics related to (non-) legislative reports and issues in Intergroup meetings. In most cases, invited guests (e.g. representatives of civil society) constituted the experts on a particular issue. Moreover, MEPs inform themselves about events, rules and routines linked to their legislative work via the Intergroup. This includes knowledge about the views and positions of parliamentary colleagues, CSOs and other EU institutions on parliamentary reports as well as knowledge about amendments, votes and majority ratios in the Parliament.

The chapter revealed further that Intergroup members as opposed to Intergroup chairs primarily gather expert knowledge in Intergroup meetings, while Intergroup chairs seek and acquire both expert and organisational knowledge. With regard to the acquisition of political knowledge, only limited evidence has been gathered. On the one hand, the set-up and maintenance of an Intergroup have been interpreted as a sign of possessing political knowledge. On the other hand, for individual Intergroup chairs displaying long-term commitment to the EP and the Intergroup, the study supports the interpretation that these MEPs already possess political knowledge, based on their seniority, and make use of it for the cause of the Intergroup. Emphasising the acquisition of expert and organisational knowledge, the chapter confirms earlier studies on Intergroups highlighting political coordination and the exchange of political information (Ringe et al., 2013). It does not support, however, the notion of Intergroups as a venue where MEPs seek compromise or consensus.

The comparison with official sources of knowledge and expertise in the EP (e.g. parliamentary committees) revealed that MEPs gain on the specific topic new and original expert knowledge. This knowledge is not available in this neat and compact form for them in the parliamentary committees or public hearings. Moreover, in terms of organisational knowledge, individual MEPs argued that they gain better knowledge about the positions and views of fellow MEPs as the result of the established trust and mutual respect among Intergroup members that does not exist in the parliamentary committees (limited to the 'Trade Union' Intergroup). Overall, the comparison has shown that the acquisition of informational capital takes place against the background of MEPs perceiving an asymmetry of themes and interests being represented in and by the EP. The upcoming Chapter 7 will show how MEPs make use of this informational capital to raise awareness for those marginalised perspectives in the EU .

Notes

1. See Interview MEP 12.
2. See Interview MEP 1.
3. See Interview MEP 13.
4. For further studies on legislative organisation, see, e.g., Weingast and Marshall (1988), Shepsle and Weingast (1987), and Cox and McCubbins (1993).
5. E.g. Yordanova (2009, 2011), Kaeding (2004), and Bowler and Farrell (1995).
6. See Interview MEP 4.
7. See Interview MEP 17.
8. See Interviews MEPs 2, 12, 14, 15, 17, 18, 19.
9. See Interview MEP 2.
10. See Interviews MEP 14; see also MEPs 4, 5, 10, 12, 13, 14, 16, 17, 19; CSO 3, 5; PG 1, 2.
11. See Interviews MEPs 4, 5, 10, 12, 13, 14, 16, 17, 19; CSO 3, 5; PG 1, 2.
12. See Interviews MEP 12; see also MEPs 13, 14, 15; CSO 6.
13. See Interviews MEPs 2, 14.
14. See Interview MEP 1.
15. See Interview MEP 19; see also MEP 18.

16. Between September 2009 and March 2013.
17. Parliamentary committees may draw-up reports on their own initiative on subjects, which they have not been consulted. These reports may refer to 'entirely new issues on the policy agenda', to a communication by the European Commission on which the EP 'has not been formally consulted' or result from a motion of resolution tabled by individual MEPs (Corbett et al., 2016, p. 180). There are various types of own-initiative reports. For an insight, see Corbett et al. (2016). Most importantly, legislative own-initiative reports may advance new legislative proposals from the European Commission. In this way, they constitute an important instrument to influence the Commission's work programme at a very early stage.
18. See Interviews MEPs 1, 12, 17, 19.
19. See Interviews MEPs 1, 9, 12, 17, 19.
20. See Interviews MEPs 2, 3, 8, 14, 15, 17, 18; CSO 2, 6.
21. For an in-depth discussion see Haas (1992).
22. See Interview MEP 2.
23. See Interviews MEPs 1, 2, 12, 14.
24. See Interviews MEP 2; CSO 1.
25. See Interviews MEP 2; CSO 1.
26. See Interview MEP 1.
27. See Interview MEP 13.
28. With the limitation that not all meeting protocols of all four selected Intergroups for the entire 7th EP could be obtained, the following numbers can only provide a partial insight.
29. See MEP Kartika Liotard (GUE/NGL, NL) announcing the deadline for tabling amendments to her draft report 'A Sustainable Development of European Aquaculture' in the Intergroup meeting on 21 January 2010 (Intergroup on the Welfare & Conservation of Animals, 2010).
30. Report on 'The introduction of measures to encourage improvements in the safety and health at work of pregnant workers and workers who have recently given birth or are breastfeeding'. For further discussion, see Kluger Dionigi (2017).
31. See Interview MEP 2.
32. See Interview MEP 1.
33. See Interview MEP 13.
34. See Interview MEP 20.
35. See Interview MEP 13.
36. See Interview MEP 17.
37. See Interview CSO 6.
38. See Interview MEP 13.
39. See Interviews MEPs 7, 18, 19; CSO 6.

40. See Interview MEP 7; CSO 6.
41. See Interview MEP 14.
42. See Interview MEP 14.
43. See Interview MEP 16.
44. For an additional insight on the 'Trade Union' Intergroup as a forum to reach compromises between MEPs and trade union representatives, see Settembri and Neuhold (2009, p. 143).
45. See Interviews MEP 13; CSO 2.
46. See Interviews MEPs 11, 13, 14, 17.
47. See overview of attended Intergroups meetings in Appendix B.
48. The majority of interviewees justified their engagement in the Intergroup with their personal interest for the policy issue, (see Interviews MEPs 2, 6, 7, 8, 10, 11, 14) which is also coupled to their previous professional occupation (see Interviews MEPs 1, 4, 5, 9, 12, 13, 17, 19, 21).
49. See Interview MEP 2.
50. See Interviews MEPs 2, 4, 8, 14.
51. See Interviews MEPs 1, 2, 5, 6.
52. See Interviews MEPs 2, 3, 4, 6, 17.
53. See Interview MEP 2.
54. See Interview MEP 14.
55. Jan Olbrycht, president of the 'Urban' Intergroup at the URBAN—CEMR working breakfast on Urban Agenda, 19 February 2014.
56. See Interview MEP 4.
57. See Interview MEP 2.
58. See Interviews MEPs 1, 14, 17
59. See Interview MEP 17.
60. See Interview MEP 13.
61. See Interview MEP 13.
62. See Interview MEP 13.
63. See Interviews MEP 13; CSO 3.
64. See Interview MEP 14.
65. See Interview MEP 20.

References

Beauvallet, W., & Michon, S. (2010). Professionalization and Socialization of the Members of the European Parliament. *French Politics, 8*(2), 145–165.

Bernhard, S. (2012). Informationelles Kapital als Transnationale Ressource. In S. Bernhard & C. Schmidt-Wellenburg (Eds.), *Feldanalyse als Forschungsprogramm 2: Gegenstandsbezogene Theoriebildung* (pp. 195–216). Wiesbaden: VS Verlag für Sozialwissenschaften.

Bernhard, S. (2015). Informational Capital: How It Is Developed and Used by CSOs and EU Institutions. In H. Johansson & S. Kalm (Eds.), *EU Civil Society: Patterns of Cooperation, Competition and Conflict* (pp. 43–60). Basingstoke: Palgrave Macmillan.
Bourdieu, P., & Wacquant, L. J. D. (Eds.). (1992). *An Invitation to Reflexive Sociology* (1st ed.). Chicago: University of Chicago Press.
Bourdieu, P., Wacquant, L. J. D., & Farage, S. (1994). Rethinking the State: Genesis and Structure of the Bureaucratic Field. *Sociological Theory, 12*(1), 1–18.
Bowler, S., & Farrell, D. M. (1995). The Organizing of the European Parliament: Committees, Specialization and Co-ordination. *British Journal of Political Science, 25*(02), 219–243.
Corbett, R., Jacobs, F., & Neville, D. (2016). *The European Parliament* (9th ed.). London: John Harper Publishing.
Corbett, R., Jacobs, F., & Shackleton, M. (2011). *The European Parliament* (8th ed.). London: John Harper Publishing.
Cox, G. W., & McCubbins, M. D. (1993). *Legislative Leviathan: Party Government in the House*. Berkeley: University of California Press.
Dutoit, L. (2009). *Parlement Européen et Société Civile: Vers de Nouveaux Aménagements Institutionnels*. Louvain-la-Neuve: Bruylant-Academia.
Haas, P. M. (1992). Introduction: Epistemic Communities and International Policy Coordination. *International Organization, 46*(1), 1–35.
Intergroup on the Welfare & Conservation of Animals. (2010). *Report of the 258th Session*. Brussels: Intergroup on the Welfare & Conservation of Animals.
Intergroup on the Welfare & Conservation of Animals. (2011a). *Report of the 271st Session*. Brussels: Intergroup on the Welfare & Conservation of Animals.
Intergroup on the Welfare & Conservation of Animals. (2011b). *Report of the 274th Session*. Brussels: Intergroup on the Welfare & Conservation of Animals.
Intergroup on the Welfare & Conservation of Animals. (2011c). *Report of the 277th Session*. Brussels: Intergroup on the Welfare & Conservation of Animals.
Intergroup on the Welfare & Conservation of Animals. (2012a). *Report of the 280th Session*. Brussels: Intergroup on the Welfare & Conservation of Animals.
Intergroup on the Welfare & Conservation of Animals. (2012b). *Report of the 281st Session*. Brussels: Intergroup on the Welfare & Conservation of Animals.
Intergroup on the Welfare & Conservation of Animals. (2013a). *Agenda: Thursday 7 February 2013—The Directive 2010/63/EU on the Protection of Animals Used for Scientific Purposes*. Brussels: Intergroup on the Welfare & Conservation of Animals.
Intergroup on the Welfare & Conservation of Animals. (2013b). *Agenda: Thursday 12 December 2013—EU Regulation on Invasive Alien Species*. Brussels: Intergroup on the Welfare & Conservation of Animals.

Intergroup on the Welfare & Conservation of Animals. (2013c). *Minutes of Working Group Meeting: Debate with Commissioner Tonio Borg on On-Going and Planned Animal Welfare Issues*. Brussels: Intergroup on the Welfare & Conservation of Animals.

Intergroup on the Welfare & Conservation of Animals. (2014). Meetings. Retrieved 28 October 2014, from http://www.animalwelfareintergroup.eu/meetings.

Kaeding, M. (2004). Rapporteurship Allocation in the European Parliament: Information or Distribution? *European Union Politics, 5*(3), 353–371.

Kauppi, N. (2005). *Democracy, Social Resources and Political Power in the European Union*. Manchester: Manchester University Press.

Kauppi, N. (2011). EU Politics. In A. Favell & V. Guiraudon (Eds.), *Sociology of the European Union* (pp. 150–171). Basingstoke: Palgrave Macmillan.

Kluger Dionigi, M. (2017). *Lobbying in the European Parliament: The Battle for Influence*. Cham: Palgrave Macmillan.

Krehbiel, K. (1992). *Information and Legislative Organization*. Ann Arbor: University of Michigan Press.

Neuhold, C. (2001). The 'Legislative Backbone' Keeping the Institution Upright? The Role of European Parliament Committees in the EU Policy-Making Process. *European Integration Online Papers (EioP), 5*(10), 1–29.

Ringe, N. (2010). *Who Decides, and How? Preferences, Uncertainty, and Policy Choice in the European Parliament*. Oxford: Oxford University Press.

Ringe, N., Victor, J. N., & Carman, C. J. (2013). *Bridging the Information Gap: Legislative Member Organizations as Social Networks in the United States and the European Union*. Ann Arbor: University of Michigan Press.

Settembri, P., & Neuhold, C. (2009). Achieving Consensus Through Committees: Does the European Parliament Manage? *Journal of Common Market Studies, 47*(1), 127–151.

Shepsle, K. A., & Weingast, B. R. (1987). The Institutional Foundations of Committee Power. *The American Political Science Review, 81*(1), 85–104.

Trade Union Intergroup. (2009). *Bureau: Minutes 11 November 2009*. Brussels: Group of the Progressive Alliance of Socialists & Democrats in the European Parliament.

Trade Union Intergroup. (2010a). *Bureau: Minutes 2 March 2010*. Brussels: Group of the Progressive Alliance of Socialists & Democrats in the European Parliament.

Trade Union Intergroup. (2010b). *Bureau: Minutes 29 June 2010*. Brussels: Group of the Progressive Alliance of Socialists & Democrats in the European Parliament.

Trade Union Intergroup. (2010c). *Bureau: Minutes 30 June 2010*. Brussels: Group of the Progressive Alliance of Socialists & Democrats in the European Parliament.

Trade Union Intergroup. (2010d). *Plenary: Minutes 17 June 2010*. Strasbourg: Group of the Progressive Alliance of Socialists & Democrats in the European Parliament.

Trade Union Intergroup. (2011). *Bureau: Minutes 1 March 2011*. Brussels: Group of the Progressive Alliance of Socialists & Democrats in the European Parliament.

Trade Union Intergroup. (2012). *Bureau: Minutes 11 April 2012*. Brussels: Group of the Progressive Alliance of Socialists & Democrats in the European Parliament.

Urban Intergroup at the European Parliament. (2014a). Events—Monthly Meetings. Retrieved 30 July 2014, from http://urban-intergroup.eu/category/meetings-events/monthly-meetings/.

Urban Intergroup at the European Parliament. (2014b). Events: Intergroup's Events and Conferences Urban-CEMR Working Breakfast on Urban Agenda 19 February 2014. Retrieved 28 October 2014, from http://urban-intergroup.eu/category/meetings-events/intetergroups-events-and-conferences/page/2/.

Weingast, B. R., & Marshall, W. J. (1988). The Industrial Organization of Congress; or, Why Legislatures, Like Firms, Are Not Organized as Markets. *Journal of Political Economy, 96*(1), 132–163.

Westlake, M. (1995). *A Modern Guide to the European Parliament* (Repr. ed.). London: Pinter.

Whitaker, R. (2011). *The European Parliament's Committees: National Party Influence and Legislative Empowerment*. London: Routledge.

Wilken, L. (2008). The Development of Minority Rights in Europe. In K. de Feyter & G. Pavlakos (Eds.), *The Tension Between Group Rights and Human Rights: A Multidisciplinary Approach* (Human Rights Law in Perspective) (pp. 89–104). Portland: Hart Publishing.

Winzen, T. (2011). Technical or Political? An Exploration of the Work of Officials in the Committees of the European Parliament. *The Journal of Legislative Studies, 17*(1), 27–44.

Wodak, R. (2009). *The Discourse of Politics in Action: Politics as Usual*. New York: Palgrave Macmillan.

Yordanova, N. (2009). The Rationale Behind Committee Assignment in the European Parliament: Distributive, Informational and Partisan Perspectives. *European Union Politics, 10*(2), 253–280.

Yordanova, N. (2011). Inter-institutional Rules and Division of Power in the European Parliament: Allocation of Consultation and Co-decision Reports. *West European Politics, 34*(1), 97–121.

CHAPTER 7

Conversion and Mobilisation of Political Capital

> [...] The more obligations you have, [sic!] more visible you are [...] so that's why politically, politically you are becoming the politicians who are known to the others and this politically speaking this is a big capital.[1]

Knowing what kind of interpersonal relations and what dimensions of knowledge Members of the European Parliament (MEPs) acquire through their participation Intergroups is only one side of the story. Social resources need to be used to be of value to their owner. Consequently, this chapter is dedicated to the questions of how MEPs convert the acquired social capital and informational capital into political capital and how they subsequently utilise these various forms of capital to influence European Parliament (EP) politics and outcomes.

Political capital, as the scarce resource for which MEPs fight in the EP, comes in two different forms. It comes as symbolic personal and objectified institutionalised political capital that is acquired individually or by delegation (Bourdieu, 1991). Symbolic personal political capital is expressed in credit and political recognition. It is reflected in reputation and prestige, that is, being known as a parliamentarian for one's own characteristics (Kauppi, 2005). The acquisition of personal political capital takes time. It results from actions conducted in times of crisis or 'institutional void' and disappears with the person (Kauppi, 2005, p. 34).

L. Landorff, *Inside European Parliament Politics*,
Palgrave Studies in European Political Sociology,
https://doi.org/10.1007/978-3-030-04206-6_7

As a form of symbolic capital, political capital constitutes a 'subtype of social capital' (Swartz, 2013, p. 65). It includes the ability 'to mobilise individuals around a common goal' (Kauppi, 2003, p. 778). Objectified institutionalised political capital is vested in collective resources such as posts, office space or facilities offered by the EP to its members, as well as the right to speak in the name of the Parliament (Kauppi, 2011). It is acquired partly 'through investiture by an institution' (i.e. by the EP and becoming an MEP) and expressed in the individual rights attached to the mandate, for instance 'to table and move amendments' to parliamentary texts, to table written declarations and motions for resolutions (Corbett, Jacobs, & Shackleton, 2011, p. 62; Kauppi, 2003, p. 780).

Fieldwork generated only scattered and limited empirical evidence for the argument that MEPs gain personal or institutionalised political capital through their Intergroup participation, as expressed by one interviewee stating 'it [i.e., being chair of the Intergroup] is not something that makes you very glamorous'.[2] In contrast, interviews revealed that it is rather MEPs collectively mobilising their institutionalised political capital attached to their mandate, in combination with the acquired social capital and informational capital, for the cause of the Intergroup. This is to shape the content of parliamentary reports and thus EP policy outcomes as well as to initiate, strengthen or reintroduce parliamentary debate on topics that MEPs perceive to be dominated on the parliamentary agenda.

The first part of the chapter is dedicated to the conversion of previously acquired social capital and informational capital into political capital, with political capital constituting the specific type of resource that agents (i.e. in the present case, MEPs) 'accumulate, and fight for, in the political field' (Kauppi, 2003, p. 778; 2011). It is mainly discussed in terms of MEPs career development as the acquired social capital and informational capital are perceived to increase MEPs visibility as well as equipping them with a reputation as an expert.

The second part of the chapter is dedicated to how MEPs individually and collectively mobilise the institutionalised political capital attached to their mandate in combination with the previously acquired forms of capital. Thereby, empirical evidence was mainly generated in connection with the Intergroup chairs. This may be due to the fact that they are the only ones who possess a post in the Intergroup and thus institutionalised political capital.

Personal Political Capital: Increased Visibility and Recognition

Arguing that 'if you have less job it means that you are marginalized [...] you are not important',[3] the membership in an Intergroup is perceived as one more obligation that increases the visibility of an individual MEP, as expressed by the statement heading this chapter. Conceptualising the Intergroup as bridging social capital, MEPs extend their interpersonal relations to colleagues beyond their parliamentary committees, political groups and member states as expressed by an MEP in the following statement:

> Well, you become better known because you are working with a much wider focus of MEPs across all the political spectrum from all the different member states than you would just in your committee.[4]

Consequently, MEPs extend their interpersonal relations to agents who move in different subfields or in circles different from their own within the transnational field, but who share the interest in the topic through the Intergroup. In doing so, the engagement in an Intergroup contributes to the fact of being known among 736 peers from 27 member states as well as to other agents in the transnational field, such as civil society actors (see Chapter 5 again). In this way, bridging social capital is used to gain political capital. This increased visibility constitutes 'big capital'[5] and thus is interpreted as political capital by and for MEPs. In the light of low attendance rates of MEPs identified for the selected Intergroups, as well as the frequency of Intergroup meetings, this statement, however, needs to be viewed critically in terms of the numbers of MEPs to which parliamentarians become more visible and known. It is important to note that these statements come from Intergroups chairs who gain institutionalised political capital as discussed in the next section. It is further important to notice that this enhanced visibility appears to play, in particular, a role for those MEPs who serve their first mandate in the EP[6] and do not occupy posts of authority (e.g. in the EP leadership, political group or parliamentary committee) immediately. As demonstrated in Chapter 4, the majority of MEPs who engage in Intergroups do not have a position in the EP leadership. By contrast, it is either MEPs in the second-row leadership or rank-and-file parliamentarians. Moreover, around one-fourth of the Intergroup chairs severed in their first EP mandate. In three out of the four selected Intergroups under scrutiny, first-time MEPs constituted the majority. Given the similarity between the professional background of MEPs and the themes of the Intergroup, the Intergroup constitutes an easy and convenient additional obligation to fulfil when MEPs enter the EP for the first time. They are familiar with the topic from their previous occupation.[7] Linking visibility to reputation and recognition, two patterns emerged: one is related to MEPs gaining a positive image which may become a valuable resource in terms of the MEP's re-election. The other one is related to MEPs being recognised as a specialist[8] which becomes a valuable asset in terms of opinion-formation in the EP.

Positive Image

To be known as a politician who is 'speaking up [...] on behalf of disabled people'[9] or who is engaging for animal welfare[10] was interpreted by MEPs as providing them with 'a very positive image'.[11] Some anecdotal evidence points to a link between this 'positive image' and the MEP's efforts towards his or her constituency, that is to create a positive image vis-à-vis one's electorate.[12] However, only a few MEPs[13] related their Intergroup commitment to their constituency. In general, the 'electoral connection' between European Union (EU) citizens and their representatives is extremely weak in the EP (Hix, Noury, & Roland, 2007). Re-election of an MEP depends in the first instance on the re-selection of the MEP as a candidate for EP elections by his or her 'local, regional and national party organs' which control the selection process (Hix, Raunio, & Roger, 1999, p. 12). In this context, two observations and possible interpretations are noteworthy to mention. The linkage between Intergroup participation and constituencies is made by either British MEPs or MEPs who are elected to the EP under open-list systems. With regard to the former, previous research has shown that British MEPs tend 'to accord a high priority to geographical representation' despite being 'elected under a closed-list system' (Farrell & Scully, 2010, p. 51). Moreover, evidence has been generated in connection with the Intergroup 'Animal Welfare'. As previously noted in Chapter 4, 25 British MEPs have been listed as members of the Intergroup in the 7th EP. In this case, the British special affection for animals has to be noted as a particular case, which is interpreted as MEPs pursuing their actions based on national cultural habits.

With regard to the latter, it is known that MEPs who are elected under open-list electoral systems[14] (i.e. those whose 'electoral fates are affected by their personal vote-chasing activities'[15]) 'are associated with a greater constituency focus' (Farrell & Scully, 2010, p. 42; 51). For a very recent insight into the linkage between MEP's re-election, constituency and Intergroup activities, see Wilson, Ringe, and van Thomme (2016). In the context of this study, none of the interviewees linked his or her national delegation to the Intergroup activities, i.e. to those organs which control the (re-)selection process of candidates for EP elections. By contrast, a couple of interviewed MEPs[16] denied explicitly a direct link to their constituency or, respectively, denied that their constituency knew about their Intergroup membership. The reason given by MEPs for this was a general lack of interest in EU affairs on the side of the constituency. This lack of interest would not justify talking about the Intergroup.[17] By contrast, it is more important to explain to the constituency what the EU is and its institutions do (e.g. European Commission, Council of Ministers and European Parliament) than talking about Intergroups.[18] These findings are supported by the discovery that only a fraction of Intergroup members and chairs publicise their Intergroup membership on their official EP profile (European Parliament, 2013b) and thus communicate their membership to the public.[19] This aspect is discussed again in the upcoming section on the Intergroup as institutionalised political capital. Denying a direct link to their constituency, however, does not mean that the constituency does not know that the MEP engages for the policy issue in general, as one interviewee emphasised.[20]

Recognition as an Expert

With regard to the recognition as a specialist, Chapter 6 demonstrated that it is both experts and non-experts sharing an interest in the topic who meet in Intergroups, with the non-experts (mostly the MEPs) learning either from external, invited experts (i.e. civil society representatives) or from their fellow MEPs who already possess expert knowledge on the topic. One interviewee referred to his or her colleagues of the 'Youth Intergroup' who present themselves in parliamentary committees as members of the respective Intergroup. They do so to show 'that they are specialised in something [...], that I have been working on this issue [...] some time, some years, I have been listening to experts, I have been giving some thought so now I want to give my input'.[21] In a similar vein, another interviewee confirmed that it is appreciated in the parliamentary committee that experts (i.e. those members of the Intergroup) are sitting in the respective committee.[22]

Initially, learning about the subject has been perceived by interviewees, particularly by those who have an interest in the topic but do not consider themselves as experts, as a prerequisite to establishing a position on a policy issue.[23] Moreover, knowing what is going on in committees other than their main committee and knowing about positions and views of fellow parliamentarians 'via the Intergroup'[24] (i.e. organisational knowledge) are perceived by MEPs as valuable assets when it comes to discussions within their transnational groups as the following statement exemplarily demonstrates:

> [...] via the Intergroup I know that something is going on in AGRI [sic!] helps me internally in my group [sic!] have a discussion in my group, to change the group position on something going on in AGRI.[25]

In a similar fashion, a member of the 'Viticulture' Intergroup elaborated on how he or she uses the acquired expert knowledge to support an opinion within the transnational political group based on the arguments heard during discussions in the Intergroup.[26] Moreover, the MEP had been asked for an opinion by colleagues from the political group because of the participation in the Intergroup.[27] This constitutes an interesting finding with regard to previous research on how MEPs make policy choices at the individual level (Ringe, 2010). From this, it is known that if MEPs 'have to make decisions outside their areas of expertise', they will 'adopt the position of their expert colleague in the respective parliamentary committee whose preferences they believe most closely match their own' (Ringe, 2010, p. 6). This is either the expert colleague from their national delegation or, in case of those being not represented in the committee, the expert colleague from the transnational political group (Ringe, 2010). Hence, through the participation in the Intergroup, the MEP appears as an expert on the policy issue to his or her colleagues in the transnational political group. As a result, the recognition as a specialist becomes a valuable asset for the MEPs in terms of opinion-formation.

Overall, evidence for the acquisition of personal political capital is only found marginally. One reason for this may be that the accumulation of personal political capital takes time. It is, for instance, built up in times of institutional crisis. Looking at the seniority of those MEPs being interviewed, eight served in their first mandate, five in their second mandate, five in their third mandate, and three interviewees had served more than three mandates in the EP. Recalling the temporal dimension of the EP, i.e. its high turnover in membership with every parliamentary term, the finding that there is no extensive long-term commitment (i.e. over various legislative terms) of Intergroup chairs (Chapter 4), and that the majority of Intergroup members attends meetings on an ad hoc basis, the argument of MEPs acquiring personal political capital becomes less likely. In this context, the Luxembourgish MEP Astrid Lulling, chair of the Intergroup Viticulture since 1999,[28] constitutes the exception. She stands out as an MEP possessing symbolic personal political capital and having built up a substantial reputation over time. Interviewees called her the 'Grande Dame' of viticulture and linked her reputation and authority in the EP to her seniority.[29] The particularity of her case is related to her comparatively long-term and continuous engagement in the Intergroup. Furthermore, Astrid Lulling is and was the only active MEP in the 7th Parliament who also served in the unelected EP from 1965 to 1974 (Corbett et al., 2011). She re-entered the directly elected EP in 1989 and continuously served as an MEP until 2014 (European Parliament, 2012). By the time of the 7th EP, she drew on nearly 35 years of membership and experience in the Parliament, as well as on 15 years as Intergroup chair by 2014. Next to her only the German MEPs Gert Pöttering and Elmar Brok, both active in the 7th EP, have served continuously in the Parliament since 1979 or, respectively, 1980 (Corbett et al., 2011).

Institutionalised Political Capital

Institutionalised political capital is vested in collective resources such as posts, office space or facilities offered by the EP to its members, as well as the right to speak in the name of the Parliament (Kauppi, 2011). It is acquired partly 'through investiture by an institution' (i.e. by the EP and becoming an MEP) and expressed in the individual rights attached to the mandate of an MEP (Kauppi, 2003, p. 780). The previous discussion of the regulation of Intergroups in Chapter 3 has shown that physical resources, i.e. rooms, interpretation and translation facilities, are highly competitive in the Parliament.

The continuous expansion of the Parliament throughout the last eight parliamentary terms and the multilingual character of parliamentary business make office spaces and facilities scarce resources. Moreover, posts such as party leadership, committee chairmanship or a senior position in the EP presidency are controlled by national delegation leaders or party group leaders (Hix et al., 1999; Mamadouh & Raunio, 2003) and require long-term investment in the Parliament (Beauvallet & Michon, 2010). For instance, to obtain the chairmanship of a transnational political group MEPs had served close to four terms in the EP (Beauvallet & Michon, 2010).

To discuss institutionalised political capital in the context of MEPs' membership in Intergroups is a double-edged sword. On the one hand, the rules on the establishment of Intergroups (see Chapter 3) deprive Intergroups from the right to speak in the name of the Parliament and thus, from collective institutionalised political capital offered by the Parliament. On the other hand, individual MEPs inhabiting the Intergroup possess through their mandate the right to speak in the name of the Parliament. Additionally, those political groups that support the official recognition of an Intergroup are also responsible for the provision of rooms and interpretation facilities for Intergroup meetings. Thus, they are responsible for the provision of institutionalised political capital. Moreover, with its organisational structure resembling those of the parliamentary committees, consisting of chairs, vice-chairs and members, MEPs are offered posts within Intergroups. Hence, obtaining a post as chair or vice-chair of an Intergroup is interpreted as obtaining institutionalised political capital. Thereby, the perceptions of how valuable these posts are differ among interviewees. While a CSO representative justified the organisational structure of the Intergroup with the reason that it sounds better for MEPs to be a vice-chair of an Intergroup than just a member,[30] MEPs themselves, however, downplayed the importance of the post as Intergroup chair or vice-chair in comparison with their posts in official parliamentary organs. By arguing, for instance, that being a committee member or a vice-president of a parliamentary committee gives an MEP more authority than a post as Intergroup chair, they attached greater meaning to their positions in official parliamentary organs.[31] Taking into account that there is also a competition for Intergroup chairs, as reported for the Intergroup 'Animal Welfare',[32] it appears that within Intergroups posts as chair or vice-chair are perceived as valuable.

In comparison with posts in formal organs of the EP their value decreases. However, referring to one's Intergroup membership in plenary meetings appears to be the exception. The analysis of parliamentary questions, debates, reports, written declarations and motions for resolutions of the interviewed MEPs, as well as of the most active members of the four selected Intergroups, revealed that none of the interviewees, nor those from the four selected Intergroups made a reference to the Intergroup or his or her Intergroup activities during the 7th parliamentary term (European Parliament, 2013b).[33] While one can detect similarities in topics (i.e. similarities in topics that have been discussed in the Intergroup and those addressed in parliamentary speeches or questions), the name of the Intergroup or membership in the Intergroup is not mentioned and thus not utilised as social capital by the interviewees. In other words, the interviewees had not 'communicated' their membership in his or her parliamentary speeches or questions. Hence, membership in the Intergroup and the political post in the Intergroup were not mobilised in official parliamentary activities. In contrast, it is perceived as something 'very internal'[34] to the parliamentarian and something of his or her own personal interest. This conclusion ties back to the discussion on the linkage between Intergroup and MEPs' constituency as well as to the finding that only nine of the 48 Intergroup chairs (e.g. around one-fifth) in the 7th EP publicised their post as Intergroup chair on their EP profiles.[35] Occasional evidence shows that the post as Intergroup chair may become valuable capital outside the European Parliament, i.e. in terms of communication with the media.[36]

Against the backdrop that the acquisition of symbolic personal and institutionalised political capital plays a marginal role in the Intergroup, the study argues that MEPs first and foremost collectively mobilise the institutionalised political capital attached to their mandate (e.g. to table and move amendments, to table written declarations or motions for resolutions and so forth) in combination with their acquired informational capital and social capital (Corbett et al., 2011). They do so to shape the content of parliamentary reports and thus EP policy outcomes as well as to initiate, strengthen or reintroduce debate on topics that they perceived to be marginalised on the parliamentary agenda. In this context, political capital in its symbolic form, including 'the capacity to mobilise individuals around a common goal', plays a central role (Kauppi, 2003, p. 778). The upcoming sections expand on the collective mobilisation of institutionalised political capital in terms of organising majorities in the Parliament to shape EP policies and parliamentary debate.

Mobilising Individuals Around a Common Goal

With no predetermined coalitions in the EP, majorities have to be formed on every single issue, and coalitions likewise vary by policy areas.[37] In line with the dominant habitus of the EP as a transnational field, the political groups 'enable MEPs to organise with like-minded' parliamentarians and to influence collectively EP policy outcomes (Hix & Høyland, 2013, p. 181). Given, however, the heterogeneity of the political groups, the policy preferences of individual MEPs may not always match those of the transnational political groups. In the 7th EP, over 176 national parties were represented (Sabbati, 2014). Moreover, this book argues that MEPs pursue primarily their own policy preferences with their Intergroup activities. Besides, the topics dealt with by MEPs in Intergroups are perceived by some parliamentarians[38] to be attributed only minor importance in the EP while still being considered as generally important and representing common and public goods (see also Dutoit, 2009; Ringe, Victor, & Carman, 2013). Additionally, the topics covered by MEPs in Intergroups stretch across the jurisdiction of various committees. As a result, this study claims that MEPs utilise the interpersonal connections regularised through Intergroups to identify and find like-minded MEPs among the social group of 736 parliamentarians. Subsequently, they aim to organise majorities for their policy preferences[39] in order to shape the content of parliamentary reports[40] or to initiate parliamentary debates and new EU legislation[41] in the long term. In this way, MEPs seek to impose their own 'principles of vision and division' of the social world (Bourdieu, 2005, p. 39).

As outlined in Chapter 5, Intergroups differ from advocacy groups as its members share the same policy priorities but not necessarily the same policy preferences. Hence, despite the shared interest in the topic, MEPs in Intergroups might not have common normative and causal beliefs with regard to the Intergroup theme. This has an impact on how they engage into collective mobilisation of (social) resources to transform their beliefs into EP policies and outcomes. The analysis revealed a distinction between MEPs in Intergroup leadership positions and MEPs attending Intergroups as 'normal' members with regard to the conversion and mobilisation of different forms of capital. Members stressed individual actions that MEPs would pursue based on the input they received during the exchange with colleagues and experts in Intergroup meetings and emphasised that it is up to the individual parliamentarians to make up their mind.[42] Collective actions, such as written declarations, letters and (oral) questions sent to the European Commission and/or to the EP president, motions for resolutions and the tabling of amendments to EP reports, were predominately listed by MEPs in Intergroup leadership positions.[43] Hence, MEPs engage to different degrees in Intergroups. They utilise the gained social capital and informational capital in different ways.

With regard to the four Intergroups under scrutiny, reported successes of collective actions were amendments to or rejections of legislative proposals coming from the European Commission. Examples from the 'Trade Union' Intergroup included the Services Directive proposed by the European Commissioner Frits Bolkestein (see also Kovacs, 2008), the REACH regulation and the Port Services Directive(European Commission, 2016b; European Parliament & Council of the European Union, 2006; European Parliament—Press Service—Directorate for Media, 2006).[44] Examples from the Intergroup 'Viticulture' were all related to the reform of the Common Organisation of the Market (COM) in wine in 2008 (European Commission, 2016a). This concerned the Commission's draft regulation on oenological practices and the withdrawal of its proposal to lift 'the ban on the blending of red and white wine to produce rosé wine' (European Parliament, 2009), and the reform of the Common Agricultural Policy (CAP) in 2013, including the liberalisation of planting rights from 2015 onwards envisaged by the European Commission.[45] Beyond the four selected Intergroups, examples of Intergroups initiating EU legislation were the Baltic Sea strategy.[46] Ringe et al. (2013) provide an in-depth discussion on this. Moreover, the rejection of the EU-Morocco fisheries agreement by the EP in December 2011 was attributed to the Intergroup 'Western Sahara'. Its members organised the cross-party support for the rejection of the agreement[47] in December 2011, and thereby, the rejection of the 'proposal by the European Commission for a one-year extension of the agreement' (Vogel, 2011).

Shaping EP Policy Outcomes

Individually, MEPs are provided with the opportunity to voice their opinion directly to rapporteurs and therewith, to those agents in the transnational field who largely shape the content of legislative acts on the specific policy issue. Through the Intergroup, the MEP perceives to exert influence in a committee which he or she is not a member of, as expressed by the following parliamentarian:

> So it is [...] good in that sense that I can get influence in a committee which I am not a member of [...] I can tell the AGRI rapporteur what I think directly [...].[48]

In this case, the Intergroup provides the MEP with access to the AGRI committee via the AGRI rapporteur. This opportunity is not given in the context of the MEPs' main committee. Likewise, a member of the 'Urban' Intergroup perceived the Intergroup as an entry to the committees on Transport and Tourism (TRAN) or on Industry, Research and Energy (ITRE).[49] All of these committees cover relevant elements for urban-related issues. Hence, the Intergroup provides the MEP with access to different perspectives and information on legislative dossiers across various committees.

Through the Intergroup, MEPs gain access to rapporteurs, who possess highly valued forms of capital in their own right (i.e. institutionalised political capital). They gain the opportunity to present their opinion on a legislative dossier directly to the rapporteur 'without having to set up a personal meeting with this person'.[50] This presents easy and convenient access to key players within the transnational field on the topic that constitutes a policy priority for the respective MEP. In this context, the Intergroup is perceived as an 'access for members to [...] legislate in committees which are not their main committees [...]'[51] but which still count as their policy priorities. However, it should be noted that interviewees also reported that whether the rapporteur adapts his or her report based on the discussions in the Intergroup is a completely different story and not a given per se.[52]

In turn, MEPs[53] who participated in Intergroup meetings in their role as rapporteur perceived the gained expert and organisational knowledge as valuable assets for the legislative work. Here, the multipositionality of MEPs comes into play, providing them with valuable resources. Interviewees highlighted the importance of hearing the opinions and views of CSO representatives on parliamentary reports, as these could make some arguments, which are important for the rapporteur 'to mention in reports or in speeches'.[54] Moreover, the exchange with civil society representatives allows the rapporteur to view the report from a range of different perspectives mediated through the presentations of CSOs,[55] and to get to know how external stakeholders evaluate the report.[56] Furthermore, rapporteurs use Intergroups to explain and inform their fellow parliamentarians, sharing the interest in the topic, about the state of the art of a parliamentary report within the legislative process. On the one hand, this is perceived as a valuable asset as not every parliamentarian has the time or the inclination to read a report in detail as done by the rapporteur.[57] On the other hand, this is perceived as a valuable asset in terms of establishing support and majorities for the report.[58] Here, social capital and informational capital interact with each other, or, respectively, social capital is converted into informational capital (e.g. into organisational knowledge). Through the Intergroup, rapporteurs receive access to MEPs across political groups and committees. In this way, they have the option to explain their report to colleagues who move in different social groups within the transnational field, but which constitute valued resources in establishing majorities for the report given their shared interest in the topic.[59]

As outlined in Chapter 6, legislative and non-legislative dossiers are frequently discussed in the Intergroups 'Trade Union', 'Animal Welfare' and 'Viticulture'. Thereby, reports subject to the ordinary legislative procedure (OLP) prevailed over own-initiative reports in the 'Trade Union' Intergroup, while the situation is reversed in the 'Animal Welfare' Intergroup as own-initiative reports dominated the discussion. The reports discussed in the Intergroup 'Viticulture' were as well subject to the ordinary legislative procedure (OLP), see, for instance, the report on a Single CMO Regulation[60] by MEP Dantin or the report on the regime of the single payment scheme and support to vine-growers[61] by MEP Dorfmann.

As a result, discussions about amendments to parliamentary reports feature frequently in Intergroup meetings. To trace amendments from Intergroup members, i.e. from discussions in Intergroups to the final legislative acts, presents a challenge. This is due to the informal character of Intergroups, the lack of documentation on the content of Intergroup meetings (i.e. Intergroup minutes) and the very fact that when tabling amendments to legislative reports, MEPs appear as members of their political groups and not as members of Intergroups. This means that they do not speak or appear on behalf of the Intergroup when tabling an amendment, but as members of the transnational political groups (e.g. as an EPP or S&D member). Moreover, in cases where MEPs share positions in parliamentary committees and Intergroups covering the same policy issue, these actions may also be the result of deliberations and negotiations taking place in parliamentary committees. Relying, however, on interview data[62] as well as on available minutes, examples of Intergroup members seeking to shape the content of parliamentary reports via amendments are provided in the following paragraphs. These examples serve illustrative purposes.

The first example refers to an amendment tabled by members of the Intergroup 'Viticulture' to an own-initiative report by the German MEP Albert Dess (European Parliament, 2015a). Dess is also enrolled as a member of the Intergroup (European Parliament, 2013a). The report deals with the EU's common agricultural policy (CAP) and very importantly for the members of the Intergroup 'Viticulture' relates to the European Commission's proposal to liberalise planting rights from 2015 onward (European Parliament—Legislative Observatory, 2011) (see Table 7.1).

The amendment was tabled by the Intergroup chair Astrid Lulling (EPP-ED, LU) as well as the members Herbert Dorfmann (EPP-ED, IT), Giancarlo Scottà (EFD, IT) and Christa Klass (EPP-ED, DE). Three of the Intergroup members are members of the European People's Party—Christian Democrats (EPP Group) and one is a member of the Europe of Freedom and Democracy Group (EFD). They come from three different member states: Italy, Germany and Luxembourg. Both MEPs Dorfmann and Scottà have been members of the AGRI committee to which the own-initiative report was tabled (European Parliament, 2013f, 2014a). The MEPs Lulling and Klass served as substitutes in the AGRI committee with their main committee being the ECON[63] or ENVI committee, respectively (European Parliament, 2012, 2013d).

The MEPs Lulling and Klass are involved in the Intergroup for several parliamentary terms.[64] The MEPs Dorfmann and Scottà just joined the EP and thus the Intergroup in 2009 (European Parliament, 2013f, 2014a). This demonstrates again the cross-party, cross-committee character of the Intergroup or rather of this initiative as it is MEPs from different political groups and parliamentary committees, with different

Table 7.1 Intergroup 'Viticulture'—Example of an Amendment

Committee Draft Report (24 November 2010–15 February 2011)	*Intergroup meetings on planting rights*	*Amendment 1032 by Astrid Lulling, Herbert Dorfmann, Giancarlo Scottà, Christa Klaß (22 March 2011)*	*Committee report tabled for plenary, single reading (31 May 2011)*	*Text adopted by Parliament, single reading (23 June 2011)*
46. Calls on the Commission to investigate whether the current arrangement whereby the wine market organisation ban on planting is to expire should be maintained, in view of anticipated market trends	22 September 2010 16 February 2011 6 April 2011 6 July 2011 19 April 2012	46. Calls on the Commission to consider maintaining planting rights in the wine sector beyond 2015 and to take account of this in its assessment report on the reform of the wine CMO to be submitted in 2012	61. Believes that the Commission should consider proposing that planting rights in the wine sector be maintained beyond 2015 and should take account of this in its assessment report, to be submitted in 2012, on the 2008 reform of the wine CMO	63. Believes that the Commission should consider proposing that planting rights in the wine sector be maintained beyond 2015 and should take account of this in its assessment report, to be submitted in 2012, on the 2008 reform of the wine CMO

Source European Parliament—Legislative Observatory (2011), European Parliament (2011), and Griesbeck (2014)

lengths of membership in the EP and the Intergroup, tabling this amendment. What they do have in common is a professional background in viticulture (e.g. Dorfmann, Klass) as well as coming from a vine-growing region (see Chapter 4 again).

As shown in Table 7.1, the draft of the report was presented in the AGRI committee in November 2010 and February 2011 (European Parliament—Legislative Observatory, 2011). Amendments to the draft report were tabled in the committee in March 2011 (European Parliament—Legislative Observatory, 2011). The topic of planting rights has been frequently discussed in the Intergroup 'Viticulture' during the 7th EP (see Appendix C). An Intergroup meeting took place right after the draft report was presented in the AGRI committee on 16 February 2011 and before the tabling of amendments to the draft report in the committee in March 2011. In their amendment, the four MEPs call on the European Commission for the maintenance of the planting rights in the EU wine sector after 2015. As shown in Table 7.1, they thereby enforce and strengthen the original formulation in the text, calling the European Commission to *consider* the maintenance of planting rights 'in the wine sector beyond 2015', and added content with regard to the Commission's assessment report. Both aspects are reflected again in the committee report tabled for the plenary session in May 2011 and in the final text adopted by the Parliament in June 2011. This example demonstrates how MEPs make use of their multiple positions and utilise their shared memberships in parliamentary committees and Intergroups, as well as the interpersonal relations regularised across political groups and committees in the Intergroup to shape the content of parliamentary reports. Additionally, individual interviewees indicated further that opinion-formation in Intergroups has been perceived as facilitating decision-making processes within parliamentary committees. In this context, the Intergroup acted occasionally as a preliminary stage of opinion-formation before committee meetings.[65] An example is the discussion of the Commission's proposal on organic wine in the AGRI committee.[66] The quick rejection of the proposal in the committee has been attributed to members of the Intergroup 'Viticulture' having formed an opinion on the legislative proposal prior to the committee meeting, and who represented similar arguments in the committee discussion and thereby, forged a rejection of the Commission's proposal.[67]

Another example originates from the 'Trade Union' Intergroup. The analysis of Intergroup minutes showed that presenting rapporteurs actively call attending MEPs and civil society representatives to send them amendments for the respective reports (Trade Union Intergroup, 2009, 2010, 2011a, 2011b, 2011c). One example is the French MEP Jean-Paul Gauzès (EPP), rapporteur on the co-decision report on 'Alternative Investment Fund Managers', who asked the present trade union representatives to send him and the S&D shadow rapporteur amendments for the legislative report (Trade Union Intergroup, 2009, p. 2). Another example is the Spanish MEP Alejandro Cercas. During the discussion of his own-initiative report on 'European Corporate Social Responsibility', the co-chair of the Intergroup called the present trade union representatives to study the amendments and 'to identify those that should be […] defended during the Committee vote […]' (Trade Union Intergroup, 2011b, p. 2). He further referred to his position as S&D group coordinator in the EMPL committee and in this context to his efforts to integrate all proposed amendments into the report (Trade Union Intergroup, 2011b). This practice clearly exemplifies how MEPs make use of their multipositionality within the transnational field on the respective issue, occupying at the same time positions as group coordinator (i.e. as those agents who play a central role in achieving consensus in the respective committees, which have been conceptualised in this study as closed subfields), committee member and Intergroup co-chair/member.

Initiating Parliamentary Debate Through Written Declarations

Written declarations allow individual MEPs to raise issues and to 'initiate or reintroduce parliamentary discussion on a matter of common concern' (Corbett et al., 2011; Tenhunen, 2012, p. 1). In this respect, they share characteristics with Intergroups representing also interests of the common good (see Chapter 3 again). They constitute a 'text of a maximum of 200 words relating exclusively on a matter falling within the competence of the European Union' and are not 'considered as an act of the Parliament representing its position, but only those of its authors and signatories' (European Parliament, 2015c). To submit a written declaration at least 10 MEPs representing at least three different political groups may need to present a text to be signed by their fellow parliamentarians (European Parliament, 2015c). If a written declaration is signed by a majority of MEPs, 'they are forwarded to the institutions named in them, without debate in committee or plenary' (Corbett et al., 2011, p. 341). While allowing 'MEPs to raise awareness on a current topic', written declarations 'have had only a limited impact in decision-making or agenda setting' (Tenhunen, 2012, p. 1). Thus, they are not comparable with legislative reports that MEPs work on in the parliamentary committees. In the past, only a few written declarations received the required number of signatures in order to be forwarded to the institution addressed in the declaration. Between 1989 and 2004, only 13 written declarations were adopted, while the number increased to 37 in the 6th EP (2004–2009) (Corbett et al., 2011). In the 7th EP,[68] 199 written declarations were initiated, of which 69 were adopted (Groffen & Lehmann, 2011, p. 5).

Written declarations have been stated as collective actions and successes by interviewees across Intergroups.[69] Given that the Intergroup 'Animal Welfare' belongs to the four chosen Intergroups of the study, the focus is on those written declarations initiated by members of this Intergroup. Reasons for why MEPs of the Intergroups 'Trade Union', 'Urban' and 'Viticulture' did not relate to written declarations may be attributed to the different workings methods of the Intergroups and the EP's legislative competences in the respective policy area. For instance, the focus of the 'Trade Union' Intergroup is on current, upcoming legislative proposals from the European Commission and thus, on parliamentary debates that are already in place. By contrast, written declarations are a means to initiate or reintroduce parliamentary debate and eventually to initiate EU legislations in the long term.

In sum, 10 written declarations were issued on behalf of or by members of the Intergroup 'Animal Welfare' during the 7th EP (2009–2014). Five of them were adopted, while five of them lapsed (see Appendix E). As it shows, it is not always the same constellation of MEPs issuing written declarations together but rather individual names that reappear, such as the Romanian MEP Daciana Octavia Sârbu (S&D), the Swedish MEP Carl Schlyter (Greens/EFA) and the Polish MEP Janusz Wojciechowski (ECR). This points to the interpretation that individual MEPs combine their institutionalised political capital with their acquired social capital in the Intergroup in order to initiate collective actions rather than the Intergroup as such acting as a coherent and uniform group. All of these written declarations have been addressed to the European Commission, and depending on the declaration, to the Council of Ministers or national parliaments and governments in the

EU member states (Appendix E). According to the study by the EP's Directorate-General for Internal Policies, the European Commission is the only institution which produces 'concrete statements referring to EP Written Declarations' (Groffen & Lehmann, 2011, p. 9). With regard to the written declarations issued by MEPs of the Intergroup 'Animal Welfare', only responses to two of the written declarations have been identified. The subsequent elaborations focus on these.

Written Declaration: On the Transportation of Horses for Slaughter (54/2009)

The first declaration to be mentioned is the one 'On the transportation of horses for slaughter' (54/2009), which has been presented as a success of the Intergroup.[70] The written declaration was initiated by the MEPs Elizabeth Lynne (S&D, GB), Sidonia Jędrzejewska (EPP-ED, PL) and Carl Schlyter (Greens/EFA, SE) and thus by MEPs from three different members states and political parties, who served at the time in their third (MEP Lynne), second (MEP Schlyter) and first mandate (MEP Jędrzejewska) in the EP (European Parliament, 2013c, 2013g, 2015b). The declaration was discussed in the Intergroup three times in November and December 2009, as well as in January 2010 (Intergroup on the Welfare & Conservation of Animals, 2009a, 2009b, 2010a). In these meetings, Caroline Lucas (Greens/EFA, GB), chair of the Intergroup, called on all MEPs present to support the declaration. The written declaration was adopted by the majority of the EP (i.e. with 405 votes) in February 2010 (Intergroup on the Welfare & Conservation of Animals, 2010b).

In the written declaration, MEPs called 'on the Commission and Member States effectively to scrutinise World Horse Welfare's dossier of evidence in the context of the Commission's review of Council Regulation (EC) 1/2005' and urged 'the Member States and the European Commission to robustly enforce Council Regulation (EC) 1/2005' (Lynne, Jędrzejewska, & Schlyter, 2009, p. 2). In reaction to the written declaration, a letter sent by the European Commission 'to all Member States in order to draw their attention to the risks associated with the transport of slaughter horses, and the need to implement a harmonised procedure regarding the treatment of animals' can be identified (Groffen & Lehmann, 2011, pp. 26–27). It is, however, not clear whether the letter can be directly attributed to the written declaration as both the letter and the written declaration were sent in February 2010 (Groffen & Lehmann, 2011).

What is noticeable in this context is the mobilisation of institutionalised political capital and bridging social capital by the Intergroup members who sought and gained support for the written declaration beyond the Intergroup and across their political groups through their different party affiliations.[71]

Written Declaration: On Support for Strengthening the European Union Ban on Shark Finning (71/2010)

The second written declaration to be mentioned is the one 'On support for strengthening the European Union ban on shark finning (71/2010)' (Besset, Davies, Pietikäinen, & Sârbu, 2010). It was initiated by the MEPs Jean-Paul Besset (Greens/EFA, FR), Chris Davies (ALDE, GB), Sirpa Pietikäinen (EPP-ED, FI) and Daciana Octavia Sârbu (S&D, RO) and thus by MEPs from four different political groups and countries, who served at the time in their third (MEP Davies), second (MEPs Pietikäinen and Sârbu) and first mandate (MEP Besset) in the EP (European Parliament, 2013e, 2014b, 2016a, 2016b). The topic of shark finning was discussed twice in the Intergroup in October and November 2010 (Intergroup on the Welfare & Conservation of Animals, 2010c, 2010d). The MEPs Sârbu and Davis called their colleagues in the Intergroup 'to promote the written declaration among the MEPs who have not yet signed' (Intergroup on the Welfare & Conservation of Animals, 2010c). The declaration was adopted on 16 December 2010 by the majority of the EP with 423 votes (Intergroup on the Welfare & Conservation of Animals, 2010e). In the written declaration, MEPs were calling the European Commission to 'deliver a proposal to prohibit the removal of shark fins onboard vessels by the second anniversary of the Community Plan of Action for Sharks' in February 2011 (Besset et al., 2010, p. 2). In its response, the European Commission referred to an already initiated public consultation process and steps taken by the Commission to amend the regulation on the removal of shark fins onboard vessels (Groffen & Lehmann, 2011). Moreover, the European Commission declared that a presentation of a legislative proposal by February 2011 as requested in the written declaration 'will not be possible' (Groffen & Lehmann, 2011, p. 26). Instead, a legislative proposal aimed at amending the regulation on shark finning was envisaged for adoption by the Commission in autumn 2011 (Groffen & Lehmann, 2011). Tracing follow-up actions by the European Commission is beyond the scope of this study (see suggestions for further research in Chapter 8). When it comes to the Intergroup, the Commission's proposal amending the current EU legislation on shark finning was discussed again in the Intergroup in March 2012 (Intergroup on the Welfare & Conservation of Animals, 2012). At this meeting, a representative of the European Commission's Directorate-General for Maritime Affairs and Fisheries (MARE) was present as well as the responsible rapporteurs from the PECH and ENVI committee (Intergroup on the Welfare & Conservation of Animals, 2012). This demonstrates the continuous engagement of MEPs in the Intergroup for the topic.

Closing this discussion it needs to be stressed that with five out of ten initiated written declarations being adopted by the majority of the EP, the success rate of these collective actions by members of the Intergroup 'Animal Welfare' is assessed as rather moderate. MEPs, however, perceive it as a success of the Intergroup that written declarations initiated by members of the Intergroup received the support of the majority of the MEPs and became an official position of the European Parliament, as for instance in the case of the ban on shark finning.[72]

Returning to the theoretical framework of this study and the conceptualisation of MEPs as goal-oriented agents, this final chapter has shown that MEPs pursue primarily their own policy objectives with their Intergroup membership. References to constituency interests and thus re-election goals occurred only sporadically. No evidence has been found for MEPs pursuing office goals in the EP with their Intergroup activities.

Conclusion

Based on the argument that political capital (both in its symbolic personal and institutionalised form) is the specific resource for which MEPs struggle in the transnational political field (i.e. the EP), this chapter explored the conversion of social capital and informational capital into political capital and the subsequent mobilisation of all three forms of capital by MEPs in the European Parliament.

The first part of the chapter showed how MEPs increase their own visibility beyond their usual work environment in parliamentary committees and political groups through their Intergroup membership. In this way, bridging social capital is used to gain political capital. Moreover, sporadic evidence points, inter alia, to the recognition as a specialist in the respective policy issue. Along those lines, informational capital is converted into political capital which is subsequently utilised in terms of opinion-formation in the parliamentary committees and political groups. Overall, the analysis revealed, however, only scattered evidence for MEPs accumulating political capital through their work in the Intergroup. Those MEPs obtaining a post as Intergroup chair are perceived to gain institutionalised political capital to which they attach, however, lesser meaning than to a post in an official parliamentary structure.

The second part of the chapter demonstrated how MEPs mobilise institutionalised political capital attached to their mandate as MEPs in combination with the social capital and informational capital acquired in the Intergroup. Being primarily driven by their own policy goals, MEPs used their resources to shape EP policies, i.e. parliamentary reports, through the collective tabling of amendments or the direct exchange with rapporteurs and thus with key agenda-setters in the European Parliament. Moreover, they used their social resources to raise awareness for a topic, to initiate debate and actions in the EP, as exemplified in the case of written declarations initiated by the members of the Intergroup 'Animal Welfare'.

Notes

1. See Interview MEP 1.
2. See Interview MEP 6.
3. See Interview MEP 1.
4. See Interview MEP 3.
5. See Interview MEP 1.
6. See Interview MEP 1.
7. See Interview MEP 1.
8. See Interview MEPs 14, 19.
9. See Interview MEP 9.
10. See Interview CSO 1.
11. See Interview MEP 9.
12. See Interview CSO 1; MEP 9.
13. See Interview MEPs 7, 8, 15.
14. These are MEPs from Denmark, Estonia, Finland, Ireland, Italy, Lithuania, Luxembourg, Malta and Northern Ireland, see Farrell, D. M., & Scully, R. (2010). The European Parliament: One Parliament, Several Modes of Political Representation on the Ground? *Journal of European*

Public Policy, 17 (Special Issue: Political Representation and European Union Governance), 36–54.

15. These are MEPs from, e.g., Estonia, Malta and Lithuania, see ibid.
16. See Interview MEPs 11, 16, 18, 19, 20.
17. See Interview MEP 20.
18. See Interview MEP 16.
19. MEPs may still communicate their Intergroup membership and activities on their personal websites. Assuming that the constituency may rather consult the personal website of the MEP than his or her EP website this finding may provide further evidence for MEPs informing their constituency about their Intergroup, and thus for the pursuit of re-election goals. To substantiate this claim further, systematic analysis is required.
20. See Interview MEP 19.
21. See Interview MEP 14.
22. See Interview MEP 19.
23. See Interview MEPs 13, 18.
24. See Interview MEP 2.
25. See Interview MEP 2.
26. See Interview MEP 18.
27. See Interview MEP 18.
28. See Interview CSO 6.
29. See Interview MEP 19. What is also noteworthy in this context is that across the interviews Astrid Lulling and the Intergroup 'Viticulture' were the most frequently mentioned other Intergroup. This provides some insight into the reputation, recognition and visibility of the person Astrid Lulling and (her engagement in) the Intergroup.
30. See Interview CSO 1.
31. See Interview MEPs 2, 9.
32. See Interview CSO 1; see also Chapter 3 again.
33. For this statement, all MEP profiles available at the European Parliament's website were analysed.
34. See Interview MEP 14.
35. These are: Struan Stevenson (Climate Change, Biodiversity and Sustainable Development), Jan Olbrycht (Urban), Claude Moraes (Anti-Racism and Diversity; Ageing and Intergenerational Solidarity), Thomas Mann (Tibet), Véronique Mathieu Houillon (Sustainable Hunting, Biodiversity, Countryside Activities and Forests), Corinne Lépage (Seas and Coastal Affairs), Jean Lambert (Ageing and Intergenerational Solidarity), Emine Bozkurt (Anti-Racism and Diversity; Disability), and Heinz K. Becker (Ageing and Intergenerational Solidarity).
36. See Interviews MEPs 2, 3, 6.

37. For an in-depth and up-to-date discussion on coalition formation in the EP, see, e.g., Hix, S., & Høyland, B. (2013). Empowerment of the European Parliament. *Annual Review of Political Science, 16*, 171–189.
38. See Interviews MEPs 2, 4, 6, 14.
39. See Interviews MEPs 2, 7, 11, 13, 17, 21.
40. See Interviews MEPs 7, 9, 13, 14, 17, 21; CSO 1.
41. See Interviews MEPs 2, 12, 13, 20.
42. See Interview MEPs 14, 16; see also MEP 12 for similar insights.
43. See Interviews MEPs 2, 7, 8, 9, 10, 11, 13, 14, 21.
44. See Interview MEP 13.
45. See Interviews MEPs 7, 18, 19; CSO 6.
46. See Interview MEP 20.
47. See Interview MEP 11.
48. See Interview MEP 2.
49. See Interview MEP 1.
50. See Interview MEP 2.
51. See Interview MEP 14.
52. See Interview MEP 16.
53. See Interviews MEPs 8, 9, 13, 16, 17, 19, and 21.
54. See Interview MEP 16.
55. See Interview MEP 17.
56. See Interview MEP 19.
57. See Interview MEP 19.
58. See Interview MEPs 17, 19.
59. See Interview MEPs 17, 19.
60. Report on the proposal for a regulation of the European Parliament and of the Council establishing a common organisation of the markets in agricultural products.
61. Report on the proposal for a regulation of the European Parliament and of the Council amending Council regulation (EC) N° 1234/2007 as regards the regime of the single payment scheme and support to vine-growers.
62. See Interview MEP 7.
63. Parliamentary committee on Economic and Monetary Affairs (ECON).
64. Since the establishment of the Intergroup in 1994 (informal talk during the Intergroup meeting on 12 September 2012, Strasbourg, France).
65. See Interview MEPs 17, 19.
66. See Interview EP official 1; MEP 19.
67. See Interview EP official 1; MEP 19.
68. As of 30 November 2011.
69. See Interviews MEPs 2, 8, 14, 21.
70. See Interview MEP 14.
71. See Interview MEP 14.
72. See Interview MEP 14.

References

Beauvallet, W., & Michon, S. (2010). Professionalization and Socialization of the Members of the European Parliament. *French Politics, 8*(2), 145–165.

Besset, J.-P., Davies, C., Pietikäinen, S., & Sârbu, D. O. (2010). *Written Declaration on Support for Strengthening the European Union Ban on Shark Finning* (Written Declaration No. DC\830420EN.doc). Brussels: European Parliament.

Bourdieu, P. (1991). *Language & Symbolic Power*. Cambridge: Polity Press in association with Blackwell Publishers.

Bourdieu, P. (2005). The Political Field, the Social Science Field, and the Journalistic Field. In R. Benson & E. Neveu (Eds.), *Bourdieu and the Journalistic Field* (pp. 29–46). Oxford: Polity Press.

Corbett, R., Jacobs, F., & Shackleton, M. (2011). *The European Parliament* (8th ed.). London: John Harper Publishing.

Dutoit, L. (2009). *Parlement Européen et Société Civile: Vers de Nouveaux Aménagements Institutionnels*. Louvain-la-Neuve: Bruylant-Academia.

European Commission. (2016a, January 8). *Agriculture and Rural Development: Wine*. Retrieved 18 March 2016, from http://ec.europa.eu/agriculture/wine/.

European Commission. (2016b, March 2). *Environment: Chemicals—Reach*. Retrieved 18 March 2016, from http://ec.europa.eu/environment/chemicals/reach/reach_en.htm.

European Parliament. (2009). Debates: Tuesday, 5 May 2009—Strasbourg—13. *Rosé Wines and Permitted Oenological Practices (Debate)*. Retrieved 30 November 2012, from http://www.europarl.europa.eu/sides/getDoc.do?pubRef=-//EP//TEXT+CRE+20090505+ITEM-013+DOC+XML+V0//EN.

European Parliament. (2011). *Committee on Agriculture and Rural Development: Amendments 819-1055 Draft Report Albert Deß: The CAP Towards 2020: Meeting the Food, Natural Resources and Territorial Challenges of the Future* (No. AM\861376EN.doc). Brussels: European Parliament.

European Parliament. (2012). *MEPs: Astrid Lulling*. Retrieved 8 September 2012, from http://www.europarl.europa.eu/meps/en/1186/Astrid_LULLING.html.

European Parliament. (2013a). *About Parliament: Organisation and Work—Intergroups*. Retrieved 24 January 2013, from http://www.europarl.europa.eu/aboutparliament/en/00c9d93c87/Intergroups.html.

European Parliament. (2013b). *European Parliament: MEPs*. Retrieved 16 December 2013, from http://www.europarl.europa.eu/meps/en/map.html.

European Parliament. (2013c). *MEPs: Carl Schlyter*. Retrieved 16 December 2013, from http://www.europarl.europa.eu/meps/en/28139/CARL_SCHLYTER_.html.

European Parliament. (2013d). *MEPs: Christa Klass*. Retrieved 24 November 2014, from http://www.europarl.europa.eu/meps/de/1929/CHRISTA_KLASS_cv.html.

European Parliament. (2013e). *MEPs: Daciana Octavia Sârbu*. Retrieved 16 December 2013, from http://www.europarl.europa.eu/meps/en/33989/DACIANA+OCTAVIA_SARBU_home.html.

European Parliament. (2013f). *MEPs: Herbert Dorfmann*. Retrieved 15 December 2013, from http://www.europarl.europa.eu/meps/de/96787/HERBERT_DORFMANN_cv.html.

European Parliament. (2013g). *MEPs: Sidonia Elżbieta Jędrzejewska*. Retrieved 14 February 2013, from http://www.europarl.europa.eu/meps/en/96782/SIDONIA+ELZBIETA_JEDRZEJEWSKA_home.html.

European Parliament. (2014a). *MEPs: Giancarlo Scottà*. Retrieved 18 November 2014, from http://www.europarl.europa.eu/meps/de/96996/GIANCARLO_SCOTTA_home.html.

European Parliament. (2014b). *MEPs: Sirpa Pietikäinen*. Retrieved 27 November 2014, from http://www.europarl.europa.eu/meps/en/40599/SIRPA_PIETIKAINEN_home.html.

European Parliament. (2015a). *MEPs: Albert Dess*. Retrieved 21 May 2015, from http://www.europarl.europa.eu/meps/de/28228/ALBERT_DESS_home.html.

European Parliament. (2015b). *MEPs: Elizabeth Lynne*. Retrieved 25 February 2015, from http://www.europarl.europa.eu/meps/en/4541/Elizabeth_LYNNE_home.html.

European Parliament. (2015c). *Plenary: Questions and Declarations—Written Declarations*. Retrieved 12 May 2015, from http://www.europarl.europa.eu/plenary/en/written-declarations.html.

European Parliament. (2016a). *MEPs: Chris Davies*. Retrieved 4 March 2016, from http://www.europarl.europa.eu/meps/en/4554/CHRIS_DAVIES_home.html.

European Parliament. (2016b). *MEPs: Jean-Paul Besset*. Retrieved 4 March 2016, from http://www.europarl.europa.eu/meps/en/96699/JEAN-PAUL_BESSET_declarations.html.

European Parliament, & Council of the European Union. (2006). *Europa: EU Law and Publications - EUR-Lex - EUR-Lex - 32006L0123 - EN - Directive 2006/123/EC of the European Parliament and of the Council of 12 December 2006 on Services in the Internal Market*. Retrieved 18 March 2016, from http://data.europa.eu/eli/dir/2006/123/oj.

European Parliament—Legislative Observatory. (2011, 16 March 2016). *Procedure File: CAP Towards 2020: Meeting the Food, Natural Resources and Territorial Challenges of the Future*. Retrieved 21 May 2015, from http://www.europarl.europa.eu/oeil/popups/ficheprocedure.do?lang=en&reference=2011/2051%28INI%29.

European Parliament—Press Service—Directorate for Media. (2006, 3 December 2007). The Port Services Directive: An Overview. *Background*, Retrieved 18 March 2016, from http://www.europarl.europa.eu/sides/

getDoc.do?pubRef=-//EP//NONSGML+IM-PRESS+20060124BKG0462 6+0+DOC+PDF+V0//EN&language=EN.

Farrell, D. M., & Scully, R. (2010). The European Parliament: One Parliament, Several Modes of Political Representation on the Ground? *Journal of European Public Policy, 17* (Special Issue: Political Representation and European Union Governance), 36–54.

Griesbeck, N. (2014). *MEP Nathalie Griesbeck: Agenda—Intergroupe Vin, Fruits, Légumes, Tradition et Produits de Qualité*. Retrieved 29 October 2014, from http://www.nathalie-griesbeck.fr/2011/02/intergroupe-vin-fruits-legumes-tradition-et-produits-de-qualite/.

Groffen, C., & Lehmann, W. (2011). *Written Declarations in the European Parliament: A Review of Process and Impact* (No. PE462.424). Brussels: European Parliament: Directorate General for Internal Policies Policy Department C: Citizens' Rights and Constitutional Affairs.

Hix, S., & Høyland, B. (2013). Empowerment of the European Parliament. *Annual Review of Political Science, 16*, 171–189.

Hix, S., Noury, A. G., & Roland, G. (2007). *Democratic Politics in the European Parliament*. Cambridge: Cambridge University Press.

Hix, S., Raunio, T., & Roger, S. (1999). *An Institutional Theory of Behaviour in the European Parliament*. Paper Presented at the Joint Sessions of the European Consortium for Political Research.

Intergroup on the Welfare & Conservation of Animals. (2009a). *Report of the 256th Session*. Brussels: Intergroup on the Welfare & Conservation of Animals.

Intergroup on the Welfare & Conservation of Animals. (2009b). *Report of the 257th Session*. Brussels: Intergroup on the Welfare & Conservation of Animals.

Intergroup on the Welfare & Conservation of Animals. (2010a). *Report of the 258th Session*. Brussels: Intergroup on the Welfare & Conservation of Animals.

Intergroup on the Welfare & Conservation of Animals. (2010b). *Report of the 259th Session*. Brussels: Intergroup on the Welfare & Conservation of Animals.

Intergroup on the Welfare & Conservation of Animals. (2010c). *Report of the 264th Session*. Brussels: Intergroup on the Welfare & Conservation of Animals.

Intergroup on the Welfare & Conservation of Animals. (2010d). *Report of the 265th Session*. Brussels: Intergroup on the Welfare & Conservation of Animals.

Intergroup on the Welfare & Conservation of Animals. (2010e). *Report of the 266th Session*. Brussles: Intergroup on the Welfare & Conservation of Animals.

Intergroup on the Welfare & Conservation of Animals. (2012). *Report of the 281st Session*. Brussels: Intergroup on the Welfare & Conservation of Animals.

Kauppi, N. (2003). Bourdieu's Political Sociology and the Politics of European Integration. *Theory and Society, 32*(5/6), 775–789.

Kauppi, N. (2005). *Democracy, Social Resources and Political Power in the European Union*. Manchester: Manchester University Press.

Kauppi, N. (2011). EU Politics. In A. Favell & V. Guiraudon (Eds.), *Sociology of the European Union* (pp. 150–171). Basingstoke: Palgrave Macmillan.

Kovacs, M. (2008). *How Do Trade Unions Interact with the European Parliament? A Descriptive Analysis*. Brussels: European Trade Union Institute for Research, Education and Health and Safety (ETUI-REHS).

Lynne, E., Jędrzejewska, S., & Schlyter, C. (2009). *Written Declaration on the Transportation of Horses for Slaughter in the European Union* (No. 0054/2009). Brussels: European Parliament.

Mamadouh, V. D., & Raunio, T. (2003). The Committee System: Powers, Appointments and Report Allocation. *Journal of Common Market Studies, 41*(2), 333–351.

Ringe, N. (2010). *Who Decides, and How? Preferences, Uncertainty, and Policy Choice in the European Parliament*. Oxford: Oxford University Press.

Ringe, N., Victor, J. N., & Carman, C. J. (2013). *Bridging the Information Gap: Legislative Member Organizations as Social Networks in the United States and the European Union*. Ann Arbor: University of Michigan Press.

Sabbati, G. (2014). *European Parliament: Facts and Figures* (No. PE 542.150). Brussels: European Parliamentary Research Service.

Swartz, D. (2013). *Symbolic Power, Politics, and Intellectuals: The Political Sociology of Pierre Bourdieu*. Chicago: University of Chicago Press.

Tenhunen, S. (2012). Reviewing the Rules for Written Declarations. *Library Briefing* (120341REV2), 1. Retrieved from http://www.europarl.europa.eu/RegData/bibliotheque/briefing/2012/120341/LDM_BRI%282012%29120341_REV1_EN.pdf.

Trade Union Intergroup. (2009). *Bureau: Minutes 13 October 2009*. Brussels: Group of the Progressive Alliance of Socialists & Democrats in the European Parliament.

Trade Union Intergroup. (2010). *Bureau: Minutes 14 September 2010*. Brussels: Group of the Progressive Alliance of Socialists & Democrats in the European Parliament.

Trade Union Intergroup. (2011a). *Bureau: Minutes 11 January 2011*. Brussels: Group of the Progressive Alliance of Socialists & Democrats in the European Parliament.

Trade Union Intergroup. (2011b). *Bureau: Minutes 12 April 2011*. Brussels: Group of the Progressive Alliance of Socialists & Democrats in the European Parliament.

Trade Union Intergroup. (2011c). *Plenary: Minutes 10 March 2011*. Strasbourg: Group of the Progressive Alliance of Socialists & Democrats in the European Parliament.

Vogel, T. (2011, 4 December 2014). MEPs Reject EU-Morocco Fisheries Pact: Fisheries Commmissioner Says She Will Ask Council to Repeal Agreement. *European Voice*. Retrieved from http://www.politico.eu/article/meps-reject-eu-morocco-fisheries-pact/.

Wilson, S. L., Ringe, N., & van Thomme, J. (2016). Policy Leadership and Re-election in the European Parliament. *Journal of European Public Policy, 23*(8), 1158–1179.

CHAPTER 8

Conclusion

The evolution of the European Parliament (EP) from a 'talking shop' to a key player within the EU institutional set-up, and the increasing importance of the informal dimension of EU politics makes the study of informal practices in parliamentary politics imperative. The continuous and increasing engagement of Members of the European Parliament (MEPs) in Intergroups shows that there is much more going on in the EP than an exclusive focus on its official organs and formal procedures may reveal. In contrast, academic research on MEPs' activities in Intergroups has only been marginally addressed in EP contemporary research and is close to non-existent. In response, this book started out to study informal practices of MEPs in EP Intergroups. Thereby, it took an explorative, interpretative and interdisciplinary approach to social science research. Presented as informal cross-party groupings in the scarcely available literature, Intergroups bring together MEPs from different political groups, parliamentary committees and member states, as well as representatives of civil society and other EU institutions, in their meetings.

Knowing that time is a scarce resource of MEPs, that Intergroups are not official bodies of the Parliament, and therefore are not part of the official legislative process, and that official parliamentary committees already cover policy issues dealt with by Intergroups, the core interest driving this study was to explore: Why do MEPs engage in Intergroups? Based on the assumption that MEPs as legislators display strategic and

L. Landorff, *Inside European Parliament Politics*,
Palgrave Studies in European Political Sociology,
https://doi.org/10.1007/978-3-030-04206-6_8

goal-oriented behaviour, it was further assumed that the engagement in Intergroups must have some benefits for MEPs.

Inspired by a fairly new research agenda in EU studies calling for a revival of sociological approaches in European integration studies, this study analysed the EP and its members from a sociological perspective. It used structural constructivism as its theoretical backbone, and developed a conceptual framework based on the three interrelated concepts of field, capital and habitus originating from the work of the French sociologist Pierre Bourdieu.

Based on its political sociological approach, this book shows how MEPs acquire and mobilise different forms of capital and regularise certain interactions to shape parliamentary practices, outcomes and organisation at the supranational level.

Key Empirical Findings

Backed by an iterative conceptual framework in which structural locations and social characteristics are linked to political strategies and actions of parliamentarians, Chapter 4 analysed the socio-demographic and political features of all Intergroup chairs in the 7th EP, as well as of the most active members in the four chosen Intergroups. In consideration of the small sample size for the four Intergroups, one important finding of the analysis is the link between prior professional occupation, educational background (partially) and Intergroup commitment in the case of the MEPs in the Intergroups 'Trade Union', 'Urban' and 'Viticulture'. This shows that MEPs sought Intergroup assignments where they could draw on previous work experience and had a substantial personal interest. Another important finding with regard to the structural positions of Intergroup chairs and most active members is that these belong either to the second row leadership with posts as vice-chairs in official parliamentary structures (e.g. political groups or parliamentary committees), or to the group of rank-and-file parliamentarians without any other post in the EP. From this it is concluded that it is mainly MEPs with less institutionalised political capital, that is with less valued or no posts in official parliamentary bodies, who join Intergroups, and thereby MEPs who are structurally disadvantaged in the field. These interpretations appear to be consistent with the research conducted by Ringe, Victor, and Carman (2013). Recalling previous findings on informal legislative organisations in the US Congress, this book shares insights with earlier studies on the caucuses, i.e., that it is mostly those legislators without formal leadership posts engaging in informal legislative organisations (e.g. Intergroups or caucuses).

Moving on, Chapter 5 explored Intergroups as social capital of MEPs. In the light of various interpretations of the concept of social capital, this chapter argued for a conceptualisation of Intergroups as bridging social capital as opposed to bonding social capital. This means, Intergroups link MEPs to colleagues who 'normally' move in different subfields of the EP (i.e. parliamentary committees and political groups) as well as to other agents in the transnational political field, i.e., to representatives of civil society (including scientific experts) and representatives of other EU institutions. In this way, Intergroups represent outward-looking, inclusive and heterogeneous networks that transcend political, social, national and institutional cleavages. They provide MEPs with access to closed subfields and key players in the EP, such as rapporteurs. Moreover, the analysis revealed that the majority of Intergroup members practices its membership on an ad hoc, flexible and sporadic basis. Consequently, the interpersonal relationships regularised in Intergroups qualify rather as ties of professional acquaintance than as close and trusted group ties.

Building on the conceptualisation of Intergroups as bridging social capital, Chapter 6 argued for a conceptualisation of Intergroups as informational capital. In this way, the chapter highlights the interplay between bridging social capital and informational capital where the former social resource is used to acquire the latter. In the context of Intergroups, the chapter offers an original modification of the Bourdieusian concept of informational capital including three types of knowledge: expert, organisational and political knowledge. In this manner, the chapter provides a more comprehensive and holistic conceptualisation of not only information but knowledge going beyond the terms of policy information and political information used in theories of legislative organisation. The analysis showed that primarily an exchange of expert and organisational knowledge among MEPs, as well as between MEPs and representatives of civil society organisations (CSOs), takes place during Intergroup meetings. In terms of political knowledge only limited evidence has been gathered which is limited to a handful of long-serving MEPs engaging in Intergroups. Moreover, the comparison with established, official knowledge bases in the EP (e.g. parliamentary committees) highlighted the advantages of Intergroups. MEPs gain original and new knowledge on a topic of their personal interest that is not available within the official structure. This is due to Intergroup themes constituting rather low profile items on the parliamentary agenda despite being of general concern. On these marginalised perspectives, Intergroups offer a neat and compact format of knowledge accumulation that does not require an intensive investment of resources on the side of the MEPs.

Based on the argument that political capital constitutes the specific resource for which MEPs compete in the transnational political field, Chapter 7 analysed the conversion of social capital and informational capital into political capital and looked at the mobilisation of all three forms of capital by MEPs in the EP. The analysis provided occasional evidence for MEPs increasing their own visibility in the Parliament, as well as gaining the reputation of being an expert in the policy issue. In this way, bridging social capital and informational capital are used to gain personal political capital. In turn, the chapter emphasised that MEPs rather mobilise the institutionalised political capital attached to their mandate in combination with the social capital and informational capital they acquired in the Intergroup. They do so to shape EP policy outcomes, i.e., legislative and non-legislative reports, and to initiate and strengthen parliamentary debates on issues that these MEPs perceive to be sidelined on the Parliament's agenda.

Embedding these findings into the context of MEPs as strategic agents displaying goal-oriented behaviour and the identified goals of legislators (e.g. re-election, policy, office, a career beyond the EP and private gains) this study points primarily to the pursuit of policy goals by MEPs in Intergroups. This is followed by sporadic evidence that points to the pursuit of re-election goals. Thereby, the pursuit of policy goals is primarily linked to a personal or professional interest, which is not necessarily mutually exclusive, of the MEPs in the topic. With regard to office goals, no evidence has been found that MEPs accommodated their Intergroup activities to the interests of those who control the assignment to positions of prestige and authority in the EP (i.e. the national delegations or political groups). Therefore, the claim that MEPs follow office goals through their Intergroup commitment cannot be supported. In contrast, the analysis revealed that some MEPs mobilise a combination of posts that they already possess (e.g. as rapporteurs or coordinators) together with the Intergroup post, or that MEPs need to have posts in the formal organs of the Parliament to be trusted by their transnational political group with an Intergroup chairmanship. To substantiate claims with regard to office goals, the study would have needed to trace actions and career trajectories of MEPs without a post in the 7th EP over several parliamentary terms, in order to gain an insight on this issue.[1]

Based on the conceptualisation of the EP as a transnational political field, the conceptual framework of the study initially suggested that political capital as the specific resource of the political field would be the form of capital that MEPs struggle for and mobilise. The findings generated in the context of MEPs' engagement in Intergroups, however, point to something else. Specifically, it is above all knowledge and information, conceptualised as informational capital in this book, which MEPs seek to acquire through Intergroups. This is either combined with social capital or institutionalised political capital to initiate individual or collective actions. In view of this finding, it appears that MEPs' practices in EP Intergroups are rather embedded within an overarching, transnational bureaucratic field in which agents struggle primarily for expert, organisational and political knowledge as opposed to an overarching, transnational political field which is characterised by partisan competition and struggles for representation. For further discussion on EU institutions as bureaucratic fields, see Georgakakis (2018). Having this said, it also needs to be noted that in this research interviewed parliamentarians explicitly distanced themselves from bureaucrats, for instance, from those in the EP leadership in the context of the regulation of Intergroups. This points again to the multiple field struggles, MEPs are involved in, and that EP and EU politics at large are a double-edged sword.

Contributions

The book makes valuable contributions along several lines:

Empirically, it provides fresh and original data to research on EP Intergroups, MEPs' behaviour and the EP's internal organisation as it sheds new light on the informal dimension of parliamentary politics. By opening up the institutional black box and zooming in on MEPs and their practices beyond the official structures, this study enriches our knowledge on the life of the Parliament beyond descriptive accounts of 'its formal, institutional position' (Priestley, 2008, p. xi).

In terms of research on EP Intergroups, the book complements existing studies by adding insights from different Intergroups and MEPs, as well as from CSOs. In this way, it contributes to a more complete picture of Intergroups in the EP. Drawing on different data and methods than previous studies (e.g. on observations and minutes), the study also contributes to a more 'realistic' picture of MEPs' engagement in Intergroups in terms of their' attendance of Intergroup meetings. It also adds to a more differentiated and nuanced picture revealing differences between Intergroup chairs and members with regard to their activities and meaning attached to the Intergroup. Moreover, the study shows that Intergroups are less informal in their set-up, resembling official parliamentary structures. Furthermore, their official recognition is regulated by the political groups in the EP, which points to a process of institutionalisation and formalisation. While interactions among MEPs in Intergroups are still perceived as informal, the setting in which these occur is becoming increasingly formalised.

In terms of research on MEPs' behaviour, the book provides new insights as it accounts for informal practices as part of MEPs' behaviour, and thereby goes beyond studying MEPs' behaviour primarily in terms of voting. While acknowledging the finding that MEPs' activities in Intergroups constitute a minor part of their day-to-day parliamentary practices in comparison with their activities in political groups and parliamentary committees, as Intergroup meetings signify at best a monthly event, this study contributes nevertheless new insights into the parliamentary processes and practices that occur at the pre-plenary or pre-committee stage. Thereby, it provides fresh insights on intra-institutional interactions occurring beyond the official structure of the EP, and how these may influence EP politics and policies. Studying what MEPs do prior to and beyond voting, as well as the meaning they attach to their actions, enhances our understanding of how MEPs practice their job, and which opportunities and constraints they face serving multiple constituents with at times (contradictory) demands. These insights deliver a valuable input for the discussion about the EU's democratic deficit as they provide insights into the practices that may or may not (re-)produce this democratic deficit.

Taking its contributions to research on MEPs' behaviour and EP Intergroups together, this book constitutes a valuable contribution to research on the EP's internal organisation and legislative organisation at large. Illustrating the interplay between MEPs and the EP in the context of Intergroups, between the individual and the organisation, has shown processes of institutionalisation beyond formal structures. It has shown how MEPs apply practices to the institution they are inhabiting, and vice versa, how the EP imposes practices on its members as seen in the case of the regulation of Intergroups through the political groups.

With the main message of this book being that Intergroups serve primarily the informational advantage of the individual MEPs, who pursue mainly their own policy priorities with their Intergroup commitment, the book supports the findings by Ringe et al. (2013) and Nedergaard and Jensen (2014). It departs, however, from the concluding proposition that Intergroups 'may serve as arenas for contestation, negotiation and coordination' (Ringe et al., 2013, p. 206). The findings generated in this study, based on interviews with MEPs covering in total 13 Intergroups and the observations made during Intergroup meetings, do not support this proposition with regard to the aspects of contestation and negotiation. In contrast, what has been observed in meetings and reported by interviewees was a mere presentation of views and positions in Intergroup meetings without necessarily engaging in an argument. That is, it was the mere exchange of expert and organisational knowledge as conceptualised in this study, which is subsequently used by MEPs to form an opinion and which may eventually lead to a consensus or compromise, but not necessarily. With the limitation that not all Intergroups were studied and that they were not exactly the same as those studied by Ringe et al. (2013), practices of negotiation and contestations have not been observed in attended Intergroup meetings. In contrast, some interviewees claimed that the reach for consensus or compromise was not necessary in the Intergroup due to the like-mindedness of its members. It further departs from the argument of signalling preference to the constituency (Nedergaard & Jensen, 2014; Ringe et al., 2013). In this study only minor evidence, limited to a particular group of MEPs (e.g. British MEPs), has been generated for this claim.

Conceptually, the book makes a valuable contribution to a very recent research strand within EU studies calling for a revival of sociological approaches in European integration studies. It draws on structural constructivism in the theoretical framework, develops an iterative political sociological conceptual framework for the study of informal practices in a supranational institution, and offers innovative conceptual refinements with regard to the Bourdieusian concepts of field and capital.

The discussion of various interpretations of the concept of field (from its antagonist to its cooperative reading), and its application to the EP showed that a pure antagonist take on social interactions as inbuilt in the Bourdieusian application of the concept does not grasp the reality of MEP's everyday parliamentary business, of EP and EU politics at large. The EP and its members do not operate in a vacuum. The Parliament is part of an institutional triangle consisting of the European Commission and the Council and operates in a system of multilevel governance. Consequently, the EP and the work of its members cannot be understood without reference to the wider institutional set-up in which it is embedded, i.e., the EU (e.g. Corbett, Jacobs, & Shackleton, 2011; Yordanova, 2011). The EU constitutes an overarching 'super-field' in which consensus-style decision-making prevails. Acting as an equal partner in EU legislation and budget requires individual MEPs across heterogeneous political groups to establish a common and collective EP position vis-à-vis other EU institutions, such as the European Commission or the Council. As a result, EP politics is characterised by a constant need and necessity for cooperation and compromise based on cross-party consensus with conflict and coalition lines changing along with the policy issue at stake. While acknowledging the presence of internal and external power struggles in the EP, as well as the dominance of some policy issues over others, to stress conflict and domination exclusively would only produce a one-sided picture of the EP. It would neglect professional motives of MEPs (e.g. to acquire expert and organisational knowledge in order to make knowledgeable decisions on highly technical dossiers) and the need for consensus. Thus, with regard to the EP a refinement of the concept of field should account for the interplay of cooperation and competition.

In this context, the modification of the concept of informational capital constitutes a further important contribution of this study. By refining informational capital as to consisting of three different dimensions of knowledge, i.e., expert, organisational and political knowledge, this book departs from previous coinages of the concept relating to statistics, to a statistical infrastructure that is used, for instance, as transnational power resource to impose a symbolic representation of Europe (Bernhard, 2012). The value added of this adaptation is perceived along the following lines. Initially, this conceptual advancement does not neglect but rather incorporates political science accounts of policy and political information present in research on legislative organisation, as they are reflected in expert and organisational knowledge. Furthermore, it combines these with a third component: political knowledge. This third component is perceived as a useful addition in connection with the two other interrelated concepts of field and habitus. Political knowledge (i.e. the know-how of how to convince others, how to build alliances and how to persuade) is argued to be of great importance within the EP conceptualised as a transnational field that is characterised by cooperation and competition between various agents. Moreover, as one dimension of informational capital, it feeds into the notion of habitus (i.e. the internalised system of dispositions that provides the basis for practices of the individual MEP). This differentiated view and development of informational capital allows to capture differences among MEPs and individuals involved in Intergroups with regard to the meaning they attached to their interactions in Intergroups.

With regard to the concept of social capital, this book argues for a differentiation of social capital into bonding and bridging forms to capture the diversity of interpersonal relations regularised in and through Intergroups. This allows to account for the different practices and meanings MEPs attach to these interpersonal relations and reveals differences across Intergroups with regard to the closeness and heterogeneity of the social relations regularised in these. Based on the findings of this study, bridging social capital is interpreted as a specialised resource. This means it is very much tied to the Intergroup context, the interactions regularised there and the time in which MEPs engage in the Intergroup. The differentiated picture provided by the distinction into bonding and bridging forms of social capital might also help on a meso-level to categorise Intergroups as, for instance, sporadic policy issue networks or as policy communities (see, e.g. Heclo, 1978; Rhodes, 2006).

Future Outlook

How does the future of Intergroups in the European Parliament look like? In the current 8th parliamentary term (2014–2019), 28 Intergroups received official recognition, which constitutes an increase in the numbers of the official registration of Intergroups (European Parliament, 2016a). This shows a continuous support of and demand for Intergroups by MEPs and points to an increasing formalisation and institutionalisation of them within the EP. A look at the list shows that five Intergroups that were listed as official Intergroups in the 7th EP are no longer listed among those in 8th EP, despite their previous chairs still being members of the 8th EP.[2] Among them is the long-established 'Tibet' Intergroup, which indicates that several terms of official recognition do not necessarily provide for an automatic renewal. Moreover, it shows that what is worth to be acknowledged with an official recognition as an Intergroup changes among MEPs and political groups. In turn, six new Intergroups appear (European Parliament, 2016a).[3] The interesting observation in this context is that with the Intergroups 'Sports' and 'Integrity - Transparency, anti-corruption and organised crime', there are two new Intergroups which made the shift from being non-registered Intergroups in the 7th EP to being officially recognised Intergroups in the 8th EP. Consequently, these two made one step further towards formalisation.

In terms of personnel turnover, only nine Intergroup chairs stayed in their office from the 7th to 8th EP (European Parliament, 2016a).[4] Nineteen of these 28 officially recognised Intergroups are chaired by an MEP who had not been an Intergroup chair in the 7th EP. With one-third staying in office, Intergroup leadership is still characterised more by change than by stability from one parliamentary term to another.

With regard to the four Intergroups whose members have been investigated in more depth in this study, they all received official recognition as an EP Intergroup in the 8th legislative term, and experienced, with the exception of the 'Urban' Intergroup, a change in their leadership. The Intergroup 'Viticulture' is now led by the Italian MEP Herbert Dorfmann, the Intergroup 'Animal Welfare' is led by the Polish MEP Janusz Wojciechowski, and the Intergroup 'Trade Union' is led now by the German MEP Jutta Steinruck (European Parliament, 2016b, 2016c, 2016d). All new chairs have been members of the Intergroup in the previous term. In line with the established practice, the chair of the 'Trade Union' Intergroup is again the S&D coordinator in the Committee on Employment and Social Affairs: the German MEP Jutta Steinruck (Group of the Progressive Alliance of Socialist and Democrats in the European Parliament, 2016). From this, it is concluded that Intergroups are said to stay and remain in the EP with their institutional set-up being more and more formalised.

Suggestions for Further Research

This book opens up further avenues for research:

First, the explorative characteristic of this research leaves ample scope for a more systematic study of Intergroups and their members covering several parliamentary terms and all registered Intergroups to reveal institutional origins of Intergroups and their development over time.

Second, based on the finding that it is primarily policy goals or their own policy priorities that MEPs pursue through their Intergroup activities, future studies could focus in more detail on tracing policy ideas and actions developed by MEPs in Intergroup meetings to committee meetings. Thereby, one suggestion is to focus on those MEPs whose membership in EP committees matches the policy issues discussed in the Intergroup, as indicated in this study for the members of the 'Trade Union' Intergroup who shared membership in the political group, parliamentary committee and Intergroup. In doing so, the developed proposition concerning, for example, opinion-formation processes in and from Intergroups to parliamentary committees or political groups could be explored in more depth and could enlighten, for instance, pre-committee processes.

Third, given the empirical evidence generated in this study with regard to the cooperation of CSOs, Intergroups and MEPs, future studies may further investigate the interactions between parliamentarians and civil society representatives in Intergroups, to systematically explore the influence of CSOs on Intergroups and thus, on EP politics and policies. These studies could shed new light on current EP Intergroup research, which is so far inconclusive regarding the role of Intergroups as lobbying vehicles or as access for lobby groups to the EP (e.g. Bouwen, 2003; Kluger Dionigi, 2017; Nedergaard & Jensen, 2014; Ringe et al., 2013). As this study briefly addressed in the context of the 'Animal Welfare' Intergroup and the involvement of the Eurogroup for Animals in the Intergroup, CSOs may play a significant role not only in terms of the organisation but also with regard to the content alignment of the Intergroup. With this focus, future studies could also link to research on interest and lobby groups in the EP.

Fourth, given previous research (e.g. Crespo Allen, 1996; Landorff, 2010; Pontier, 1982) and interview partners pointing to similar phenomena in national parliaments in EU member states, future studies may aim for a comparative study of Intergroups or informal cross-party groups across various national parliaments. A comparative perspective could provide new insights to questions concerning to what extent MEPs upload their own cultural and political practices to the EP. Moroever, it could contribute to the discussion of the EP as a unique or increasingly 'normal' parliament, or of the MEP being 'a new type of politician' (Kauppi, 2003, p. 782). A comparative perspective focusing on national parliaments in EU member states (e.g. France, Germany, Austria, and Great Britain) (see Crespo Allen, 1996; Dutoit, 2009) may also complement already existing comparative studies which focus, however, on the caucuses system of the US Congress (see Nedergaard & Jensen, 2014; Ringe et al., 2013).

Fifth, future research may also aim for a comparison of officially registered Intergroups with those non-registered Intergroups. For the 7th EP, 29 non-registered Intergroups are documented, among them the well-known and long-standing Kangaroo Group as well as the Spinelli Group (Corbett et al., 2011, p. 212). Given that these non-registered Intergroups are not subject to the EP regulation on Intergroups, and thus do not require the support of at least three political groups and are not subject to the rules prescribing meetings times and places, they constitute an interesting research object with regard to the questions of how these groupings shape EP politics and policies, and what meaning MEPs attach to these.

Notes

1. Furthermore, no empirical evidence has been generated in this study for the claim that MEPs pursue a career beyond the EP or private gains with their engagement in Intergroups.
2. These are the Intergroups: 'Water', 'New Media', 'Media', 'Tibet' and 'Baltic-Europe'. Except for the former chair of the Intergroup 'Water', Richard Seeber (EPP-ED), all other former chairs of these Intergroups are still MEPs in the 8th EP (2014–2019).
3. These are the Intergroups: 'Sports', 'Creative Industries', 'Digital Agenda', 'Freedom of religion and belief and religious tolerance', 'Integrity - Transparency, anti-corruption and organised crime', and 'Long-term investment and reindustrialisation'.
4. These are: Norbert Neuser (Western Sahara), Othmar Karas (SMEs), Sylvie Goulard (Extreme Poverty and Human Rights), Jan Olbrycht (Urban), Ulrike Lunacek (LGBTI), Eider Gardiazabal Rubial (Youth Issues), Ádam Kósá (Disability), Lambert van Nistelrooij (Active Ageing and Intergenerational Solidarity) and Kinga Gál (Traditional Minorities).

References

Bernhard, S. (2012). Informationelles Kapital als Transnationale Ressource. In S. Bernhard & C. Schmidt-Wellenburg (Eds.), *Feldanalyse als Forschungsprogramm 2: Gegenstandsbezogene Theoriebildung* (pp. 195–216). Wiesbaden: VS Verlag für Sozialwissenschaften.

Bouwen, P. (2003). A Theoretical and Empirical Study of Corporate Lobbying in the European Parliament. *European Integration Online Papers (EioP), 7*(11), 1–17. Retrieved from http://eiop.or.at/eiop/texte/2003-011a.htm.

Corbett, R., Jacobs, F., & Shackleton, M. (2011). *The European Parliament* (8th ed.). London: John Harper Publishing.

Crespo Allen, M. (1996). *Rules on Lobbying and Intergroups in the National Parliaments of the Member States*. Luxembourg: European Parliament.

Dutoit, L. (2009). *Parlement Européen et Société Civile: Vers de Nouveaux Aménagements Institutionnels*. Louvain-la-Neuve: Bruylant-Academia.

European Parliament. (2016a). *About Parliament: Organisation and Rules—Intergroups*. Retrieved 5 April 2016, from http://www.europarl.europa.eu/aboutparliament/en/20150201PVL00010/Organisation-and-rules.

European Parliament. (2016b). *About Parliament: Organisation and Rules—Intergroups—Trade Unions—List of Members*. Retrieved 5 April 2016, from http://www.europarl.europa.eu/pdf/intergroupes/VIII_LEG_22_Trade_Unions.pdf.

European Parliament. (2016c). *About Parliament: Organisation and Rules—Intergroups—Welfare And Conservation of Animals—List of Members*. Retrieved 5 April 2016, from http://www.europarl.europa.eu/pdf/intergroupes/VIII_LEG_25_Welfare_20160204.pdf.

European Parliament. (2016d). *About Parliament: Organisation and Rules—Intergroups—Wine, Spirits and Quality Foodstuffs—List of Members*. Retrieved 5 April 2016, from http://www.europarl.europa.eu/pdf/intergroupes/VIII_LEG_27_Wine_spirits.pdf.

Georgakakis, D. (2018). Conclusion: Entre technocratie et démocratie? Ce qu'une analyse structurale (du champ de l'Eurocratie) nous dit du Parlament européen, et le contraire. In S. Michon (Ed.), *Le Parlament européen au travail: Enquêtes sociologiques* (pp. 187–200). Rennes: Presses Universitaires de Rennes.

Group of the Progressive Alliance of Socialist and Democrats in the European Parliament. (2016). *Home: S&D Members—Co-ordinators*. Retrieved 5 April 2016, from http://www.socialistsanddemocrats.eu/coordinators?title=&name_list=All&shs_term_node_tid_depth=All&sort_bef_combine=field_mep_group_role_value%20ASC&sort_order=ASC&sort_by=field_mep_group_role_value&page=1.

Heclo, H. (1978). Issue Networks and the Executive Establishment: Government Growth in an Age of Improvement. In A. King (Ed.), *The New American Political System* (pp. 87–124). Washington, DC: American Enterprise Institute.

Kauppi, N. (2003). Bourdieu's Political Sociology and the Politics of European Integration. *Theory and Society, 32*(5/6), 775–789.

Kluger Dionigi, M. (2017). *Lobbying in the European Parliament: The Battle for Influence*. Cham: Palgrave Macmillan.

Landorff, L. (2010). *The Role and Function of Intergroups in the European Parliament: A Study on the Intergroup for Traditional National Minorities, Constitutional Regions and Regional Languages in the 6th Parliamentary Term (2004–2009)* (Unpublished MA thesis). Aarhus: University of Aarhus.

Nedergaard, P., & Jensen, M. D. (2014). The Anatomy of Intergroups: Network Governance in the Political Engine Room of the European Parliament. *Policy Studies*, 1–19.

Pontier, J.-M. (1982). Le Rôle, des Intergroupes au Parlement Français. *Revue Française de Science Politique, 32*(4–5), 810–836.

Priestley, J. (2008). *Six Battles That Shaped Europe's Parliament*. London: John Harper Publishing.

Rhodes, R. A. W. (2006). Policy Network Analysis In M. Moran, M. Rein & R. E. Goodin (Eds.), *The Oxford Handbook of Public Policy* (pp. 423–445). Oxford: Oxford University Press.

Ringe, N., Victor, J. N., & Carman, C. J. (2013). *Bridging the Information Gap: Legislative Member Organizations as Social Networks in the United States and the European Union*. Ann Arbor: University of Michigan Press.

Yordanova, N. (2011). Inter-institutional Rules and Division of Power in the European Parliament: Allocation of Consultation and Co-decision Reports. *West European Politics, 34*(1), 97–121.

Appendix A

L. Landorff, *Inside European Parliament Politics*,
Palgrave Studies in European Political Sociology,
https://doi.org/10.1007/978-3-030-04206-6

27 Officially Recognised Intergroups in the 7th EP (2009–2014)

Name of the Intergroup	*Year of Foundation*	*Chairs & Co-Chairs*[a]	*Registered Members*[b]	*Meetings*
1. Sustainable Hunting, Biodiversity, Countryside Activities and Forests	1985	Mathieu Houillon, Véronique	129	4 per year
2. Ways of Saint James/Caminos de Santiago	1997	Millán Mon, Francisco José	67	Every 2nd month
3. Media	1994/2010	Cavada, Jean-Marie	34	3 per year
4. Urban	2005	Olbrycht, Jan	61	Monthly
5. Public Services (SGI-SSGI)	1994/2010[c]	Castex, Françoise	14	Monthly (2010)
6. Trade Union	1979	Cercas, Alejandro; Morin-Chartier, Elisabeth	20	Monthly
7. Western Sahara	1985	Neuser, Norbert	59	Upon demand; every six weeks
8. TIBET	1989	Mann, Thomas	102	Monthly
9. Disability	1980	Kósa, Ádám	69	Once a month, every two month, upon demand
10. Water/Wasser	2009	Seeber, Richard	110	Monthly
11. Traditional Minorities, National Communities and Languages	1983	Gàl, Kinga (2009–2011); Haglund, Carl (until 2012); Tabajdi, Csaba; Alfonsi François	41	Monthly
12. Mountains, Islands and Sparsely Populated Regions	2010	Sonik, Bogusław	59	3 per year (2010)
13. Baltic-Europe	2004/2005	Kelam, Tunne	52	4 per year
14. Lesbian, Gay, Bisexual & Transgender Rights—LGBT	1997/1999[d]	Cashman, Michael; Lunacek, Ulrike	113	4–5 per year
15. Social Economy/Economie Sociale	1990	Tarabella, Mark; Mauro, Mario (until 2013	73	4 per year; monthly (2007–2009)
16. Mers et Zones Côtières/Seas and Coastal Areas	2010	Lépage, Corinne	38	3–4 per year
17. Sky and Space/Ciel et Espace	2001	Prodi, Vittorio	110	Not specified

Name of the Intergroup	*Year of Foundation*	*Chairs & Co-Chairs*[a]	*Registered Members*[b]	*Meetings*
18. Anti-Racisme & Diversity	2000	Bozkurt, Emine	52	Not specified
19. Youth Issues/Jeunesse	2010	Abad, Damian (until 2012); Gardiazábal Rubial, Eider	33	Every 2nd month, at irregular intervals
20. Family and the Rights of the Child & Bioethics	1994/2000	Záborská, Anna; Mikolášik, Miroslav; Auken, Margrete	106	Not specified
21. Wine, Fruits and Vegetables, Tradition and Quality Food/ Viticulture	1994	Lulling, Astrid	95	Every 2nd month
22. Welfare & Conservation of Animals	1983	Poc, Pavel (2014); Schlyter, Carl (2010–2012); Jørgensen, Dan (2012–2013); Lucas, Caroline (2009–2010)	44	Monthly
23. SME 'Small and Medium-Sized Enterprise'	2005	Karas, Othmar	112	Every 2nd month
24. Ageing and Intergenerational Solidarity	1982	Moraes, Claude; Cabrnoch, Milan; Gutiérrez-Cortines, Cristina; Lambert, Jean; Liotard, Kartika Tamara; Van Nistelrooij, Lambert; Becker, Heinz K.; Lynne, Elisabeth (until 2012)	37	3 or more per year
25. Climate Change, Biodiversity and Sustainable Development/ Changement Climatique, Biodiversité et Développement Durable	1994	Stevenson, Struan	126	Monthly
26. Extreme Poverty and Human Rights	1980	Goulard, Sylvie (from 2011); Méndez de Vigo, Íñigo (until 2011)	12	Upon demand
27. New Media, Free Software, Open Information Society	2011	Schaake, Marietje; Lichtenberger, Eva	31	Not specified

(continued)

(continued)

Name of the Intergroup	*External/Internal Secretariat*	*Website*	*Sources*
1. Sustainable Hunting, Biodiversity, Countryside Activities and Forests	External/European Federation of Associations for Hunting and Conservation (FACE), European Landowners' Organisation (ELO)	www.face.eu/about-us/face-the-eu/hunting-intergroup	www.face.eu/about-us/face-the-eu/hunting-intergroup, last accessed 25 July 2013
2. Ways of Saint James/Caminos de Santiago	Internal/MEPs' office	–	Interview MEP
3. Media	Internal/MEPs' office	–	http://jeanmariecavada.eu/?s=Intergroup, last accessed 2 October 2011; (Jacobs, Corbett, & Shackleton, 1995)
4. Urban	Internal/MEPs' office	http://urban-intergroup.eu/	http://urban-intergroup.eu/
5. Public Services (SGI-SSGI)	Internal/MEPs office	http://services-publics-europe.eu/	Castex, F. (2011). Public Services Intergroup—Activity Report 2010; EP Public Service Intergroup (2011). EP Public Service Intergroup—Meetings—Meetings 2010—Draft program adopted the 20 January 2010. Retrieved 3 October 2011, from http://pro.union-habitat.org/structu/m-europe.nsf/62569fb6fa5eb929c12566e20077b9ba/47135a6ad3d13a6ac12576be004f2e8b?OpenDocument; (Jacobs et al., 1995)
6. Trade Union	Political Groups (EPP and S&D)	–	Interview CSO, MEPs
7. Western Sahara	Internal/MEPs' office	–	Interview MEP
8. TIBET	Internal/MEPs' office	Blog: http://eutibet.typepad.com/	(Mann & Reuter, 2010)

Name of the Intergroup	*External/Internal Secretariat*	*Website*	*Sources*
9. Disability	External/European Disability Forum (EDF)	http://www.edf-feph.org/Page_Generale.asp?DocID=18390	http://www.edf-feph.org/Page_Generale.asp?DocID=18390, last accessed 1 March 2013
10. Water/Wasser	External/European Federation of National Associations of Water Services (EUREAU)	http://epwatergroup.eu/	http://epwatergroup.eu/, last accessed 22 July 2013
11. Traditional Minorities, National Communities and Languages	Internal/MEPs' office	Facebook: http://de-de.facebook.com/pages/Intergroup-for-Traditional-Minorities-National-Communities-and-Languages/125934977420371	(Gál & Hicks, 2010; Gál, Hicks, & Eplényi, 2011)
12. Mountains, Islands and Sparsely Populated Regions	External/European Assembly of Elected Representatives from Mountain Regions (AEM)	http://intergroup174.com/ until December 2012	http://intergroup174.com/, last accessed 16 December 2012
13. Baltic-Europe	Internal/MEPs' office	–	Interview MEP
14. Lesbian, Gay, Bisexual & Transgender Rights—LGBT	Internal/MEPs' office	http://www.lgbt-ep.eu/	http://www.lgbt-ep.eu/, last accessed 18 April 2016
15. Social Economy/Economie Sociale	External/Social Economy Europe	http://www.socialeconomy.eu.org/social-economy-intergroup	http://www.socialeconomy.eu.org/social-economy-intergroup, last accessed 18 April 2016
16. Mers et Zones Côtières/Seas and Coastal Areas	Mixed/MEPs' office & Conference of Peripheral Maritime Regions of Europe (CPMR)	http://www.mersetzonescotieres.eu	(Saint Martin & Thomas, 2012)

(continued)

(continued)

Name of the Intergroup	*External/Internal Secretariat*	*Website*	*Sources*
17. Sky and Space/Ciel et Espace	Internal/MEPs' office	–	(European Parliament, 2002, 2003)
18. Anti-Racisme & Diversity	External/European Network against Racism (ENAR)	–	(European Parliament, 2002, 2003)
19. Youth Issues/Jeunesse	Internal/MEPs' office	http://de-de.facebook.com/pages/Youth-Intergroup-of-the-European-Parliament/182628841757687	http://de-de.facebook.com/pages/Youth-Intergroup-of-the-European-Parliament/182628841757687, last accessed 18 July 2013
20. Family and the Rights of the Child & Bioethics	Internal/MEPs' office	–	(European Parliament, 2002, 2003; Jacobs et al., 1995)
21. Wine, Fruits and Vegetables, Tradition and Quality Food/Viticulture	Internal/MEPs' office	Blog until 2008: http://intergroupevin.blogspot.de/	Interview CSO, MEP; (Jacobs et al., 1995)
22. Welfare & Conservation of Animals	External/Eurogroup for Animals	http://www.animalwelfare-intergroup.eu/	http://www.animalwelfareintergroup.eu/, last accessed 18 April 2016; (Intergroup on the Welfare & Conservation of Animals, 2012)
23. SME 'Small and Medium-Sized Enterprise'	Internal/MEPs' office	–	(European Parliament, 2005)
24. Ageing and Intergenerational Solidarity	External/Age Platform Europe	http://www.age-platform.eu/en/age-and-the-eu-institutions/european-parliament/intergroup-on-ageing-and-intergenerational-solidarity	http://www.age-platform.eu/en/age-and-the-eu-institutions/european-parliament/intergroup-on-ageing-and-intergenerational-solidarity, last accessed 22 December 2011

Name of the Intergroup	External/Internal Secretariat	Website	Sources
25. Climate Change, Biodiversity and Sustainable Development/Changement Climatique, Biodiversité et Développement Durable	External/European Bureau for Conservation and Development (EBCD), International Union for Conservation of Nature (IUCN)	http://ebcd.org/intergroup/	http://ebcd.org/intergroup/, last accessed 15 May 2013
26. Extreme Poverty and Human Rights	External/ATD Fourth World	–	(Comité Quart Monde Européen, 2004–2009); Interview CSO
27. New Media, Free Software, Open Information Society	Internal/MEPs' office	–	European Parliament—About Parliament—Organisation and Work—Intergroups, available at http://www.europarl.europa.eu/aboutparliament/en/00c9d93c87/Intergroups.html, last accessed 19 May 2014

Source Author's own table based on sources listed in the right column and in footnotes

[a]European Parliament. (2011). *About the Parliament: Organisation and Work—Intergroups*. Retrieved 11 May 2011, from http://www.europarl.europa.eu/aboutparliament/en/00c9d93c87/Intergroups.html, European Parliament. (2013). *About Parliament: Organisation and Work—Intergroups*. Retrieved 24 January 2013, from http //www.europarl.europa.eu/aboutparliament/en/00c9d93c87/Intergroups.html, European Parliament. (2014). *About Parliament: Organisation and Work—Intergroups*. Retrieved 19 May 2014, from http://www.europarl.europa.eu/aboutparliament/en/00c9d93c87/Intergroups.html

[b]European Parliament. (2013). *About Parliament: Organisation and Work—Intergroups*. Retrieved 24 January 2013, from http://www.europarl.europa.eu/aboutparliament/en/00c9d93c87/Intergroups.html

[c]Jacobs et al. (1995) already list an Intergroup on 'Public Services' in 1994. MEP Castex established the Intergroup 'Public Services', including services of general interest (SGI) and Social Services of General Interest (SSGI), in 2010 in response to the Lisbon Treaty

[d]Date of informal establishment: 1997; date of formal establishment: 1999 (e-mail correspondence Laura Landorff—Bruno Selun/secretary of LGBT Intergroup, 13 February 2013 18:39 CET)

Most Active MEPs of the Four Intergroups

Intergroup 'Viticulture'	*Intergroup 'Urban'*	*Intergroup 'Animal Welfare'*	*Intergroup 'Trade Union'*
• Astrid Lulling (EPP, LU) • Christa Klass (EPP, DE) • Herbert Dorfmann (EPP, IT) • Michel Dantin (EPP, FR) • Françoise Grossetête (EPP, FR) • Elisabeth Morin-Chartier (EPP, FR) • Nathalie Griesbeck, (ALDE, FR) • Giancarlo Scottà, (EFD, IT) • Catherine Grèze (Greens/EFA, FR) • Georges Bach (EPP, LU)	• Jan Olbrycht (EPP, PL) • Oldřich Vlasák (ECR, CZ) • Lambert van Nistelrooij (EPP, NL) • Karima Delli (Greens/EFA, FR) • Marie-Thérèse Sanchez-Schmid (EPP, FR) • Peter Simon (S&D, DE) • Joachim Zeller (EPP, DE) • Arlene McCarthy (S&D, GB) • Cristina Gutiérrez-Cortines (EPP, ES) • Ramona Mănescu (ALDE until 2013/EPP from 2014, RO) • Sophie Auconie (EPP, FR) • Rui Tavares (GUE/NGL 2009–2011/Greens/EFA, PT)	• Carl Schlyter (Greens/EFA, SE) • Dan Jørgensen (S&D, DK) • Nadja Hirsch (ALDE, DE) • Elisabeth Jeggle (EPP, DE) • Marit Paulsen (ALDE, SE) • Anna Rosbach (EFD 2009–2011; ECR from 2011, DK) • Daciana Octavia Sârbu (S&D, RO) • Janusz Wojciechowski (ECR, PL) • Andrea Zanoni (ALDE, IT)	• Alejandro Cercas (S&D, ES) • Elisabeth Morin-Chartier (EPP, FR) • Stephen Hughes (S&D, GB) • Georges Bach (EPP, LU) • Richard Falbr (S&D, CZ) • Frédéric Daerden (S&D, BE) • Evelyn Regner (S&D, AT)

Source Author's own table

Appendix B

Semi-Structured Interview Guide for MEPs

Prior the interview/organisational issues:

- Do you allow me to record the interview?
- Would you like to remain anonymously?
- What is the study about?

1st Block:

- What was your main/primary motivation for joining the Intergroup? Where there any additional aspects?
- How did you become aware of the Intergroup?
- Why is it (so) important to you to stand up for this particular [topic/issue/group]?
- How do you participate in the Intergroup?

Optional: Do you

- Suggest topics/issues, and/or invite guests for discussion in Intergroup?
- Initiate statements, written declarations by the Intergroup?
- Make own presentations?
- Contribute your own (work) experience or expertise?
- Other?

L. Landorff, *Inside European Parliament Politics*,
Palgrave Studies in European Political Sociology,
https://doi.org/10.1007/978-3-030-04206-6

2nd Block:

- How would you describe the Intergroup?/What are the central characteristics of an Intergroup? Is it more like
  Follow-up questions:

  - A political group, a friendship group, or debate club or … ?
  - Being [insert the description of the interviewee] is it a rather of formal or informal character?

- As a [insert description of interviewee] how does the Intergroup relate to the overall work of the European Parliament?
- Being more concerned with/active in [insert answer to Question 8] does that correspond to your own understanding of what the main tasks of an MEP are (e.g. that MEPs represent a particular group or interest or are primarily concerned with policy-preparation/formulation/making?
- Why cannot you discuss this topic/issue in the committee and/or public hearing?
- To what extend does the work in the Intergroup differ from your work in your committee? Is it different? How?
- Have there been situations where you/several members did not share the same opinion or did not agree with the decision made by your colleagues in the Intergroup? How was the situation solved in the IG?

Since 1999 Intergroups are subject to rules established by the Conference of Presidents. According to these rules, Intergroups are not official organs of the EP, and therefore, are not allowed to express the opinion of the Parliament. Moreover, Intergroups are only allowed to meet on Thursdays during the Strasbourg plenary session. To become officially recognized, an Intergroup needs the signature of three political groups.

- What is your opinion on the regulation of Intergroups?

3rd Block:

- If you would need to assess the achievements of the Intergroup, what do you say is your personal success in the Intergroup and that of the Intergroup itself? Were the expectations met you had when you joined the Intergroup?
- In retrospect, have you ever wished to spend more time on the Intergroup? Why?
- Will you compete again for the next EP elections?
- Is there any other thing I should know about the Intergroup, is there any other person I should talk to?
- Is there any written material on the Intergroup available, e.g. minutes, statements that could be of interest to me?

Thank you very much for the conversation!

List of Interviews June 2012–February 2014

	Date	*Interview*	*Length of interview*	*Place*	*Reference in the study*
1.	25/06/2012	MEP	51:30	Germany	
2.	29/06/2012	MEP	42:27	Germany	
3.	11/09/2012	Assistant/IG Traditional National Minorities	Not recorded/42:00	Strasbourg	
4.	24/09/2012	MEP	45:07	Germany	
5.	02/10/2012	MEP	26:47	Brussels	MEP 1
6.	03/10/2012	MEP	47:29	Brussels	MEP 2
7.	03/10/2012	MEP	58:38	Brussels	MEP 3
8.	03/10/2012	MEP	01h 04	Brussels	
9.	04/10/2012	MEP	23:51	Brussels	
10.	08/10/2012	MEP	31:52	Brussels	MEP 4
11.	09/10/2012	MEP	24:41	Brussels	MEP 5
12.	09/10/2012	MEP	15:00	Brussels	MEP 6
13.	10/10/2012	MEP	47:16	Brussels	MEP 7
14.	10/10/2012	MEP	39:24	Brussels	MEP 8
15.	11/10/2012	MEP	30:41	Brussels	MEP 9
16.	11/10/2012	MEP	32:44	Brussels	

(continued)

(continued)

	Date	*Interview*	*Length of interview*	*Place*	*Reference in the study*
17.	16/10/2012	MEP	50:20	Brussels	MEP 10
18.	17/10/2012	EP Bureau	44:02	Brussels	
19.	17/10/2012	MEP	Not recorded/1h 30 min	Brussels	
20.	17/10/2012	MEP	44:25	Brussels	MEP 11
21.	18/03/2013	Assistant/IG Trade Union	Not recorded/~1h	Brussels	Ass 1
22.	18/03/2013 + Follow-up	MEP	53:41	Brussels	MEP 12
23.	19/03/2013	MEP	47:39	Brussels	MEP 13
24.	19/03/2013	MEP	40:21	Brussels	MEP 14
25.	20/03/2013	MEP	55:12	Brussels	MEP 15
26.	21/03/2013	Political Group Official	45:57	Brussels	PG 1
27.	26/03/2013	MEP	38:03	Brussels	MEP 16
28.	26/03/2013	MEP	35:16	Brussels	MEP 17
29.	27/03/2013	MEP	1h 01	Brussels	MEP 18
30.	27/03/2013	MEP	1h 06	Brussels	MEP 19
31.	28/03/2013	Assistant/IG Urban	1h 05	Brussels	Ass 2
32.	06/05/2013	CSO	55:40	Brussels	CSO 1
33.	08/05/2013	EP Official Committee Secretariat	28:53	Brussels	EP Official 1
34.	10/05/2013	CSO	52:22	Brussels	CSO 2
35.	13/05/2013	Political Group Official	40:42	Brussels	PG 2
36.	14/05/2013	CSO	1h 06	Brussels	CSO 3
37.	14/05/2013	MEP	59:51	Brussels	MEP 20
38.	15/05/2013	CSO	1h 03	Brussels	CSO 4
39.	16/05/2013 + Follow-up 29 July 2013	CSO	51:38	Brussels	CSO 5
40.	16/05/2013	Assistant/IG Urban	47:05	Brussels	Ass 3
41.	17/02/2014	CSO	01h 39	Strasbourg	CSO 6
42.	27/02/2014	MEP	39:06	Strasbourg	MEP 21

List of Attended Intergroup Meetings September 2012–February 2014

	Date	*Intergroup*	*Topic*	*Time and Place*
1.	12/09/2012	Viticulture	• 'Single CMO' Discussion of the report of Mr. Dantin and the tabled amendments, Michel Dantin, rapporteur • Vinissima—Women and Wine, Presentation, Christa Jüngling, regional responsible for Moselle and Ahr • EuroFoieGras—Presentation of the Federation and its animal welfare charter, Jean Schwebel, President EuroFoieGras	5:00–6:00 pm plus Wine Tasting 6:00–7:00 pm EP Strasbourg, France
2.	13/09/2012	Traditional Minorities, National Communities and Languages	• Situation of the Alsatian culture and language • Situation of the Hungarian national community in Romania	10:00–11:30 am EP Strasbourg, France
3.	13/09/2012	Animal Welfare	• The Non-Commercial movement of Pets—Presentation of the related draft report, Dr. Horst Schnellhardt, MEP Rapporteur in the ENVI-Committee • The animal health and welfare related aspects, Claire Calder, Policy Officer Companion Animals, Eurogroup for Animals	11:00 am–12:00 pm EP Strasbourg, France
4.	16/10/2012	Trade Union	• 'Erasmus for all'—Programme for Education Training, Youth and Sport 2014–2020 • Groundhandling services at Union airports	9:00–10:00 am EP Brussels, Belgium
5.	27/03/2013	Water	• Water and Regional Policy, Innovation and Research in the Context of Smart Specialisation	5:00–6:30 pm EP Brussels, Belgium
6.	07/05/2013	Climate Change, Biodiversity and Sustainable Development/ Sub-group: Islands	• European Islands' challenges	4:00–6:30 pm EP Brussels, Belgium
7.	06/02/2014	Traditional Minorities, National Communities and Languages	• Situation of Catalan language in Spain • Possible ratification of the European Charter for Regional or Minority Languages by France	10:00–11:30 am EP Strasbourg, France

Appendix C

L. Landorff, *Inside European Parliament Politics*,
Palgrave Studies in European Political Sociology,
https://doi.org/10.1007/978-3-030-04206-6

Meetings of the Intergroup 'Animal Welfare' in 7th EP (2009–2014)

	Date	*Topics*
2014	13 March	CETACEANS IN CAPTIVITY • Dolphinaria, a summary of captive dolphin facilities Daniel Turner, Born Free Foundation—EU • The impact of captivity on the welfare of cetaceans Dr. Naomi Rose, Animal Welfare Institute • Behind the scenes—A former trainer's perspective on marine mammal training Samantha Berg, Voice of the Orcas • Managing dolphins under human care; the zoo point of view Niels van Elk, European Association of Zoos and Aquaria, Bottlenose dolphin EEP coordinator
	6 February	THE CLONING OF ANIMALS FOR FOOD SUPPLY • The motion for a resolution of the Committee on Environment, Kartika Tamara Liotard MEP, (GUE/NGL, NL), Co-rapporteur • Animal welfare remains a concern, Kirsty Reid, Policy Officer, Research Animals, Eurogroup for Animals
	16 January	DAIRY COWS: STEPS NEEDED TO IMPROVE WELFARE Peter Stevenson, *Chief Policy Advisor, Compassion in World Farming (CIWF)* CONSUMER DEMAND FOR MANDATORY METHOD OF PRODUCTION LABELLING, UNDERPINNED BY ROBUST OUTCOME-BASED ASSESSMENTS ffinlo Costein, *Labelling Matters EU Project Manager*
2013	12 December	THE EU REGULATION ON INVASIVE ALIEN SPECIES • Presentation of the ENVI-draft report Pavel Poc MEP (S&D, CZ) Rapporteur in the ENVI—Committee & Vice-President of the AW Intergroup • The NGOs' position—Prevention is better than cure (for animals & the environment) Staci McLennan, Policy Officer Wildlife, Eurogroup for Animals • Case studies: The Muskrat, the American Mink, the Grey Squirrel, Canada Geese, the Red-Eared Terrapin Dr. Andrew Kelly, Wildlife Policy Advisor, Humane Society International
	21 November	• Animal Welfare and Education—Can one go without the other? Monika Hametter, Deputy Director, 'Tierschutz macht Schule' (Association for Animal Welfare Education), Austria • Education: A key component of the EU Animal Welfare Strategy, James Pirnay, EU Policy Officer for Companion Animals and Animal Action Education, IFAW-International Fund for Animal Welfare

Date	*Topics*
24–29 October	Study trip to the Cheetah Conservation fund in Namibia
24 October	• The EU-Regulation on the protection of animals at the time of killing • Enforcement in the Member States Denis Simonin, Evaluation Officer—Legislative Veterinary Officer, DG SANCO, European Commission • The NGO's position Dr. Michel Courat, Policy Officer Farm Animals, Eurogroup for Animals
18 September Brussels	Commissioner Tonio Borg on ongoing animal welfare related issues—On-going and planned animal welfare issues
12 September	THE ANIMAL HEALTH LAW—The AGRI-draft report Marit Paulsen MEP, Rapporteur in the Committee on Agriculture and Rural Development • Recognising Animal Welfare & Health Inter-linkages Chris Gallasch, Policy Officer—Sustainable Farming, Eurogroup for Animals
4 July	• EAZA's views on the guidelines for zoos and on the accreditation system, Dr. Lesley Dickie Executive Director EAZA • The EU Zoo Inquiry: Outcomes and future actions, Daniel Turner Born Free Foundation
13 June	LIVING WELL WITH WOLVES IN THE EU—The state of play, the problems and solutions • The migrations of wolves from Italy to neighboring countries Prof. Luigi Boitani, Dept. Biology and Biotechnologies, 'Sapienza' University of Rome, Italy • The situation in Poland and Scandinavia, Małgorzata Czyżewska General Directorate of the Polish State Forests Poland
23 May	• European elections 2014: The animal welfare challenges for the next term, Reineke Hameleers, *New Director of Eurogroup for Animals* • Consistency approach in vaccines testing, Ian Ragan, *Project leader, European Partnership for Alternative Approaches to Animal Testing (EPAA)* • With short introductory and closing remarks by Gwenole Cozigou &Florian Vernay, *EPAA—Industry Vice-chair of the Steering Committee*
18 April	• Pigeon Control in a Humane Way, François Tisserant, *President of the SPA Upper Alsace* • Guiding principles in the Humane Control of Pests, Frederic Verwilghen, *Executive Board Member, CEPA—Confederation of European Pest Management Associations*

(continued)

(continued)

	Date	*Topics*
	14 March	THE WELFARE OF PIGS • The enforcement of the legislation, Denis Simonin DG SANCO • Pig castration, Patrick Chevillon *IFIP, the French Pork Institute*
	7 February	THE DIRECTIVE 2010/63/EU ON THE PROTECTION OF ANIMALS USED FOR SCIENTIFIC PURPOSES • EURL ECVAM—A broader role to achieve greater impact, Maurice Whelan *Head of Unit, EURL ECVAM-European Union Reference Laboratory on Alternatives to Animal Testing, Joint Research Centre, European Commission* • Focus on implementation—The key to success, Susanna Louhimies, *Policy Officer—Use of animals for scientific purposes, DG ENV, European Commission*
	17 January	ANIMAL WELFARE IN POLAND • The Welfare of pigs, Anna Kowalska Klockiewiscz, First Secretary Veterinary Affairs, Permanent representation of Poland to the EU • Current animal welfare issues in the farming sector: Slaughter, transport, animal markets, Prof. Andrzej Elzanowski Polish Academy of Sciences
2012	13 December	THE PROTECTION OF PUBLIC HEALTH & WILDLIFE FROM ENDOCRINE DISRUPTORS • The Human Toxome project and endocrine disruption testing, Prof. Thomas Hartung, *Director of CAAT, Centre for Alternatives to Animal Testing, John Hopkins University, Baltimore, USA* • The Environment Committee draft report, Carl Schlyter *(Greens/EFA, SE) Shadow rapporteur in the ENVI Committee*
	22 November	BRIEFING ON KEY ISSUES FOR CITES COP 16 • Polar bears, sharks, manta rays and rhinos, Dr. Joanna Swabe, *EU Director, Humane Society International-HIS* • Elephants, e-commerce and implementing decisions, Satyen Sinha, *Political and Campaigns Officer, IFAW*
	25 October	CONSERVATION EFFORTS OF BIG FELINES IN AFRICA • Strategies for Cheetah Conservation in its Natural Habitat, Dr. Laurie Marker *Cheetah Conservation Fund* • The big cats sanctuary, Lionsrock in South Africa, Katja Brunner, *Director of Communications Vier Pfoten*

Date	*Topics*
13 September	HEALTH REQUIREMENTS FOR THE NON-COMMERCIAL MOVEMENTS OF PETS • Presentation of the draft report on the non-commercial movements of pets, Dr. Horst Schnellhardt MEP, *rapporteur* • The animal welfare related aspects of the non-commercial movements of pets, Claire Calder, Policy Officer Companion Animals, Eurogroup for Animals
5 July	THE INTERNATIONAL DIMENSION OF ANIMAL WELFARE • The World Organisation for Animal Health (OIE) and animal welfare, Dr. Karin Schwabenbauer, *German Chief Veterinary Officer and OIE President* • DG SANCO's animal welfare related work on international level, Dr. Judith Krommer *Legislative Officer, Animal Welfare, DG SANCO, European Commission*
14 June	PUBLIC PROCUREMENT • The proposal for a Directive on public procurement & Animal welfare in Swedish procurement schemes, Åsa Westlund MEP (S&D, SE), *Rapporteur in the Environment Committee* • The benefits of including animal welfare in EU-public procurement policy, Effiong Essien, *Project Officer Sustainable Food Chain & CSR, Eurogroup for Animals*
24 May	ANIMAL TESTING • An update on the Cosmetics Directive, Food and Feed and ECVAM, Roman Kolar, *Deputy Director, Akademie für Tierschutz, Deutscher Tierschutzbund* • The implementation of Dir. 2010/63 on the protection of animals used for scientific purposes, Nicolas Dudoignon *Vice Chair of EFPIA research & animal welfare working group*
19 April	ANIMAL WELFARE AND HORIZON 2020—THE FRAMEWORK PROGRAMME FOR RESEARCH AND INNOVATION • Research opportunities on Farm Animal Welfare and trends for Horizon 2020, Danièle Tissot, *Programme Officer, European Commission, DG Research and Innovation* • Advancing Safety Science & Health Research with modern, Non-Animal Tools, Dr. Joanna Swabe, *EU Director, Humane Society International (HSI)* • Report on the Elephant Slaughter in Cameroon and the Global Ivory Trade, Julie Landry, *Communications Officer for West Africa (IFAW)* & Satyen Sinha, *Political and Campaigns Officer (IFAW)*

(continued)

(continued)

	Date	Topics
	15 March	SHARK FINNING • The Commission proposal amending the current EU legislation, Christos Theophilou, *Policy Officer, DG MARE, European Commission* • The PECH draft report, Maria do Céu Patrão Neves (EPP, PT), *Rapporteur in the Committee on Fisheries* • The animal welfare and conservation concerns, Susie Watts, *Shark Consultant, Humane Society International (HSI)* • The Animal Welfare Strategy 2012–2015—The AGRI draft report, Marit Paulsen (ALDE, SE), *Rapporteur in the Committee on Agriculture*
	29 February	ANIMAL WELFARE RELATED PRIORITIES OF THE DANISH PRESIDENCY Mette Gjerskov, Danish Minister for food, agriculture and fisheries
	7 February	THE NEW ANIMAL WELFARE STRATEGY 2012–2015 John Dalli, EU Commissioner for Health
	19 January	HALF TERM • Election of the new President and new Vice-President • Our life insurance, our natural capital: An EU biodiversity strategy to 2020, Presentation of the ENVI draft report by Gerben Gerbrandy (ALDE, NL), Rapporteur in the Committee on Environment
2011	15 December	THE CAP AND ANIMAL WELFARE CONCERNS *Elisabeth Jeggle (EPP, DE) Intergroup Vice-President, Member of the Agriculture Committee* • The Commission's point of view, *Juan Alvarez de la Puente, DG Agriculture, European Commission* • The new CAP: Better conditions for the farmers and the animals?, *Veronique Schmit, Executive Officer Policy, Eurogroup for Animals* • Implications of the CAP proposals on the livestock sector: Estimated effects and alternative approaches, Henk Westhoek, *Pbl Netherlands Environmental Assessment Agency*

Date	*Topics*
17 November	• Update on the battery cage ban for laying hens, Sonja Van Tichelen, *Director Eurogroup for Animals* • Report on the impact of EU regulation on the protection of animals during transport, Denis Simonin, Evaluation Officer—Legislative Veterinary Officer, DG SANCO, European Commission • The latest evidence on the welfare of horses during transport, Joanne White, Campaigns Adviser at the World Horse Welfare • New written declaration on animal transport, Dan Jørgensen MEP (S&D, DK), Vice-President of the Intergroup
27 October	WILDLIFE TRADE: HEALTH AND INVASIVE RISKS ENFORCEMENT • Health Risks from new Companion Animals, Staci McLennan, *Policy officer Wildlife, Eurogroup for Animals* • Invasive Alien Species and an EU Strategy, Valentina Bastino, *European Commission, DG Environment* • INTERPOL's Response to the Threat of organised Wildlife Crime, Justin Gosling *Interpol, Intelligence Officer, Environmental Crime Project*
11 September	• Written declaration 26/2011 on dog population management in the European Union, Daciana Sârbu MEP, (S&D, RO) Vice-President of the Intergroup • Animal Welfare and its position in the humanitarian sphere—Presentation and film footage James Sawyer, *Head of Disaster Management, World Society for the Protection of Animals (WSPA)*
7 July	• Footage from the 2011 sealing season in Canada, Lesley O'Donnell *Director EU Office, International Fund for Animal Welfare (IFAW)* • Challenges to the EU ban on seal products at the WTO, Dr. Joanna Swabe, *EU Director, Humane Society International (HSI)*
9 June	• Written declaration 26/2011 on dog population management in the European Union, Daciana Sârbu MEP, (S&D, RO) Vice-President of the Intergroup • Identification and registration: A pillar of Companion animal health and welfare, Paolo Dalla Villa, *Head of Human-Animal Relationship and Animal Welfare Laboratory, Instituto G. Caporale, Teramo, Italy* • Adequate Guardianship: Aspects of a humane Companion Animal Management Plan, Kate Natrass Atema, *Program Director Companion Animals, IFAW*
24 May Brussels	Jane Goodall, Reason for Hope

(continued)

(continued)

Date	*Topics*
4 May Brussels	ENFORCEMENT OF THE LIVE ANIMAL TRANSPORT LEGISLATION • The positive aspects of the implementation of Regulation (EC) 1/2005, Piet Thijsse, Vice-President, European Livestock and Meat Trading Union (UECBV) • How can better enforcement contribute to higher quality transports, Marc Billiet, Head—EU Goods Transport, International Road Transport Union • The veterinary role in the proper enforcement to prevent disease risks, Nancy de Bryne Deputy Executive Director, Federation of Veterinarians of Europe (FVE) • FVO findings on enforcement of the Transport Regulation, Terence Cassidy, Head of Sector Animal Welfare, FVO—European Food and Veterinary Office, EC • The principal welfare problems arising from poor enforcement of the Transport Regulation', Peter Stevenson, Chief Policy Advisor, Compassion in World Farming • Official Members States reports and poor enforcement of the transport regulation, Dr. Michel Courat, Policy Officer Farm Animals, Eurogroup for Animals • Checking compliance with Regulation (EC) 1/2005 on German roads: Options and problems in the practical work of an official veterinarian, Claudia Eggert, Official Veterinarian, Unit for Animal Health, Lahn-Dill-Kreis, Germany
7 April	• Novel Foods and the cloning of animals for food supply: The outcome of the negotiations in the Conciliation Committee, Intergroup Vice-President Kartika Liotard (GUE/NGL, NL) • Live plucking of Geese, Marcus Müller VIER PFOTEN/FOUR PAWS International • Foie gras production, an animal welfare perspective
10 March	European declaration on the alternatives to surgical castration of pigs, Michel Courat, *Eurogroup for Animals* • Animal welfare friendly pig production, Thierry Schweitzer, *Alsatian pig farmer and pork butcher*
16 February	COSMETICS AND ANIMAL TESTING • Advancing the Science on Alternatives to Animal Testing, *Introduction*: Bertil Heerink, *Director-General Colipa-the European Cosmetics Association, Presentation*: Dr. Horst Wenck, *Chair of the Colipa Program on Alternatives to Animal Testing & Corporate Vice President Research for Beiersdorf* • Ending Animal Testing for Cosmetics, Emily McIvor, *Senior Policy Advisor, Research and Toxicology Department, HSI Humane Society International / Europe*

	Date	*Topics*
	20 January	THE CAP TOWARDS 2020: WAYS FOR A MORE SUSTAINABLE LIVESTOCK FARMING • Animal welfare in the future CAP, Elisabeth Jeggle MEP, *(EPP, DE) AGRI-Committee Member* • The position of the farmers' organization ECVC—European Coordination Via Campesina, Christian Boisgontier, *Farmer in Lower Normandy,& representative of the European Coordination, Via Campesina*
2010	16 December	EU AGRICULTURE AND INTERNATIONAL TRADE—THE ANIMAL WELFARE CONCERNS • The Papastamkos draft report of the Agriculture Committee by *Marit Paulsen MEP, ALDE Shadow Rapporteur* • How to promote EU animal welfare standards on a global level by *Paul van Geldorp, Head of Unit for international questions (bilateral), DG SANCO, European Commission*
	25 November	• Whaling in the Faroe Islands, Lamya Essemlali, *President of Sea Shepherd France,* • François-Xavier Pelletier, *President of Homme-Nature,* Christophe Marie, *Director Animal Protection Office, Fondation Brigitte Bardot* • Shark Finning and the EU: Time for change • Susie Watts, *Shark Consultant, Humane Society International*
	21 October	• Ensuring EU animal welfare legislation is implemented, Terence Cassidy, *Head of Sector Animal Welfare, FVO—European Food and Veterinary Office, European Commission* • The EU cage ban for laying hens in 2012: Current situation and possible consequences, Peter van Horne, *Poultry economist, Agricultural economics Institute, Wageningen, The Netherlands*
	8 July	MARINE BIOTOXINS AND SEAFOOD SAFETY • Animal testing for the detection of biotoxins in shellfish: The Commission's position, Judit Krommer, *Legislative Officer—Animal Welfare, DG SANCO, European Commission* • Open forum for MEPs to raise specific animal welfare concerns
	17 June	WILDLIFE TRADE AND ENFORCEMENT • Wildlife Trade in the EU: Impacts and related policies, Staci McLennan, *Policy Officer Wildlife, Eurogroup for Animals* • Role of Sanctuaries in Enforcement—The Barbary macaque as a case study, David van Gennep, *Director, Stichting Aap, Netherlands*

(continued)

(continued)

Date	*Topics*
19 May	THE PROBLEM OF DOPING IN EQUESTRIAN SPORT • Introduction by Sabine Verheyen MEP (EPP, DE) • The position of the EEF—The European Equestrian Federation, Dr. Hanfried Haring, President of the EEF—European Equestrian Federation • The position of the International Equestrian Federation—FEI, Dr. Graeme Cooke, Director of the FEI Fédération Equestre Internationale • Open discussion
22 April (cancelled)	THE INTERNATIONAL WHALING COMMISSION—IWC AND THE PROPOSED COMPROMISE TO LEGITIMIZE COMMERCIAL WHALING • Vassili Papastavrou, Honorary Research Associate, University of Bristol (consultant whale biologist) • Open forum for all MEPs to raise specific animal welfare concerns
10 March	• Evaluation and assessment of the animal welfare action plan 2006–2010, An update, Marit Paulsen MEP *(ALDE, SE), Rapporteur in the Committee on Agriculture* • Animal welfare in the development countries, David Bowles, *Head of External Affairs, RSPCA* • Dog meat trade in the Philippines, Andrew Plumbly, *Head of Operations, Network for Animals*
10 February	• Need for improved enforcement of the Pigs Directive, Peter Stevenson, *Consultant for Compassion in World Farming* • Alternatives to castration: An overview, Stéphan Martin, *DVM, Director, Swine Marketing—Europe, Africa and Middle-East, Pfizer Animal Health* • "Alternatives to castration: Practical experience", Georg Freisfeld, *Agricultural Engineer, Pig Farmer in Westphalia, Germany*
20 January	• A Sustainable Development of European Aquaculture, Kartika Liotard MEP *(GUE/NGL, NL), Draftswoman in the Environment Committee* • Conservation efforts for Bluefin Tuna, Gerben Gerbrandy MEP *(ALDE, NL)* • Revision of the Common Fisheries Policy—The animal welfare and conservation aspects, Dr. Joanna Swabe, *EU Director HSI (Humane Society International)*

	Date	Topics
2009	16 December	• Renewal of the EU—Animal Welfare Action Plan—The views and expectations of the animal welfare groups, *Sonja Van Tichelen, Director Eurogroup for Animals* • The EP report: Evaluation and Assessment of the Animal Welfare Action Plan (2006–2010), *Marit Paulsen MEP, ALDE, SE, AGRI- rapporteur* • Preparatory work for a renewed Action Plan after 2011, Andrea Gavinelli, *DG SANCO European Commission*
	25 November	ENDANGERED SPECIES: LOOKING TO CITES—The 15th Conference of the Parties (COP15) • What is CITES, *Lesley O'Donnell, Director IFAW Europe* • The motion for a resolution of the Environment Committee, *Chris Davies, ALDE, UK* • The species and issues of concern: Polar bears, Bobcats, Sharks, Blue Fin Tuna, *Dr. Joanna Swabe, EU Director, HSI and* Elephants, Tigers, Reptiles, Internet Trade, Eve Abe PHD, Campaign Officer, IFAW
	21 October	THE PROTECTION OF ANIMALS USED FOR SCIENTIFIC PURPOSES • The current state of play, *Elisabeth Jeggle MEP, Rapporteur in the Agriculture Committee* • The Animal welfare policy objectives for the second reading, *Emily McIvor, Dr. Hadwen Trust* • Presentation of the petition *'Make Animal Testing History', Emily McIvor, Dr. Hadwen Trust* • THE ANIMAL WELFARE PRIORITIES OF THE SWEDISH PRESIDENCY, *Rolf Eriksson State Secretary to the Swedish Minister for Agriculture*
	16 September	• Introduction of the new Members of Bureau, Carl Schlyter MEP (Greens/EFA, SE) Vice-President of the Intergroup • The upcoming animal welfare issues, Andreas Erler Intergroup Secretariat • The Welfare Quality Project—Overall assessment of animal welfare: Towards a scoring system, Isabelle Veissier INRA—Institut National de la Recherche Agronomique, France

Source Intergroup on the Welfare & Conservation of Animals (2014b)

Meetings of the Intergroup 'Trade Union' in the 7th EP (2009–2014)

Year	*Dates*	*Topics*
2013	4 July (Plenary, Strasbourg)	No minutes
	26 June	No minutes
	5 June (Brussels)	No minutes
		State of play: Enforcement directive on the posting of workers
	14 May (Brussels)	Joint meeting of the 'Youth' and 'Trade Union' Intergroups: 'Tackling youth unemployment: Possible ways out' MEP Eider Gardiazabal Rubial, President of the 'Youth' Intergroup MEP Alejandro Cercas, Co-chair of the 'Trade Union' Intergroup MEP Pablo Zalba Bidegain (EPP, ES), Vice-President of the 'Youth' Intergroup • MEP Johanna Szrzydlewska (EPP, PL), Rapporteur of the draft report on tackling youth unemployment, possible ways out • MEP Evelyn Regner (S&D, AU) • MEP Csaba Öry (EPP, HU) (tbc) • MEP Kinga Göncz (S&D, RO) • MEP Raül Romeva i Rueda (Greens/EFA, ES) • Patrick Itschert, Deputy Secretary General, European Trade Union Confederation • Thiébaut Weber, Chair of the Youth Committee, European Trade Union Confederation • Giuseppe Porcaro, Secretary General, European Youth Forum
		No minutes
	14 March (Plenary, Strasbourg)	No minutes
	5 March	Proposal for a directive of the European Parliament and of the Council on conditions of entry and residence of third-country nationals in the framework of an intra-corporate transfer Proposal for a regulation of the European Parliament and of the Council on the protection of individuals with regard to the processing of personal data and on the free movement of such data (General Data Protection Regulation)
	29 January	No minutes

Year	Dates	Topics
	22 January	The impact of the economic crisis on gender equality and women's rights The proposal for a directive of the European Parliament and of the Council on public procurement
2012	13 November (Brussels) 9.00–10.00	No minutes
	16 October	'Erasmus for all'—Programme for Education, Training, Youth and Sport 2014–2020 Main speakers: MEP Doris Pack (EPP) MEP Katarina Nevedalova (S&D) Mrs. Agnes Roman, ETUC Letter by ETUC with proposed amendments to Pack report Groundhandling services at Union airports Main speakers: MEP Artur Zasada (EPP) MEP Knut Fleckenstein (S&D) Mr. Enrique Carmona, EFT Civil Aviation Section President
	25 September	No minutes
	5 September	The enforcement of Directive 96/71/EC concerning the posting of workers in the framework of the provision of services Information and consultation of workers, anticipation and management of restructuring
	15 May	No minutes
	11 April	Council Regulation (Monti II) on the exercise of the right to take collective action within the context of the freedom of establishment and the freedom to provide services Directive of the European Parliament and of the Council on the enforcement of Directive 96/71/EC concerning the posting of workers in the framework of the provision of services
	15 March	Modernisation of EU public procurement legislative framework – Report of MEP Marc TARABELLA, S&D Group
	6 March	No minutes

(continued)

(continued)

Year	Dates	Topics
	2 February	Modernisation of EU public procurement legislative framework – Report of MEP Marc TARABELLA, S&D Group
		Jurisdiction, recognition and enforcement of judgments in civil and commercial matters (repeal. Regulation (EC) No 44/2001, 'Brussels I'). Recast
2011	29 November	Minimum health and safety requirements regarding the exposure of workers to the risk arising from physical agents (electromagnetic fields) Report of Morin-Chartier (MEP in EMPL)
	17 November (Plenary)	Structural Funds
	8 November	Directive on the conditions of entry and residence of third-country nationals for the purposes of seasonal employment
		Directive on conditions of entry and residence of third-country nationals in the framework of an intra-corporate transfer (ICT)
	18 October	Fundamental Labour Rights
	20 September	Eurobonds
	7 July (Plenary)	Athens Manifesto and the ETUC programme for the coming years
	28 June	Directive on the conditions of entry and residence of third-country nationals for the purposes of seasonal employment
		Directive on conditions of entry and residence of third-country nationals in the framework of an intra-corporate transfer (ICT)
	1 June	Economic governance package:
		The implementation of the excessive deficit procedure
		Requirements for budgetary frameworks of the Member States
		Effective enforcement of budgetary surveillance in the euro area
		Enforcement measures to correct excessive macroeconomic imbalances
		Strengthening of the surveillance of budgetary positions and the surveillance and coordination of economic policies
		Revention and correction of macroeconomic imbalances
	12 April	The external dimension of social policy, promoting labour and social standards and the European Corporate Social Responsibility

Year	*Dates*	*Topics*
	10 March (Plenary)	Social services of general interest
	1 March	Single Market Act: Sustainable and equitable growth for business Rapporteurs: Cristian Busoi (IMCO, ALDE), Raffaele Baldassarre (EMPL, EPP) Restoring confidence by putting Europeans at the heart of the Single Market Rapporteurs: António Correia de Campos (IMCO, S&D), Liisa Jaakonsaari (EMPL, S&D) Dialogue, partnership, evaluation: The keys to good governance of the Single Market Rapporteurs: Sandra Kalniete (IMCO, EPP), Jürgen Creutzmann (EMPL, ALDE)
	11 January	Economic governance package: The implementation of the excessive deficit procedure Requirements for budgetary frameworks of the Member States Effective enforcement of budgetary surveillance in the euro area Enforcement measures to correct excessive macroeconomic imbalances Strengthening of the surveillance of budgetary positions and the surveillance and coordination of economic policies Prevention and correction of macroeconomic imbalances
2010	7 December	Directive on the conditions of entry and residence of third-country nationals for the purposes of seasonal employment Directive on conditions of entry and residence of third-country nationals in the framework of an intra-corporate transfer Proposal for a Council Directive on a single application procedure for a single permit for third-country nationals to reside and work in the territory of a Member State and on a common set of rights for third-country workers legally residing in a Member State
	25 November (Plenary)	Green Paper 'Towards adequate, sustainable and safe European pension systems' Commission's Green Paper
	12 October	Green Paper 'Towards adequate, sustainable and safe European pension systems'
	14 September	Demographic challenge and solidarity between generations Future for social services of general interest

(continued)

(continued)

Year	*Dates*	*Topics*
	30 June	A single application procedure for a single permit for third-country nationals to reside and work in the territory of a Member State and on a common set of rights for third-country workers legally residing in a Member State
	29 June	Introduction of measures to encourage improvements in the safety and health at work of pregnant workers and workers who have recently given birth or are breastfeeding
		Organisation of working time
	17 June (Plenary)	The Future of Pensions in the EU: Funding and future for next generations better enforcement, cooperation and compliance of existing EU-rules
	11 May	Alternative investment fund managers
	13 April	Debate on the proposal for a directive of the European Parliament and of the Council on Working Time for Road Transport Workers
	2 March	Debate Conclusions of the exceptional Heads of State and Government's Council on the part related to the promotion of employment and growth in the EU 2020 future strategy
	12 February (Cancelled)	Debate on the proposal for a directive of the European Parliament and of the Council amending Council Directive 92/85/EEC on the introduction of measures to encourage improvements in the safety and health at work of pregnant workers and workers who have recently given birth or are breastfeeding
	10 February (Plenary)	Debate: Future of Trade Unions: Achievements, challenges and opportunities
	12 January	Debate on the proposal for a directive of the European Parliament and of the Council on Working Time for Road Transport Workers
2009	25 November (Plenary)	Debate: Future of Trade Unions: Achievements, challenges and opportunities
	11 November	Proposal for a directive of the European Parliament and of the Council amending Council Directive 92/85/EEC on the introduction of measures to encourage improvements in the safety and health at work of pregnant workers and workers who have recently given birth or are breastfeeding
	13 October	The reform of the hedge funds and the social consequences
	8 September	Handover-Meeting

Source Minutes and Agenda of Trade Union Intergroup September 2009–May 2013, in possession of the author, interviews CSO 5 (May 2013), Händel (2015), Jazłowiecka (2013)

Meetings of the Intergroup 'Urban' in the 7th EP (2009–2014)

Year	*Date*	*Topic*
2014		Not specified
2013		
	21 November	Presentation of the MAIA report (Metropolitan Areas in Action) by the Eurocities Metropolitan Areas Working Group
	23 May	'International cooperation in regional urban development policy' presentation by Ronald Hall, principal advisor of the Director General, European Commission, DG Regional and Urban Policy, Inclusive Growth
	14 March	Study 'Urban development in the EU. 50 projects supported by ERDF during the 2007–2013 period' presentation by Peter Ramsden, Freiss Ltd and Stephen Duffy, European Commission, DG Regional and Urban Policy, Inclusive Growth, Urban and Territorial Development
	7 February	European Commission's activities on the European Innovation Partnership in Smart Cities and Communities presentation by Dr. Henriette VAN EIJL, European Commission, DG Mobility and Transport, Research and Innovative Transport Systems
	17 January	The development of the negotiations of the post-2013 cohesion policy with relation to urban development
2012	13 December	European Capital of Culture presentation by MEP Marie-Thérèse Sanchez-Schmid, Vice President of the Intergroup
	13 September	Discuss the state of play concerning the urban dimension of the cohesion policy after 2013
	5 July	Findings of the joint URBAN-EMI questionnaire on the urban dimension of cohesion policy presentation by Ries Kamphof, European Metropolitan network Institute
	14 May	Housing situation in Europe and different EU policy instruments supporting social housing "Affordable housing for all—Policy implications of shrinking budget" presentation by Barbara Steenbergen, International Union of Tenants (IUT), Head of EU office
	24 April	Urban dimension of Cohesion Policy 2014–2020—Urban elements in the EC Common Strategic Framework Staff Working Document

(continued)

(continued)

Year	*Date*	*Topic*
	15 March	First results of the RURBAN study on urban-rural partnership in Europe presentation by Christian Huttenloher, Secretary General of the German Association for Housing, Urban and Spatial Development
		Władysław Piskorz, Head of Unit Urban Development and Territorial Cohesion/European Commission
		Betty-Ann Bryce, OECD Rural and Regional Development Unit
2011	17 November	Findings of the EMI Knowledge and Research Agenda on 'Sustainable Urban mobility'
	26 October	Urban dimension in the legislative package for the cohesion policy 2014–2020
	22 June	Urban dimension in the White Paper on transport presentation by Sandro Santamato from the DG Mobility and Transport at the European Commission
	17 February	Role of cities in the implementation of the EU 2020 Strategy
		Report by MEP and Intergroup Vice-President Oldřich Vlasák on 'European Urban Agenda and its Future in Cohesion Policy'
	20 January	Consequences of demographic change in cities presentation by Muriel Boulmier from Cecodhas
2010	16 December	JESSICA—'An EU policy vehicle for the sustainable transformation of European city areas' presentation by Eugenio Leanza, Head of JESSICA and Investment Funds at EIB
	25 November	Urban dimension in the 5th Cohesion Report by the European Commission & ex-post evaluation of the URBAN II Community initiative presentation by Alexander Ferstl from the DG Regio at the European Commission
	21 October	Preparation of cities for natural catastrophes presentation by MEP Rui Tavares—Vice-President of the Intergroup
	8 July	Betahaus project (creation of attractive working spaces in cities) presentation by Daniela Marzavan
		EC proposal to grant more funds to projects in the field of energy
	17 June	Convenant of Mayors with the participation of Pedro Ballesteros Torres from the DG Energy at the European Commission
	20 May	Urban related issues in the next cohesion policy programming period
		'Learning from the URBAN initiative experience' presentation by Lothar Blatt, President of the German-Austrian URBAN Network

Year	*Date*	*Topic*
	11 March	'The housing dimension in the EU2020 strategy' presentation by Claire Roumet, Secretary General of Cecodhas
	11 February	Urban related issues in the current parliamentary work (social services of general interest, public procurement and sustainable transport)
		Conference 'Building on 20 Years of Community Support to Urban Development' presentation by MEP Jan Olbrycht, President of the Intergroup
	21 January	Organisational matters related to set-up of Intergroup
		Discussion of urban issues in the current work of parliamentary committees
2009	17 December	Choice of Intergroup President and members of the URBAN Bureau; organisational matters, discussion of upcoming events and conferences
	22 October	Characteristics, spatial development and current urban development related issues in the City of Strasbourg with the participation of Mme Anne Pons, executive director of ADEUS (Agency for development and urbanism of the Strasbourg Agglomeration)
	17 September	Activities of the 'Housing' Intergroup in the previous parliamentary term presentation by MEP Jean Marie BEAUPUY, former President of the 'URBAN—Housing' Intergroup

Source Urban Intergroup at the European Parliament. (2014) available at http://urban-intergroup.eu/category/meetings-events/monthly-meetings/, last accessed 30 July 2014

Meetings of the Intergroup 'Viticulture' in 7th EP (2009–2014) Strasbourg, France (Incomplete)

Year	*Dates*	*Topics*
2009	16 September	Meeting (no minutes)
2010	22 September[a]	Reform of the common market organisation (CMO) for wine—removal of controls on planting rights in 2015
2011	16 February[b]	Planting rights
		EU agriculture and international trade
	6 April[c]	CAP reform
		Planting rights
		Food labelling and nutritional labelling
	8 June[d]	Agricultural product quality policy
	23 June[e]	Agricultural product quality policy
	6 July[f]	Automatic liberalisation of planting rights in 2014
	16 November[g]	Presentation of the Green paper on promotion measures and information provision for agricultural
	5–6 pm	products
	Strasbourg	• Hans-Erwin Barth, Head of Unit—Promotion of Agricultural Products DG ARGI, European Commission
		• Anne Velluet, French Federation of Wine and Spirits Exporters (FEVS) and General Association of Wine Business (AGEV)
		Luc Sougné, Domaine Boyar International—Presentation and Testing of Bulgarian Wine
		The meeting will be followed by a tasting of wines from Bulgaria from 6pm on
2012	15 February	Meeting (no minutes)
	19 April[h]	How to improve market access and create new opportunities for EU wines and spirits
		• Marie Audren, External Trade & Economic Affairs Director, European Spirits Organisation (CEPS)
		• Nicolas Ozanam, President External Trade committee of CEEV, General Delegate Federation of French Wine and Spirits Exporters (FEVS) & General Association of Wine Enterprises (AGEV)
		High level group on planting rights
		• Astrid Lulling, President of the Intergroup 'Wine, Fruits and Vegetables, Tradition and Quality foodstuffs'
		European Sommelier Diploma
		• Thierry Corona—President of the Association of European Sommeliers

Year	Dates	Topics
	13 June[i]	Common organisation of agricultural markets (CMO): Regime of the single payment scheme and support to vine-growers • MEP Herbert Dorfmann, rapporteur Improved Single CMO and the CMO Fruit and vegetables and crisis management • Carolina Gario, Assembly of European Fruit and Vegetable Growing and Horticultural Regions (AREFLH) Improve the position of quality products in the future CAP • Laurent Gomez, Association of European Regions for Products of Origin (AREPO)
	12 September[j] 5–6 pm Strasbourg	'Single CMO' Discussion of the report of Mr. Dantin and the tabled amendments • Michel Dantin, rapporteur Vinissima—Women and Wine • Presentation Christa Jüngling, regional responsible for Moselle and Ahr EuroFoieGras • Presentation of the Federation and its animal welfare charter, Jean Schwebel, President EuroFoieGras Foie Gras and wine tasting in the WIC members restaurant
	25 October[k]	Use of traditional designations for wines (château and clos) from the USA • Pascal Bobillier-Monnot, director of La Confédération Nationale des producteurs de vins et eaux de vie de vin à Appellations d'Origine Contrôlées (CNAOC) Common Organisation of the markets in agricultural products 2014–2020
2013	16 January[l] 5–6 pm Strasbourg	Common organisation of the markets in agricultural products 2014–2020/Conclusion on High Level Group on planting rights • Michel Dantin, MEP and rapporteur on single CMO State of play in the wine sector • Georges Haushalter, Chairman Le Conseil interprofessionnel du vin de Bordeaux (CIVB) Strategy for promoting the tastes of Europe • Daniel Rameau, President of Euro-Toques International The meeting will be followed by a tasting offered by the Chefs from Euro-Toques International

(continued)

(continued)

Year	*Dates*	*Topics*
	13 March[m]	Planting rights
		Distance selling of wine
	22 May[n]	Control of PDO/PGI (protected designation of origin/protected geographical indications) products/ agricultural products
		Common organisation of the markets in agricultural products /'Single CMO'
	4 July[o]	Removal of controls on planting rights in 2015
		• Michel Dantin, MEP and rapporteur on single CMO presents on progress on reform on planting rights
		Delegation of wine and vin internet domain names to private companies
		• Pascal Bobillier-Monnot, director of La Confédération Nationale des producteurs de vins et eaux-de-vie de vin à Appellations d'Origine Contrôlées (CNAOC)
	21 November[p]	Vine wood diseases (Jean Pierre van Ruysenvelde)
		Legislative acts concerning the implementation of CAP reform (Paolo de Castro)
2014	5 February	Development of wine and vin internet domain names
	5–6 pm[q]	Information on legislative acts concerning the new 'system of authorisation of vine plantings'
		Resumé of Intergroup activities in 7th legislature (2009–2014)
		Jerez: European City of Wine 2014
	12 March[r]	Meeting (no minutes) (Association des Sommeliers d´Europe)
	16 April[s]	Meeting (no minutes)

[a]European Commissioner for Agriculture Dacian Cioloş at the Viticulture Intergroup meeting of the European Parliament—22 September 2010, available at http://www.arev.org/spip.php?article1983, last assessed 30 September 2011; http://www.vinomedia.fr, last accessed 31 July 2014

[b]MEP Nathalie Griesbeck—Agenda, http://www.nathalie-griesbeck.fr/2011/02/intergroupe-vin-fruits-legumes-tradition-et-produits-de-qualite/, last accessed 29 October 2014

[c]MEP Nathalie Griesbeck—Agenda, http://www.nathalie-griesbeck.fr/2011/04/intergroupe-vin-fruits-legumes-tradition-et-produits-de-qualite-2/, last accessed 29 October 2014

[d]MEP Nathalie Griesbeck—Agenda, http://www.nathalie-griesbeck.fr/category/agenda/page/50/?y=2011, last accessed 29 October 2014; Original Quote: '*Les discussions porteront notamment sur la politique de qualité des produits agricoles*'

[e]MEP Nathalie Griesbeck—Agenda, http://www.nathalie-griesbeck.fr/2011/06/intergroupe-vin-fruits-legumes-tradition-et-produits-de-qualite-4/, last accessed 29 October 2014

[f]MEP Nathalie Griesbeck—Agenda, http://www.nathalie-griesbeck.fr/2011/07/intergroupe-vin-fruits-legumes-tradition-et-produits-de-qualite-5/, last accessed 29 October 2014

[g]Hans-Peter Martin—Email from MEP Astrid Lulling to Invitation Intergroup meeting 16/11 sent on 31 October 2011, available at http://www.hpmartin.net/content/8112011-wine-tasting-ep-intergroup-wine, last accessed 28 July 2014

[h]Hans-Peter Martin—Email from MEP Astrid Lulling to Invitation Intergroup meeting 19/04 sent on 12 April 2012, available at http://www.hpmartin.net/content/1942012-wine-and-spirits-tasting-intergroup-wfvtqf, last accessed 28 July 2014

[i]Intergroup Wine, Fruits and Vegetables, Tradition and Quality foodstuffs—'Agenda' obtained during attendance of Intergroup meeting on 12 September 2012; in possession of Laura Landorff

[j]Intergroup Wine, Fruits and Vegetables, Tradition and Quality foodstuffs—'Agenda' obtained during attendance of Intergroup meeting on 12 September 2012; in possession of Laura Landorff

[k]MEP Nathalie Griesbeck—Agenda, http://www.nathalie-griesbeck.fr/2012/10/intergroupe-viticulture-fruits-et-legumes-tradition-alimentation-de-qualite/, last accessed 29 October 2014

[l]Hans-Peter Martin—Email from MEP Astrid Lulling to Invitation Intergroup meeting 'Intergroup-16/01 updated agenda' sent out 11 January 2013, available at http://www.hpmartin.net/content/1612013-food-and-wine-tasting-ep-intergroup-wine-fruits-and-vegetables-tradition-and-quality, last accessed at 28 July 2014

[m]MEP Nathalie Griesbeck—Agenda, http://www.nathalie-griesbeck.fr/2013/03/intergroupe-vin-fruits-legumes-tradition-et-produits-de-qualite-7/, last accessed 29 October 2014 (Original Quote: '*L'ordre du jour portera entre autres sur les droits de plantation et la vente à distance du vin*')

[n]MEP Nathalie Griesbeck—Agenda, http://www.nathalie-griesbeck.fr/2013/05/intergroupe-vin-fruits-legumes-tradition-et-produits-de-qualite-8/, last accessed 29 October 2014 (Original Quote '*L'ordre du jour portera entre autres sur un projet de surveillance des produits AOP/IGP et sur l'Organisation Commune des Marchés agricoles (« OCM unique »)*

[o]MEP Nathalie Griesbeck—Agenda, http://www.nathalie-griesbeck.fr/2013/07/intergroupe-viticulture-fruits-et-legumes-tradition-alimentation-de-qualite-2/, last accessed 29 October 2014

[p]MEP Nathalie Griesbeck—Agenda, http://www.nathalie-griesbeck.fr/2013/11/intergroupe-viticulture-fruits-et-legumes-tradition-alimentation-de-qualite-3/, last accessed 29 October 2014

[q]MEP Nathalie Griesbeck—Agenda, http://www.nathalie-griesbeck.fr/2014/02/intergroupe-viticulture-fruits-et-legumes-tradition-alimentation-de-qualite-4/, last accessed 29 October 2014

[r]MEP Nathalie Griesbeck—Agenda, http://www.nathalie-griesbeck.fr/2014/03/intergroupe-vin/, last accessed 29 October 2014

[s]MEP Nathalie Griesbeck—Agenda, http://www.nathalie-griesbeck.fr/2014/04/intergroupe-vin-2/, last accessed 29 October 2014

Intergroup Wine, Fruits and vegetables, Tradition, Quality foodstuffs

AGENDA

Wednesday 12 September 2012
European Parliament
STRASBOURG
Room SDM.S7
5.00 – 6.00 pm
Translation: EN, FR

On the agenda of this meeting:

1. **"Single CMO" Discussion of the report of Mr Dantin and the tabled amendments, *Michel Dantin*,** *rapporteur*

2. **Vinissima - Women and Wine, Presentation, *Christa Jüngling*,** *regional responsible for Moselle and Ahr*

3. **EuroFoieGras - Presentation of the Federation and its animal welfare Charter, *Jean Schwebel*,** *Président EuroFoieGras*

4. **Any other business**

5. **Foie Gras and wine tasting in the WIC members restaurant**

Contact: astrid.lulling@europarl.europa.eu

Agenda of Intergroup 'Viticulture' – Intergroup meeting on 12 September 2012 in Strasbourg, France; in possession of the author

Appendix D

L. Landorff, *Inside European Parliament Politics*,
Palgrave Studies in European Political Sociology,
https://doi.org/10.1007/978-3-030-04206-6

Overview of Parliamentary Reports Discussed in the Intergroup 'Trade Union' in the 7th EP (2009–2013)

		Name of the Report (Date of Intergroup meeting and discussion)
(Draft) Reports IMCO (4)	INI	REPORT on a Single Market for Enterprises and Growth (01/03/2011)
		REPORT on a Single Market for Europeans (01/03/2011)
		REPORT on Governance and Partnership in the Single Market (01/03/2011)
	COD	REPORT on modernisation of EU public procurement legislative framework (12/2/2012, 15/3/2012, 22/1/2013)
(Draft) Reports ECON (2)	INI	–
	COD	REPORT on Alternative Investment Fund Managers (13/10/2009, 11/05/2010)
		REPORT on the strengthening of the surveillance of budgetary positions and the surveillance and coordination of economic policies (01/06/2011)
(Draft) Reports FEMM (2)	INI	REPORT on the impact of the economic crisis on gender equality and women's rights (22/01/2013)
	COD	REPORT on the introduction of measures to encourage improvements in the safety and health at work of pregnant workers and workers who have recently given birth or are breast-feeding (11/11/2009, 29/06/2010)
(Draft) Reports LIBE (5)	INI	–
	COD	REPORT on the conditions of entry and residence of third-country nationals for the purposes of seasonal employment (08/11/2011, 28/06/2011, 07/12/2010)
		REPORT on conditions of entry and residence of third-country nationals in the framework of an intra-corporate transfer (05/03/2013, 08/11/2011, 28/06/2011, 07/12/2010)
		REPORT on a single application procedure for a single permit for third-country nationals to reside and work in the territory of a Member State and on a common set of rights for third-country workers legally residing in a Member State (07/12/ 2010, 30/06/2010)
		REPORT on working time for road transport workers (12/01/2010, 13/04/2010)
		REPORT on the protection of individuals with regard to the processing of personal data and on the free movement of such data (05/03/2013)

		Name of the Report (Date of Intergroup meeting and discussion)
(Draft) Reports EMPL (8)	INI	REPORT on 'Towards adequate, sustainable and safe European pension systems' (12/10/2010)
		REPORT on the demographic challenge and solidarity between generations (14/09/2010)
		REPORT on the future of social services of general interest (14/09/2010, 10/03/2011)
		REPORT on the external dimension of social policy, promoting labour and social standards and European corporate social responsibility (12/04/2011)
		REPORT on Information and consultation of workers, anticipation and management of restructuring (05/09/2012)
	COD	REPORT on minimum health and safety requirements regarding the exposure of workers to the risks arising from physical agents (electromagnetic fields) (29/11/2011)
		REPORT on posting of workers in the framework of the provision of services (11/04/2012)
		REPORT on the exercise of the right to take collective action within the context of the freedom of establishment and the freedom to provide services (Monti II) (11/04/2011)

Source Author's own table based on minutes and agenda of 'Trade Union' Intergroup September 2009–May 2013 in the possession of the author, interviews CSOs (May 2013)

Overview of Parliamentary Reports Discussed in the Intergroup 'Animal Welfare' in the 7th EP (2009–2014)

		Name of the Report (Date of Intergroup meeting)
(Draft) Reports PECH (1)	INI	–
	COD	REPORT on the removal of fins of sharks on board vessels (15/03/2012)
(Draft) Reports AGRI (6)	INI	REPORT on evaluation and assessment of the Animal Welfare Action Plan 2006–2010 (16/12/2009)
		REPORT on EU agriculture and international trade (16/12/2010)
		REPORT on the new Animal Welfare Strategy (2012–2015) (19/01/2012, 15/03/2012)
		REPORT on animal transport (19/01/2012)
	COD	REPORT on recommendation for second reading on the Council position at first reading with a view to the adoption of a directive of the European Parliament and of the Council on the protection of animals used for scientific purposes (21/10/2009)
		REPORT on the Animal Health Law (12/09/2013)
(Draft) Reports ENVI (4)	INI	REPORT on 'Our life insurance, our natural capital: An EU biodiversity strategy to 2020' (19/01/2012)
		REPORT on the protection of public health from endocrine disrupters (13/12/2012)
	COD	REPORT on the proposal for a regulation of the European Parliament and of the Council on the non-commercial movement of pet animals (13/09/2012)
		REPORT on the proposal for a regulation of the European Parliament and of the Council on the prevention and management of the introduction and spread of invasive alien species (12/12/2013)

Source Intergroup on the Welfare & Conservation of Animals (2014b)

Appendix E

L. Landorff, *Inside European Parliament Politics*,
Palgrave Studies in European Political Sociology,
https://doi.org/10.1007/978-3-030-04206-6

Intergroup 'Animal Welfare': Written Declarations in the 7th EP (2009–2014)

	Written Declarations	*Initiating MEPs*	*Adopted/Not adopted*	*Number of Signatories*	*Addressee/Named Institution*
1.	On the transportation of horses for slaughter (54/2009)	Elizabeth Lynne, Sidonia Jędrzejewska, Carl Schlyter	Adopted	405—11-02-2010	Council of Ministers, European Commission, parliaments and government of the Member States
2.	On support for strength-ening the European Union ban on shark finning (71/2010)	Jean-Paul Besset, Chris Davies, Sirpa Pietikäinen, Daciana Octavia Sârbu	Adopted	423—16-12-2010	European Commission
3.	On dog population management in the EU (26/2011)	Daciana Octavia Sârbu, Elisabeth Jeggle, Raül Romeva i Rueda, Adina-Ioana Vălean, Janusz Wojciechowski,	Adopted	400—13-10-2011	European Commission, Governments of the Member States
4.	On fish as a common good (47/2011)	Guido Milana, Kriton Arsenis, Corinne Lépage, Maria do Céu Patrão Neves, Raül Romeva i Rueda	Adopted	390—29-03-2012	Council of Ministers, European Commission, parliaments and government of the Member States
5.	On the establishment of a maximum 8 hours journey limit (49/2011)	Carl Schlyter, Dan Jørgensen, Esther de Lange, Andrea Zanoni, Pavel Poc	Adopted	395—15-03-2012	European Commission, Governments of the Member States
6.	On the silent slaughter of rhinoceros in Southern Africa (74/2010)	Aldo Patriciello, Alfredo Pallone, Gabriele Albertini, Barbara Matera, Licia Ronzulli	Not adopted	92 —20-01-2011	Parliaments of the Member States

	Written Declarations	*Initiating MEPs*	*Adopted/Not adopted*	*Number of Signatories*	*Addressee/Named Institution*
7.	On the marketing of eggs from hens housed in outlawed cages (87/2010)	Nicole Sinclaire, Mike Nattras	Not adopted	51—17-02-2011	Council of Ministers, European Commission
8.	On the welfare of pets (26/2010)	Carl Schlyter, Marit Paulsen, Caroline Lucas, Janusz Wojciechowski, Daciana Octavia Sârbu	Not adopted	226—09-09-2010	Parliaments of the Member States, Council of Ministers, European Commission
9.	On the implementation of the ban on individual sow stands (06/2012)	George Lyon, Esther de Lange, Dan Jørgensen, Marit Paulsen, Janusz Wojciechowski	Not adopted	165—14-06-2012	Council of Ministers, European Commission and the national authorities concerned
10.	On the promotion of alternatives to animal research and testing (53/2009)	Raül Romeva i Rueda, Daciana Octavia Sârbu, Sirpa Pietikäinen, Gerben-Jan Gerbrandy and Caroline Lucas	Not adopted	159—21-01-2010	Council of Ministers, European Commission, parliaments of the Member States

Source Intergroup on the Welfare & Conservation of Animals (2014a)

References

Castex, F. (2011). Public Services Intergroup: Activity Report 2010. Retrieved 04 December 2014, from http://web.ensie.org/LinkClick.aspx?fileticket=7031346457334177666C343D&tabid=1461&language=en-US&stats=false.

Comité Quart Monde Européen. (2004–2009). *Comité Quart Monde Européen: Intergroup au Parlament Européen – Bilan Législature 2004–2009*. Brussels: Comité Quart Monde Européen.

European Parliament. (2002). *Activities: 12/A-2002—Bulletin*. Brussels: European Parliament: Directorate for the Planning of Parliamentary Business

European Parliament. (2003). *Activities: 03/A-2003—Bulletin*. Brussels: European Parliament: Directorate for the Planning of Parliamentary Business.

European Parliament. (2005). *Activities: 08/A-2005—Bulletin*. Brussels: European Parliament: Directorate for the Planning of Parliamentary Business.

European Parliament. (2011). *About the Parliament: Organisation and Work—Intergroups*. Retrieved 11 May 2011, from http://www.europarl.europa.eu/aboutparliament/en/00c9d93c87/Intergroups.html.

European Parliament. (2013). *About Parliament: Organisation and Work—Intergroups*. Retrieved 24 January 2013, from http://www.europarl.europa.eu/aboutparliament/en/00c9d93c87/Intergroups.html.

European Parliament. (2014). *About Parliament: Organisation and Work—Intergroups*. Retrieved 19 May 2014, from http://www.europarl.europa.eu/aboutparliament/en/00c9d93c87/Intergroups.html.

Gál, K., & Hicks, D. (2010). The European Parliament Intergroup for Traditional Minorities, National Communities and Languages, 2009–2014. *Europäisches Journal für Minderheitenfragen, 3*(3–4), 236–250.

Gál, K., Hicks, D., & Eplényi, K. (2011). *Traditional Minorities, National Communities and Languages: The Issues Raised in the European Parliament Intergroup, 2009–2011*. Brussels, Budapest: Kinga Gál.

Händel, T. (2015). Thomas Händel: Mitglied des Europäischen Parlaments – Vergangene Termine-5. Juni 2013—Trade Union's Intergroup. Retrieved 17 February 2015, from http://www.thomas-haendel.eu/de/topic/18.html?viewpassed=1.

Intergroup on the Welfare & Conservation of Animals. (2012). *Press Release: New President Takes Helm at Intergroup on the Welfare & Conservation of Animals* Brussels: Intergroup on the Welfare & Conservation of Animals.

Intergroup on the Welfare & Conservation of Animals. (2014a). Actions: Written Declarations. Retrieved 18 August 2014, from http://www.animalwelfareintergroup.eu/action/written-declarations/

Intergroup on the Welfare & Conservation of Animals. (2014b). Meetings. Retrieved 28 October 2014, from http://www.animalwelfareintergroup.eu/meetings.

Jacobs, F., Corbett, R., & Shackleton, M. (1995). *The European Parliament* (3rd ed.). London: Cartermill.

Jazłowiecka, D. (2013, November 28). MEP Danuta Jazłowiecka: What's Happening in European Parliament? 3–8 June 2013. Retrieved 17 February 2015, from http://www.jazlowiecka.pl/686/whats-happening-in-europe-an-parliament-3-8-june-2013.html.

Mann, T., & Reuter, M. (2010). Die außenpolitische Funktion der Tibet Intergroup. In D. Dialer, E. Lichtenberger & H. Neisser (Eds.), *Das Europäische Parlament: Institution, Vision und Wirklichkeit* (1st ed., Vol. 2, pp. 405–423). Innsbruck: Innsbruck University Press.

Saint Martin, F., & Thomas, C. (2012). *Seas and Coastal Areas Intergroup: Mid-Term Progress Report.* Available from http://www.mersetzonescotieres.eu/uploads/bilan-mi%20mandat2012/Bilanmi-mandatIntergroupe-final06052012.pdf.

Urban Intergroup at the European Parliament. (2014). Events—Monthly Meetings. Retrieved 30 July 2014, from http://urban-intergroup.eu/category/meetings-events/monthly-meetings/.

Index

L. Landorff, *Inside European Parliament Politics*,
Palgrave Studies in European Political Sociology,
https://doi.org/10.1007/978-3-030-04206-6

CPSIA information can be obtained
at www.ICGtesting.com
Printed in the USA
LVHW080400210219
608282LV00009B/29/P

9 783030 042059